# DogLife ❖ Lifelong Care for Your Dog™

# GERMAN SHEPHERD DOG

**tfh**

**Cindy Victor**

# GERMAN SHEPHERD DOG

Project Team
Editor: Stephanie Fornino
Indexer: Elizabeth Walker
Design: Mary Ann Kahn
Series Design: Mary Ann Kahn, Angela Stanford

T.F.H. Publications
President/CEO: Glen S. Axelrod
Executive Vice President: Mark E. Johnson
Publisher: Christopher T. Reggio
Production Manager: Kathy Bontz

T.F.H. Publications, Inc.
One TFH Plaza
Third and Union Avenues
Neptune City, NJ 07753

Printed and bound in China

10 11 12 13 14    1 3 5 7 9 8 6 4 2

**Library of Congress Cataloging-in-Publication Data**
Victor, Cindy.
  German shepherd dog / Cindy Victor.
    p. cm.
  Includes bibliographical references and index.
  ISBN 978-0-7938-3606-2 (alk. paper)
  1.  German shepherd dog.  I. Title.
  SF429.G37V53 2011
  636.737'6--dc22
                        2010011366

This book has been published with the intent to provide accurate and authoritative information in regard to the subject matter within. While every reasonable precaution has been taken in preparation of this book, the author and publisher expressly disclaim responsibility for any errors, omissions, or adverse effects arising from the use or application of the information contained herein. The techniques and suggestions are used at the reader's discretion and are not to be considered a substitute for veterinary care.
If you suspect a medical problem consult your veterinarian.

Note: In the interest of concise writing, "he" is used when referring to puppies and dogs unless the text is specifically referring to females or males. "She" is used when referring to people. However, the information contained herein is equally applicable to both sexes.

*The Leader In Responsible Animal Care for Over 50 Years!*®
**www.tfh.com**

# CONTENTS

# INTRODUCTION

# INTRODUCING THE GERMAN SHEPHERD DOG

Hailing from the Alsatian region of Germany in 1899, the German Shepherd Dog has enjoyed a spectacular history and today continues to be recognized and respected throughout the world. The relatively young breed's resume of herding, guarding, policing, tracking, search and rescue, and being a superb guide for the blind fairly astounds. German Shepherds can sniff out drugs and intruders and underground mines as reliably as they can catch a tennis ball tossed to them in the back yard. They can detect gas leaks 15 feet (4.5 m) underground and will never put anything before their owner's safety and well-being. For many years the German Shepherd Dog was the only breed shown at American Kennel Club (AKC) shows that had the word "Dog" as a separate word in its name. This seems right to me, as if the AKC was acknowledging that the German Shepherd Dog—also known as the German Shepherd, GSD, or just plain Shepherd—was *the* dog.

## A BRIEF HISTORY OF THE DOG

*And the guard dog, whether a mongrel roaming a junkyard or a German Shepherd partnered with a human police officer, is not unlike the wolf that protected our caves. Our faith in such dogs surely began with an early trust in the wolf/dog.* —Jim Brandenberg, *Brother Wolf: A Forgotten Promise*

Recent studies in dog history using mitochondrial DNA suggest that wolves and dogs split into different species some 100,000 years ago. Archaeology places the earliest known domestication of the dog at possibly close to 30,000 B.C. and with certainty at 7,000 B.C.E. A burial site in Germany, dated to 14,000 years ago, was found to contain both human and dog interments. (The earliest known dog burial in America took place in Utah around 11,000 years ago.)

Archaeological dates may shift with the sands of time, but scientists agree that all dogs—whether formidable in size or small enough to be carried in a woman's handbag—evolved from wolves, and that domestication of the dog (*Canis lupus familiaris*) from the gray wolf (*Canis lupus*) began tens of thousands of years ago. It's also agreed that dogs are closer to wolves physically and in behavior than to any other member of the family Canidae. Moreover, no evidence exists in the fossil record of any other animal that may have developed into man's best friend: the dog.

The German Shepherd is endowed with the wolf's superior sight, smell, and hearing.

It's a stretch to think of the Pug or Pekingese as bearing a resemblance to any wolf, yet all dog breeds retain characteristics of wolves, and the German Shepherd—from his long muzzle and large erect ears, to his long and strong legs and long hanging tail—looks like one. The German Shepherd is also endowed with the wolf's superior sight, smell, and hearing.

Like their brother wolf, dogs are predators who defend their territory. And like the wolf, they howl and whimper and exhibit both anger and fear, dominance and submission. They are affectionate with their family but bark at intruders. Able to judge hierarchy and status in their pack, they show loyalty to the leader. They communicate with their voice, facial expression, and physical positioning—

as wolves do. Some behaviors displayed by wolves are not found in today's dogs; one is regurgitation of partially digested food for the young. But a dominant wolf will sometimes hold the muzzle of a subordinate wolf between its jaws to show who's boss—a behavior I've seen replicated in my living room by German Shepherds. And when your dog greets you with a wagging tail, he's showing both affection and that he recognizes your status. It's a smart move that he unknowingly learned from brother wolf.

## EARLY DEVELOPMENT OF THE GSD

The German Shepherd Dog was derived from assorted breeds dating back to medieval times, when the regions of Europe had herding dogs to fill their own unique needs. Subject to ongoing development, the German Shepherd Dog we know today originated in Karlsruhe, Germany, in 1899—for which we can thank the rise of nationalism and two determined dog lovers. Nationalism created a "necessity" for a single sheepdog worthy of representing the German Empire. Consequently, many passionate dog enthusiasts combined various local types in the hope of developing the ideal shepherd. But it was Captain Max von Stephanitz who, with his friend Artur Meyer, culled from the best breeds the outstanding qualities in each and gave the world the German Shepherd Dog.

The journey to this achievement had begun in 1891, with the formation of the Phylax Society—its purpose being to standardize dog breeds. The society lasted just three years, but von Stephanitz and some other members continued its vision. Then, at a dog show in 1899, a dog named Hektor Linksrhein so impressed von Stephanitz with his intelligence, obedience, and strength that von Stephanitz purchased Hektor on the spot, then quickly formed the Verein für Deutsche Schäferhunde—or SV, which translates closely to "Society for the German Shepherd Dog." Von Stephanitz changed Hektor's name to Horand von Grafrath and made him the focus of the new society's breeding programs.

Horand von Grafrath, born January 1, 1895, became the first registered German Shepherd Dog, with the number SV1. Some sources give Horand's registration number as SZ-1. Either way, Horand von Grafrath was the foundation sire of his breed and will always be Number 1. As for Max von Stephanitz, his mission of creating the ideal herding dog had been achieved. Now, realizing that industrialization was reducing the demand for herding, the captain had the foresight to take the German Shepherd Dog to the next level: policing and military work.

## BREED HISTORY IN GERMANY

In part, what had brought the Phylax Society to an end was disagreement over which traits were most desired in the evolving German Shepherd Dog. These differences of opinion surfaced in the SV as well. Von Stephanitz's position was that a dog's working ability was what the dog should be judged by, not aesthetics. To avoid arguments that might impede his desires for the SV, the first German Shepherd breed standard—written by von Stephanitz with Meyer's help—acknowledged that "a pleasing

The German Shepherd Dog was derived from assorted breeds dating back to medieval times, when the regions of Europe had herding dogs to fill their own unique needs.

appearance" was desirable. Yet it emphasized that looks were not the first consideration. "German Shepherd breeding is working dog breeding," wrote von Stephanitz, "or it is not German Shepherd breeding." The SV adopted the standard and later held its first specialty show at Frankfurt-am-Main.

Horand von Grafrath fathered a number of pups, the most celebrated of whom was named Hektor von Schwaben. Hektor, in turn, fathered three outstanding dogs who were used in later breeding programs. Their progeny, all descended from Horand, became the ancestors of all modern German Shepherd Dogs. Moreover, von Stephanitz trialed the German Shepherd in a variety of roles to ensure its survival as a working breed. The SV, as guided by the captain's vision, was to become the largest single breed club in the world. Most importantly, the German Shepherd Dog's versatility and trainability ensured his value and stature through the years.

## BREED HISTORY IN THE UNITED STATES

There can be no story of any breed's coming in force to America more powerful than that of the German Shepherd Dog during World War II. Were we able to go back in time to watch the action unfold, we would be on the edge of our seats.

But it was prior to World War I, in 1908, when an import from Germany named Queen of Switzerland became the first German Shepherd Dog registered in the United States. Her story did not end well, as poor breeding

The German Shepherd Dog is an elegant and noble breed.

resulted in her offspring suffering defects. More disappointments with the breed occurred after World War I, when America's desire for sterling German Shepherds—such as they'd read about or seen in films—resulted in haphazard breeding, often of unregistered dogs brought home by American soldiers. The noble breed seemed less noble now, and the demand for Shepherds spiraled downward.

Two years after Queen of Switzerland was registered and shown in New York, Ernest Loeb was born in Germany. His father was a Rottweiler breeder. The family was Jewish. Ernest, training with his all-breed local dog club, was taken by the German Shepherd Dog. As told by Loeb to Gail Sprock, editor of the *German Shepherd Dog Review,* he soon was showing German Shepherds—sometimes under Max von Stephanitz. With his passion for and skills in handling the breed, his reputation spread throughout Germany.

Loeb's destiny was set but not in the way he'd imagined. In 1933, Adolf Hitler, a huge fan of German Shepherds, began seizing entire kennels of dogs belonging to Jewish breeders. By 1934 Loeb's world was shattered. He was banned from SV membership. People were afraid to be seen talking to him. Realizing that Germany was no longer a place for German Jews and that the situation was worsening, Loeb emigrated to America. In New York he found both acceptance and work. He sent to Germany for his dogs, one of whom was named Brando von Heidelbeerberg.

In February 1935, Loeb entered Brando in the Westminster Kennel Club Dog show. Out of 87 entries, Brando von Heidelbeerberg took Best of Breed. Suddenly, Ernest Loeb was famous in his new country, and he had a new role to play. Fanciers paid him to import well-bred Shepherds from Nazi Germany. Loeb did this by going to Germany himself,

beginning in 1936, and he did it over and over again—knowing the danger but not willing to abandon his mission. This incredible bravery was matched by that of his German friends who in Nazi Germany sought out quality dogs for a Jew to take to America.

The war ended but not Loeb's mission. By 1966 he had imported more than 200 dogs of outstanding quality to his adopted country. His friends called him Ernie. The world called him "Mr. German Shepherd."

## RECOGNITION OF THE GSD BY MAJOR CLUBS

The German Shepherd Dog enjoys formal acceptance by all major clubs having recognizable names such as the American Kennel Club—the largest purebred dog registry in the world.

But while the German Shepherd's status has always been assured, for a number of reasons the breed has gone by different names. The one chosen by Captain Max von Stephanitz is "Deutscher Schäferhund," which translates into English as "German Shepherd Dog." In America, though, the name became German Sheep Dog. Then in the wake of World War I, negative associations with Germany by America and the British Commonwealth resulted in both "German Shepherd Dog" and "German Sheep Dog" being very unfavorable. Alternatives were chosen. America came up with "Shepherd Dog." Some international clubs, including the UK's prestigious Kennel Club, decided on "Alsatian Wolf Dog"—after the German-French border area of Alsace-Lorraine. This didn't last long, because of the negative association with the word "wolf." However, the Kennel Club stayed with "Alsatian" until 1977, when once again the breed could be registered as "German Shepherd Dog." But for clarity it is entered in shows as "German Shepherd Dog (Alsatian)." And finally, many people use the name "Police Dog," which is said with respect and pride or with a nuance of fear—depending on the character of the person saying it.

## The American Kennel Club (AKC)

The AKC, founded in 1884, sponsors the annual two-day conformation show that famously takes place at Madison Square Garden in New York City every year. The first Westminster show was held in 1877, and to date the German Shepherd Dog has had the most Group wins, with a total of 14. This total includes results from before 1983, when the herding breeds were part of the Working Group. The German Shepherd, although used far more in guarding and other activities than in herding, was one of the working breeds reassigned to the Herding Dogs Group. Certainly some GSD people were nonplussed by this switch. But as noted by the late Roger Caras, long the voice of the Westminster Kennel Club Dog Show, "There can only be one group to a customer."

## The German Shepherd Dog Club of America (GDCA)

The GDCA (www.gsdca.org) was founded in 1913 by Anne Tracy and Benjamin Throop. In 1923, a group of fanciers formed the Shepherd Dog Club of New England. This became a strong and successful club. With the desire of having one unified and strong organization to safeguard the interests of the breed, a trial merger of the two clubs was undertaken in 1948. The merger became permanent in 1950, with the membership and assets of the Shepherd Dog Club of New England turned over to the German Shepherd Dog Club of America. Today the club provides an ever-widening educational program and truly is

The German Shepherd Club of America was founded in 1913.

nationwide in scope, with over 100 regional clubs cooperating with the parent club.

Beginning in 1990, the GSDCA has given the Award of Excellence (AOE), a title awarded a dog who has reached "the highest of all goals—to become the Total German Shepherd Dog." Along with other achievements, a Total German Shepherd Dog has superior conformation and trainability and is "sound in both mind and body." Offering the AOE—which is awarded for life but may be won repeatedly, is just one way in which the GSDCA helps German Shepherds, their breeders, and their owners through promoting breed improvement. As described by the club, the AOE "is an enhanced attachment to the Select Award, which recognizes the superior mature dog or bitch with certified hips and elbows." Needless to say, a breeder can use the title in advertising his or her dogs, discerning buyers will take note, and everyone wins—including the dogs.

Today the GSDCA is the top German Shepherd Dog organization recognized by both the AKC and the World Union Organization of German Shepherd Dogs (WUSV). But what does this have to do with you?—you might ask. The answer: everything! The GSDCA holds obedience trials, herding tests and trials, and agility trials, as well as sponsoring conformation shows and tracking tests. It supports search and rescue training, therapy dog training, and since 1984 has supported GSDs through a separate entity—the American German Shepherd Dog Charitable Foundation, Inc., which allows tax-deductible gifts to be made for projects beneficial to the German Shepherd Dog. The GSDCA is also a founding member–parent club in the AKC's Canine Health Foundation. So if you're looking for mentorship and fellowship with like-minded people and would enjoy taking part in the breed's future, consider joining the GSDCA.

## INFLUENTIAL PEOPLE

It seems unlikely that anyone could have a greater influence on the German Shepherd Dog than Captain Max von Stephanitz, who brought the breed into being, or Ernest Loeb, who brought the best of the breed to America. But through the years, many dedicated people have played immense roles in keeping the German Shepherd true to type, as well as working to eradicate known health problems and prevent new ones from cropping up. This is continuing to be done by professional breeders, trainers, handlers, and show judges who appreciate the seriousness of their judging and the consequences of their choices. And finally, German Shepherd owners who give their dogs ongoing training as well as a purpose in life beyond being Mommy's sweetums are the reason why the breed is third in popularity in America, and why television audiences pay attention when a German Shepherd enters the ring at the AKC Eukanuba National Championship, Crufts International Dog Show in England, or the Westminster Kennel Club Dog Show.

Some people influence the breed by happenstance. Lee Duncan, an American who served in World War I, did this by bringing a German Shepherd puppy he named Rin Tin Tin home with him. Some have influenced the breed by putting dogs to their best possible use. In 1927, Dorothy Harrison Eustis wrote an article on GSDs in Switzerland that were being trained to lead the blind. Inspired by hearing Eustis's article, a young blind man named Morris Frank, from Nashville, Tennessee, went to Switzerland to train with Eustis and a female German Shepherd named Buddy. Frank brought Buddy home with him, and she became the first formally trained guide dog in America. With Eustis and others, Frank worked to establish the country's first guide dog school: The Seeing Eye, based in Morristown, New Jersey.

Some people exert influence by devoting their entire lives to working to improve the breed. An example of this is the team of James and Sheree Moses, both of whom grew up with German Shepherds. James Moses, a breeder, trainer, and handler, has shown many champion Shepherds and had the distinction of taking Champion Covy Tucker Hill's Manhattan to the pinnacle of dog-show success. The top-winning male of *all* breeds in the American Kennel Club's history, Manhattan won 201 All-Breed Best in Shows and took the Herding Group three times at Westminster. In 1987 he capped his career by taking Best in Show at Westminster—making him the only Herding Group dog to take top honors at Madison Square Garden. Happily for "Hatter" and his human loved ones, including James Moses, he lived to the ripe old age of 13.

Some people devote their entire lives to working to improve the breed.

## MEMORABLE DOGS

Three other German Shepherds have won the Herding Group at Westminster: Champion Altana's Mystique in 1993 and 1994; Champion Windwalker's Yes Virginia in 1999; and Champion Kismet's Sight For Sore Eyes in 2003. But as with humans, being a champion isn't the only way for a dog to go down in history or live forever in people's hearts. Here are descriptions of just some memorable GSDs:

**Filax of Lewanno:** A German Shepherd named Filax of Lewanno, who in World War I brought 54 wounded American soldiers to safety, returned home safely himself, and was exhibited at Westminster in 1917.

**Tommy:** A German Shepherd who served in World War I as the mascot of a Scottish regiment, was wounded three times, gassed, captured, and finally rescued. At the end of the war, in November 1918, Tommy received the Croix de Guerre medallion for gallantry.

**Etzel von Oeringen:** A GSD born in Germany in 1917 and trained as a police dog, he was brought to the United States by the husband and wife filmmaking team Laurence Trimble and Jane Murfin. Renamed Strongheart, this early canine movie star appeared in the 1925 adaptation of *White Fang* and *The Return of Boston Blackie*, released in 1927. He had other successful roles, but alas, most of Strongheart's films have been lost. His line survives to this day, however, and he paved the way for a new star: Rin Tin Tin.

**Rin Tin Tin:** One of the shell-shocked puppies found by American serviceman Lee Duncan in a bombed-out dog kennel in

Lorraine, France, less than two months before the Great War ended, was named for a puppet that French children gave to American soldiers for good luck. At war's end, Duncan took "Rinty" home to Los Angeles, where he became a wildly famous Hollywood star who in some years earned more money for Warner Brothers Film Studio than any human actor. Rinty's success catapulted the German Shepherd Dog to become the United States' most popular breed. But by the year he died, 1932, registrations of GSDs had plummeted. Two of Rinty's descendants played Rin Tin Tin in a television series. His line has carried through the years. Today he has descendants working in search and rescue and as service dogs for disabled children through the A Rinty for Kids Foundation.

**Afra of Cosalta:** Of much lesser fame than Strongheart or Rin Tin Tin, but with a better-known owner, was Afra of Cosalta, a German Shepherd who took second in the Westminster Kennel Club's Open Bitch class in 1933. Her owner was Lou Gehrig.

**Major and Meg:** These GSDs, owned by President Franklin Delano Roosevelt, were not as affable as FDR or as well trained as the White House staff. Major bit Arkansas Senator Hattie Caraway and ripped the trousers off Prime Minister James Ramsay MacDonald of Great Britain. Meg bit newspaperwoman Bess Fujrman on the nose.

**Blondi:** In 1942, Adolf Hitler stated during one of his table talks that if he were to get a new dog, "it could only be a German Shepherd, preferably a bitch." Unfortunately,

Captain Max von Stephanitz had a tremendous influence on the breed.

dogs can't choose their owners. Blondi, Hitler's female Shepherd, was a gift from Martin Bormann. Polish-born Gunter Grass, who won the Nobel Prize for Literature in 1999, wrote in his novel *Dog Years*—published in 1965—about the beautiful German Shepherd Dog Harras, whose offspring became the favorite dog of Adolf Hitler.

**Chips**: On July 10, 1943, Chips, a German Shepherd mix, landed in Sicily with Patton's Seventh Army. As Chips and his handler approached a grass-covered hut, a machine gun opened fire. Chips broke loose and ran to do combat. He overpowered four armed Italian soldiers and for his valor and a wound to his scalp was awarded the Silver Star and Purple Heart. But his decorations were rescinded when the national commander of the Military Order of the Purple Heart objected that giving a medal to a dog demeaned the men who received it. Chips went home to his family, which was all the reward a dog could want.

**Bullet:** The singer and cowboy actor Roy Rogers and his wife Dale Evans owned a GSD called Bullet. To his fans he was Bullet the Wonder Dog, and he appeared regularly on the 1950s television series *The Roy Rogers Show.*

**London:** *The Littlest Hobo*, starring a German Shepherd called London, was originally created by Dorrell McGowen for a television movie in 1958. Following the huge success of the movie, a Canadian television series was filmed in black and white between 1963 and 1965. In each of the 65 episodes, London arrived in a new place and solved people's problems, then left. Remade in 1979, the series became a family favorite for years to come.

**Clipper:** John F. Kennedy owned a German Shepherd Dog named Clipper. Photographer Cecil Stoughton's picture of the Kennedy

family and their dogs at Hyannis Port, Massachusetts, on August 14, 1963, is in the John Fitzgerald Kennedy Presidential Library and Museum in Boston. It can be viewed at www.jfklibrary.org.

**Nemo:** In 1966, Nemo, a German Shepherd serving in Vietnam, lost an eye to gunfire but saved his handler's life by throwing himself at the enemy. Nemo was one of few Vietnam war dogs given passage home to America.

**Radar:** A GSD called Radar, who nearly died from distemper in puppyhood, went on to become a top television star in Brazil. Twenty thousand fans showing up to bid him bon voyage when he left South America for a career in Europe testified to the impact a once-sickly dog could have on people. In England, Radar was the star in series 2 and 3 of the TV show *Softly Softly,* which aired from 1970 to 1972.

**Trakr:** On September 11, 2001, a German Shepherd named Trakr found the last survivor of the World Trade Center attack.

**Lex:** In March, 2007, Lex, a Shepherd trained to sniff out hidden explosives, was seriously injured in the Al Anbar province of Iraq, alongside his human partner, Corporal Jerome Lee of the 2nd Marine Expeditionary Force. Lex climbed on top of Lee to protect him from further harm and to lick his wounds, but Lee perished from his injuries. Lex attended Lee's funeral service in Mississippi, and at war's end the valiant dog was discharged from duty to live out his life with Lee's family.

**Buddy:** In September of 2008, a German Shepherd named Buddy saw his owner, Joe Stalnaker, lying on the floor and called 911. Buddy had been trained by Stalnaker—who suffered from seizures after being impaired in a military accident—to call 911 anytime Stalnaker was lying on the floor. Buddy, whom Stalnaker got from Paws With a Cause, has

called 911 three times. Paws With A Cause (www.pawswithacause.org) trains Assistance Dogs nationally for people with disabilities, provides lifetime team support to encourage independence, and promotes awareness through education.

**Champ:** As a child, Vice President Joe Biden was called Champ by his dad. Before the 2008 election, Jill Biden promised her husband that they would get a dog if he and Obama won. Enter Champ, a German Shepherd Dog puppy whose name was chosen by Biden's granddaughters.

**Tulip:** *My Dog Tulip*, an independent feature film released in 2009, is based on *My Dog Tulip: Life With an Alsatian*, the 1956 novel by J. R. Ackerley that tells the story of Ackerley's 14-year friendship with a German Shepherd Dog.

Memorable German Shepherd Dogs who may not be celebrities by way of heroic feats, show wins, literature, or movie or television roles are the amazing dogs that you and I know intimately because we share our homes and sometimes an apple with them. Many people single out the most memorable dog of their lives and proclaim that this dog is (or was) my heart dog. Calling a dog your heart dog affirms that he means the most to you. Other dogs may have slept in your bed, comforted you in times of sorrow, made you smile when you were down, and looked up joyfully every time you walked in the door. But with your heart dog, you share an indescribable chemistry that can't exist between you and any other dog. I hear and read this term, heart dog, often. And I don't buy it. Having lived with many dogs, including three German Shepherds, and sharing an understanding of the soul with each of them, I couldn't possibly name one as my heart dog. Live with a few German Shepherds and see whether you don't agree with me.

# PART I

# PUPPYHOOD

# CHAPTER 1

# IS THE GERMAN SHEPHERD RIGHT FOR YOU?

If you are considering bringing a German Shepherd Dog into your home, you may be on the verge of entering a profoundly rewarding chapter of your life. But be mindful that you are choosing an extremely intelligent and self-confident breed that bears a distinct personality and cannot be left to lie around the house all day, bored and with nothing to do. The German Shepherd is a dog who bonds quickly with his family and would gladly give his life to save theirs. In turn, you—the owner of his heart and soul—must commit to giving him an abundance of love, exercise, and obedience training both when he is a puppy and when he reaches emotional maturity, which occurs between one and a half and three years of age. You must also provide him with a high-quality diet, excellent health care, and opportunities to use his brain. Do you think you're up to it? Good. Let's see whether you still feel that way at the end of the chapter. I think you will.

## BREED CHARACTERISTICS

An observation made by the late American author, commentator, and syndicated newspaper columnist William F. Buckley, Jr. that "industry is the enemy of melancholy" applies not only to humans but to the German Shepherd Dog as well. This noble and highly intelligent dog needs to use his mind and energy to excel at something: obedience, police work, conformation, search and rescue, guiding the visually impaired, tracking, drug and bomb detection—or simply guarding his property; protecting his family; or getting his people out on brisk, health-sustaining walks. To be happy, the German Shepherd needs a job. And to do his job he needs a partner at his side who works and plays as hard as he does. So if his job is to be your faithful family companion, you must be his as well. This doesn't mean that you will be equals. You're the boss, or in your dog's "language," the pack leader.

## *Want to Know More?*

For more on where to find the puppy of your dreams, see Chapter 2: Finding and Prepping for Your German Shepherd Puppy.

The German Shepherd is a dog who bonds quickly with his family and would gladly give his life to save theirs.

## Temperament

The German Shepherd has a reputation for being fearless, and he is. But he is not inclined to be hostile, as some people erroneously think, most likely because of the breed's typical self-confidence and aloofness toward strangers. The Shepherd is, in fact, highly successful in a wide variety of endeavors—including conformation—because of his strong desire to please. He's wonderful to look at too, but looks are one thing and character is everything. The German Shepherd is known for his courage, dignity, poise, and loyalty. As described in *The*

*Complete Dog Book: Official Publication of the American Kennel Club,* this faithful dog has the "ability to assimilate and retain training for a number of special services." A well-bred, well-trained Shepherd is not high strung and doesn't go looking for fights. Rather, his nerves are under control and he possesses a steady disposition. And he is a better dog if his owner is equally composed and of an unvarying disposition. The German Shepherd must respect his owner and the owner respect the dog, or there will be chaos.

## Common Behavioral/ Personality Traits

The behavior of a well-trained German Shepherd is stellar. He knows what's expected of him and performs accordingly, whether he is playing in the yard with children or stacking (the art of standing in the best position) while looking attentively at the show-ring judge. This is an approachable and aim-to-please dog, which is largely the reason for his consistently being one of America's most popular breeds.

I have mentioned the German Shepherd's intelligence twice, and it will come up again in this book—along with other favorable qualities the breed is known for, such as courage and dignity. This simply can't be helped when talking about Shepherds. But perhaps we should also look at what a Shepherd should not be. He shouldn't be timid or nervous: a shrinking dog who looks around himself with an anxious facial expression and tucked-under tail. Are you likely to meet a German Shepherd such as this? No. But it can happen if you get a dog from a disreputable breeder whose purpose in bringing Shepherd puppies into the world is monetary gain, not a love of the breed.

An honest summation of a well-bred Shepherd's personality is that of what we respect in our own species: attentiveness, desire to learn, politeness, self-confidence, poise, not forcing oneself on strangers unless in the line of duty. And not least—*joie de vivre*.

## PHYSICAL DESCRIPTION

The German Shepherd can be a smiling goofball when he feels like it, but he will never look clumsy; he can't, as he is fluid in motion and above all personifies strength of character and body. He is muscular, agile, slightly elongated, more curvaceous than angled, and his gait is a dignified trot with no sway in it. Words that come to a dog lover's mind on seeing a German Shepherd, whether he is sitting, lying down, standing, or in motion are "handsome," "beautiful," or "gorgeous."

"Dignified" is often heard, as is "noble." But to someone who does not love dogs and who perhaps is in a place where he or she ought not be, the German Shepherd will look imposing and stern—very possibly dangerous. This makes the Shepherd a deterrent—which is not a bad thing but another reason to value his looks.

### General Body Structure

The Shepherd's entire body, which is deep-chested and slightly elongated, gives the impressions of depth and solidity. The withers are higher than the back, which is straight, strongly developed, and not overly long but longer than the dog is tall. In any

The GSD is muscular, agile, slightly elongated, more curvaceous than angled, and his gait is a dignified trot with no sway in it.

position—whether standing at attention or at rest, walking, running, or sleeping on his side or belly—he looks fit and agile. But for the German Shepherd fancier, few things are more pleasing to the eye than a Shepherd in motion. This dog is a trotter, and his gait, both smooth and rhythmic, seems effortless. The standard describes this fluidity as outreaching and "covering the maximum amount of ground with the minimum number of steps." Even walking, the Shepherd strides out and covers much ground. (Don't worry that his moving like a well-lubricated machine means that you'll have a hard time keeping up. Once trained, he will be happy to heel at your side on walks.) The German Shepherd moves, according to standard, with the feet traveling close to the ground on both the forward reach and backward push. This is achieved through good muscular development and ligamentation. It is strength combined with self-assuredness, purpose, and elegance, and it is one of the pleasures of living with a Shepherd.

## Size

Proportionate to the work he is meant to do, the Shepherd is large but not overly so. Rather, the breed is of a weight and height that keeps him lithe instead of bulky. The breed standard for a male is 24 to 26 inches (61 to 66 cm) at the withers (top of the highest point of the shoulder blade), and 22 to 24 inches (56 to 61 cm) for a female. This standard applies to GSDs raised in Germany as well as in America. The ideal weight for both males and females is generally stated as between 62 and 80 pounds (28 and 36.5 kg). However, they are often considerably bigger, especially males—even with a good diet and ample exercise. Interestingly, in Nova Scotia the male Shepherd is expected to weigh between 80 and 95 pounds (36.5 and 43 kg).

## By the Numbers

Socializing your Shepherd assures that he will become a good citizen. Socialization should begin the day you bring him home—which may be as early as 8 weeks—and continue through his lifetime.

## Coat Type

The American Kennel Club (AKC) standard gives a big thumbs up to Shepherds born with a standard medium-length double coat. Typically, the outer coat is quite dense, with the hair straight, harsh, and lying close to the body. However, the outer coat may be slightly wavy, and a wiry texture is permissible according to the standard. All of the head, including the inner ear, has short hair, as do legs and paws, while the hair on the neck is longer and thicker. The rear of the forelegs and hind legs also has somewhat longer hair, and the lustrous bushy tail reaches at least to the hocks and hangs down when the dog is at rest. Faults for show dogs include the outer coat being soft, silky, wooly, curly, or just too long. Keep in mind, though, that faults for show dogs aren't faults for dogs who are only family pets, who will never be scrutinized by a judge. Some people prefer the long-coated Shepherd because of his cuddly appearance. If you like silky, woolly, long, or curly—go for it. Conversely, if showing your dog is a goal, pass up the fuzzy, long-haired puppy and choose a dog with short hair.

## Coat Color

While the coat can be many colors, most usually it is black and tan or black and red—

with a black mask and saddle. Most colors are permissible for showing, but washed-out colors and blues or livers are serious faults. Shepherds with white coats are disqualified from the show ring in the United States and some other countries, the reason being that white dogs are hard to see on snow-covered hills and are too easily seen when functioning as nighttime guards. But because of their uniqueness and striking appearance (long-coated "whites" usually have lovely shades of cream), white Shepherds have gained popularity as pets. There is even a club, the American White Shepherd Association (AWSA), which is working to promote recognition and acceptance of the white-coated Shepherd as a separate and distinct breed. The goal might be met but most likely not soon.

A Shepherd whose nose is not predominantly black, but blue or liver, also cannot be shown. Max von Stephanitz noted that no good dog can be a bad color. This was true in his time and it's true today. But breed clubs have the right to create a standard, and so they do.

## Head and Neck

The Shepherd's head is noble (here's that word again!) and in proportion to the body. As described by the breed standard, it is "cleanly chiseled, strong without coarseness, but above all not fine." (That's "fine" as in "fragile" or "dainty." But everything about the German Shepherd's head and neck is "fine" as in "solid" and "pleasing to the eye.") Standing in front of the dog, you will see that the forehead is moderately arched and that the skull slopes into a long muzzle but without an abrupt "stop" (the point where skull and muzzle meet). As with body structure, the head of the male is distinctly masculine, and that of the female is unmistakably feminine. The muzzle is strong as well as long, with its topline

White Shepherds are disqualified from the show ring in the US, but make wonderful pets.

parallel to the topline of the skull. Both jaws and teeth are strongly developed, the lips are firmly fitted, and the absence of any teeth other than first premolars is a serious fault in the show ring—which is just one reason why you will brush your Shepherd's teeth. (See "Dental Care" in Chapter 6.) As to the dog's expression, in conformation trials it is keen, intelligent, and composed. But at home it is all of that plus happy and playful.

The relatively long, muscular neck is proportionate in size to the head and has no loose folds of skin. It is a strong neck, carried high when the dog is excited or at attention. At other times, especially when the dog is in motion, the head and neck are carried forward instead of up.

## Eyes

The eyes, usually very dark, are almond shaped, medium in size, and do not protrude. They have a lively, intelligent expression and show a wide range of emotions. You'll know by the eyes when a German Shepherd is feeling playful, sad, or suspicious. James Thurber, the celebrated author and cartoonist whose work often included dogs, wrote, "If you look into a German Shepherd's eyes and he looks away, you need to examine your conscience."

## Ears

Wide at the base, the adult Shepherd's ears are long, moderately pointed, and in proportion to the skull. They stand erect and are open in front—which accentuates the dog's alertness.

The eyes, usually very dark, are almond shaped, medium in size, and do not protrude.

The ears become even more erect when the dog is excited. Puppies under six months may have slightly drooping ears, but a dog with cropped or hanging ears is disqualified from shows.

## LIVING WITH A GERMAN SHEPHERD

You already know that owning a dog and giving him a good life is time consuming, expensive, and restrictive of the owner's freedom. This is true of any breed. And the German Shepherd, being of good size and high intelligence—plus requiring daily grooming and exercise and ongoing socializing and training—is not the easiest breed to own. But it certainly is one of the most satisfying. As long as the dog's needs can be met and the owner's lifestyle allows for lots of time with him, the Shepherd can be an ideal companion for either a single person or a family.

Meet German Shepherds before buying or adopting one. Get to know the breed in person, not just in books. And ask questions about the breed. You won't always get the same answer, as no two dogs are exactly alike—even in a two-Shepherd family with both dogs having the same bloodlines and breeder. Also decide whether a male or a female would be best for you, considering that males are larger and that unspayed females come in heat twice a year. It's been said that the German Shepherd is one of the best security systems a person can buy. That's absolutely true but not a good reason to get a GSD. The Shepherd is at heart a friendly dog who likes the human species. He's just not a glad-hander.

### Environment

When provided with ample exercise, socialization, and training, a German Shepherd should be able to thrive and be welcomed in either an urban, suburban, or rural environment. A house with a fenced yard and nearby walking paths and parks would be ideal. But an apartment that isn't too small, or a townhouse or condominium, certainly can be a good environment for a Shepherd if its owner is committed to making it so. GSDs actually tend not to be very active indoors. I've never had one run through the house except when we played an indoor game of "Go get Daddy! Go get Mommy!"—alternatively called "Running down the hall." However, while an apartment or other type of home in which neighbors are on the other side of the wall can be suitable for a GSD, a noisy dog isn't suitable for this environment. How much noise the dog makes usually is related to three things: how much he's left alone, the amount of exercise he gets (remember that a tired dog is a good dog), and whether he's being aroused by other noisy animals. Shepherds are highly social dogs, deeply attached to their owners, and loneliness can create problems of excessive barking or destructiveness. Even when a multi-unit residential building has thick walls and ceilings for noise control, a barking dog can be a nuisance. In 2009, a four-year-old GSD named Daz was named "loudest barker" by the Guinness World Records—with a bark recorded at 108 decibels. According to BBC News, the noise made by a jet plane 100 feet (30.5 m) away is louder than Daz by just 22 decibels. However, your Shepherd isn't likely to come near this remarkable record.

As with the single-family suburban home, a rural environment provides great opportunities for exercise. But a fenced yard that the dog can't escape from is essential unless the dog is never allowed outside alone. Having originated as herding dogs, Shepherds retain the instinct for herding—although perhaps not as keenly felt as by the Border Collie. A loose dog,

Without exception, a healthy German Shepherd must have positive ways to direct his physical energy, and that means lots of exercise.

though, is at risk in any environment, and the wide-open spaces of farm or ranch land are no exception. In some states it's legal for a dog harassing livestock to be shot by the owner of the property the dog has entered.

## Exercise

Without exception, a young and healthy German Shepherd must have positive ways to direct his physical energy, and that means lots of exercise. Deprived of exercise, he will become bored, and a bored dog, desperate for activity, is likely to engage in destructive chewing indoors, barking (as we have discussed), or tearing up the yard when he's left alone there. However, until he is 18 months old and is past his period of rapid bone growth, he must not engage in strenuous exercise, which includes long walks and jogging. While your Shepherd's bones are still growing, vigorous exercise can cause serious

and lifelong joint disease. (See Chapter 3: Care of Your German Shepherd Dog Puppy.)

Still, this is a large dog that thrives on physical as well as mental activity. Your Shepherd doesn't have to be on the go or played with many hours of the day. Indeed, he will be very happy to lie at your side while you read a book, watch television, or listen to music. But his exercise needs will not be met with one short walk and a few outings in his back yard each day—that is, unless you adopt a senior Shepherd, which is a wonderful thing to do. (See Chapter 12: Finding Your Senior German Shepherd.)

When your Shepherd puppy becomes old enough, take him on long walks. Play fetch with him; he will love your tennis-ball sessions together. Play is more than exercise—it is an integral part of the relationship between human and dog. If you find a sport for the two of you to do together, such as agility or

Shützhund, your bond with your Shepherd will be all the stronger for it.

## Sociability

A sociable dog is comfortable with himself and the world. He's curious and loves to play. Sociability may begin with breed and bloodlines, but it comes to fruition through positive interaction with others, both human and canine.

### With Children

Energetic, fun-loving, and by nature protective, the German Shepherd makes an excellent companion for children. But here again, you, the owner—or in the dog's mind, the pack leader—must set and enforce rules. Teach children not to run up to or pet a newly met Shepherd or any other unfamiliar dog, for that matter. And do socialize your Shepherd to children even if you don't have any.

A GSD will usually take his time getting to know a person, but he may speed up the process for a child and be more patient with the child than with an in-your-face adult. However, a young puppy can be unintentionally hurt by a child who doesn't know the proper way to handle or lift a dog. Conversely, a puppy will nip at everything that gets too close to his face, including the little

### Multi-Dog Tip

You can successfully have a two-Shepherd household, but it would be best to wait until the first dog has bonded with the family and had obedience training before bringing the second one home.

hands and feet of small children. The pup may even think of little kids as littermates. So don't leave a child alone with your new Shepherd for even a minute, as neither has the etiquette skills to know how to treat each other. Monitor your child and puppy's interaction until they both understand how to play nicely together. And never let a young child play tug-of-war with a dog of any age.

### With Strangers

The German Shepherd has too much dignity and suspicion of strangers to give affection lightly. But with ample socialization he will see that each new person in his life is a potential friend—and his friendship, once given, is lifelong. Socialization, like training, is an absolute must for this breed. Start when the dog is a puppy. Socialize him to people of varying ages and, if possible, to dogs of various breeds. The AKC allows that the GSD is known as a "one-man" breed. But it doesn't have to be this way. Whether your dog will have few friends or many is up to you.

A well-trained, well-socialized German Shepherd can display an amazing concern for people outside his family, including total strangers. I learned this one day when my Charlie was three years old. It was a blustery winter afternoon, with snow piled almost to the top of our picket fence. I went out, leaving the dogs home but forgetting to lock the doggy door. While I was out, my husband received a phone call at his place of business from a woman we didn't know—but who obviously knew us. She called to say what happened when she and her two young children walked down our street. As they passed our house, one of our dogs climbed the snow bank, leapt the fence, and walked beside them until they reached the intersection at the end of the block. There he sat and waited until they had crossed the street. The woman then turned and watched as Charlie stood, looked at her a long moment, and finally went home. "I'm certain he waited to make sure we crossed the street safely," the woman told my husband.

I'm certain, too.

### With Other Dogs and Pets

A German Shepherd will generally do well with other dogs as long as he is socialized early and trained properly. Being spayed or neutered is another factor in raising a dog-friendly GSD, but this is not an option if you intend to show your dog. Pack position is also important and will affect each dog's acceptance of a new canine family member. I know of families with multiple Shepherds or Shepherds and other breeds all living in harmony. Bear in mind, though, that a male may be put off by another of his kind moving in, even if his pack position is respected. If you intend to have more than one GSD, tell your breeder, who will know which lines to select from for optimum congeniality. If the breeder doesn't have the right dog for you, she will refer you to another breeder. The breeder may also encourage you to wait at least a year before getting a second dog and to get one of the opposite sex.

Along with many dog breeds possessing a prey drive, the GSD can live compatibly with cats, and some Shepherds and cats living together will form a close bond. But both animals have to be accepting for this to happen, not just the dog. A well-trained adult Shepherd may be easier than a puppy to bring into a home with a cat, as a puppy's energy level is extremely high; he wants to play with everything in sight, and his intelligence hasn't quite kicked in yet. Also, an adult dog that you adopt from an animal shelter or breed rescue can be tested for cat safety and may even have lived with a cat before. However, just because a dog is respectful of one cat does not mean all cats are safe with him. Nor does a dog's seeming indifference or fondness for a cat mean that the two will always be amicable or that the cat will always be safe with the dog. Make certain that the cat has escape routes in all levels of the home. A means of escape can be a cat door leading to another room, floor-to-ceiling climbers, or ledges onto which the cat can jump. At times your dog will want privacy from the cat too, so provide a retreat for him.

The American Society for the Prevention of Cruelty to Animals (ASPCA) recommends that a dog living with a cat or other small animal be crated or otherwise confined away from other family pets when the family people aren't home—even when the other pets are crated. This applies to both a dog who adores the family kitty or hamster and the one who politely tolerates noncanine pets. Trust in a dog is deeply satisfying except when it leads to tragedy.

## Grooming Needs

When it comes to grooming needs, the German Shepherd falls in the moderate range unless he spends a lot of time in the rugged outdoors. But the Shepherd does have a dense double coat, so on a daily basis the time you will spend brushing your dog is about five minutes—much more than a Greyhound requires and much less than a Briard. Daily brushing is necessary to keep your Shepherd from shedding all over the house. Not only does the coat require daily brushing with a slicker brush (a type of brush with short bent wire teeth), but twice a year your Shepherd will blow his coat. Then you will use a shedding rake and, weather permitting, you will do it outside or in the garage if there's rain. Bathing needn't be frequent for a mostly indoor dog unless the dog gets very dirty when playing outside. But the Shepherd's teeth should be brushed daily, for the sake of his health.

## Health Issues

As with many other breeds, and perhaps especially those that rank at the top of popularity charts, the German Shepherd has a number of both serious and minor health issues. Among those that come first to mind of seasoned Shepherd lovers are hip and elbow dysplasia, and degenerative myelopathy (also called chronic degenerative radiculomyelopathy), which we will discuss along with other breed-specific and general illnesses in Chapters 3 and 8. It is because of breed-specific health issues that conscientious breeders stay mindful of selecting good lines from conformation or working stock. Those breeders faithfully test dogs for genetic weaknesses before breeding them. The goal, always, is to protect the breed.

## Trainability

German Shepherds are extremely trainable. It is surprising how quickly they can learn some commands. Frankly, taking your Shepherd to puppy kindergarten and basic obedience classes will probably make you feel like a proud parent. But as with grooming your dog, training must be a daily priority or the time spent in class will have been wasted. Moreover, the GSD must be properly trained if he is to be happy in his own mind and body—as well as being a good citizen. Training is time consuming even when the dog enjoys being trained, which the German Shepherd does. How much time you will spend will vary, depending on your dog, the method used, and how far up the ladder of success you want your dog to go. Watching your dog train in an agility class is exciting. Watching him receive the Canine Good Citizen Certificate is a thrill. So, yes, the German Shepherd is trainable, and the more training you give him—always using positive methods—the closer your bond will be.

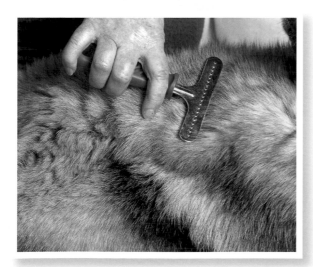

When it comes to grooming needs, the German Shepherd usually falls in the moderate range.

# CHAPTER 2

# FINDING AND PREPPING FOR YOUR GERMAN SHEPHERD PUPPY

You have made up your mind to get a German Shepherd Dog. It's an exhilarating feeling but a feeling also tinged with a bit of anxiety. You may even still be wondering whether you should get a puppy or an adult dog. And if you do get a puppy, how can you make sure that it's a dog with good lines and one who will be right for your family? These questions and many more will be talked about in this chapter—including what needs to be done before bringing "baby" home.

## WHY GETTING A PUPPY IS A GOOD IDEA

There are very good reasons for getting a puppy *or* an adult dog, and we will talk about reasons to get an adult dog in Chapter 5. Pluses on the puppy's side of the scale include that puppies are irresistibly cute and they haven't had time to pick up bad habits. No one has trained them using negative methods that make a dog fearful or suspicious. No one has spoiled them rotten. In effect, you're getting a clean slate when you get a puppy. You'll not only be able to train him using positive methods that enhance your bond with each other, but you'll be able to socialize him so that he'll see the world as a good place. And then there's life expectancy. If all goes well, a puppy will be with you many years. If you have young children, their beloved canine companion will see them through school and perhaps even college. On the other hand, life expectancy for any species is only a prediction, not a guarantee. So calculating the number of years you might enjoy with your German Shepherd should not drive the decision to get a puppy. Nor should being able to choose the puppy's name, as mature dogs are able to adjust to new names.

Rather, get a puppy because you are young at heart yourself and will love playing with and exercising your dog every single day. Get a German Shepherd puppy because you have always wanted a superbly trained dog, and now you have the time to make it happen. If you are certain that your commitment will remain as strong through the years as your desire for a puppy is now, go for it. I promise that however long he lives, you will be glad that you shared those years with him.

Puppies are irresistibly cute, and they haven't had time to pick up bad habits.

## Show-Quality Versus Pet-Quality Dogs

Fanciers often specialize in dogs suited for the show ring, but not all dogs bred in their kennels will turn out to be show quality. Those who don't are deemed pet-quality dogs—which is a high calling in itself. A conscientious breeder will be as determined to place her pet-quality dogs in good homes as she is with her show-quality dogs. In fact, a good breeder who doesn't have the right dog for you at the moment or who has a long waiting list for her dogs (as good breeders so often do) may refer you to another breeder who can offer a puppy to meet your needs without your having to wait.

Pet-quality puppies usually are sold at seven or eight to ten weeks of age, whereas show-quality puppies may be kept longer so that the breeder can better judge whether they really

are destined for a successful show career. As much for the sake of the puppy as for the buyer, the breeder does not want to go wrong in this, so she bases judgment on many factors (such as the angle of the shoulder when the puppy moves) that you and I wouldn't notice. A very fortunate moment in my life, although I couldn't know about it at the time, was when my German Shepherd breeder determined that a pup she had named Chapstick—because she was a "stick off the old Chaps," one of her successful show dogs—really wasn't destined to see Westminster. One of the easiest and most cheerful dogs I've ever owned, Chapstick came to me when she was 12 weeks old, already socialized and well behaved, and virtually housetrained.

Oftentimes a breeder will pick out a puppy that *does* have show-dog qualities and might do fairly well in the ring, but she doesn't foresee him doing as well as his littermates—as with my Chapstick. It is because the breeder doesn't want the buyer looking for a show dog to be disappointed that the puppy is placed with someone wanting a companion dog, and this is one of the reasons why such a breeder is highly regarded in the profession.

Show-dog breeders put a great deal of their time, energy, and money into the ongoing effort of breeding future champions. It's a labor of love, as they are not likely to get rich by breeding dogs. Moreover, they back up their efforts with a written contract guaranteeing no blood deficiencies or inherited breed-specific diseases in the puppy you are purchasing. And the guarantee also often goes for the little guy who gets placed as a companion dog, not a show dog.

## WHERE TO FIND THE PUPPY OF YOUR DREAMS

Of course you realize that the puppy of your dreams is not likely to be found at a puppy mill or a commerical source that uses puppy mills. This isn't to say that puppies at these sources don't need homes. They do. But a conscientious breeder would never sell a puppy by such means. Puppy mills can harbor infectious diseases, and worst of all is that irresponsible breeding has caused GSDs (and other breeds) to have serious health and temperament problems. A commercial source that uses a puppy mill doesn't know what it's getting when it purchases a puppy, and the future owner won't know anything about the puppy's background. The AKC strongly recommends that you get your GSD puppy "from a responsible, ethical breeder whose primary concern is to produce dogs of high quality, good health, and stable temperament." Following this suggestion is

your vital first step in finding the puppy of your dreams.

### Breeders

One way to locate a responsible GSD breeder is to contact the German Shepherd Dog Club of America's (GSDA) regional club in your area. You can do this by visiting www.gsdca.org and clicking on Regional Clubs. Another good way to locate a breeder is to phone veterinarians in your area and ask whether they can recommend a breeder. If the veterinarian has GSD patients, she may provide you with lots of tips on choosing your dog and even caring for your dog. If this is the case, then in addition to having found your breeder, you may also have found your vet.

If there are several GSD breeders in your vicinity, talk with each of them. Ask any questions on your mind about the breed. A good breeder should be accessible and will not rush you off the phone. If too busy to talk when you call, she will be happy to phone you back, and the breeder will have questions to ask you as well, both on the phone and when you go to meet the puppies. When you visit, ask to meet the puppies' mom.

One way to locate a responsible GSD breeder is to contact the German Shepherd Dog Club of America's (GSDA) regional club in your area.

One thing that all good breeders have in common is that they select dogs for their breeding program with soundness of temperament and bone structure who are also known to be intelligent and trainable, with loving personalities. In essence, all legitimate AKC-registered German Shepherd breeders are striving for the perfect dog.

## Show Quality

If your intent is to get a show-quality puppy, the breeder may wish to retain breeding rights and the right to show the dog, in which case you would sign a co-ownership agreement. What this agreement really means is that you, having purchased the puppy and given him a home, are the real owner. You are responsible for the dog, you have the right to move across the country with the dog, and you choose whether or not he dresses up for Halloween. You have the final say in everything *except* the dog's availability for breeding or showing, unless there is a good reason for him not to be available.

## Pet Quality

A puppy deemed as pet quality rather than show quality may be registered by your breeder under the AKC's Limited Registration, a tool the AKC offers responsible breeders so that

### *Want to Know More?*

In Chapter 3 we will talk about how a buyer can ruin a puppy's health through improper care.

they can protect their breeding programs. By opting for Limited Registration, the breeder is assured that the puppy won't be used for breeding purposes or shown in conformation. Does this mean that the breeder thinks this particular puppy is defective in any way? Heavens, no. It's just that the breeder's long experience in breeding and showing dogs tells her that this pup isn't meant for the show ring. The breeder may assure you, though, that your wonderful GSD pup will be eligible, when he grows up, to enter other competitions such as obedience, tracking, and agility tests. He might earn a title or two or three. It just won't be a conformation title.

### Paperwork

In purchasing your puppy, you may be asked to sign a contract that includes health guarantees, spay-neuter agreements, terms of co-ownership if you are entering one, restrictions on breeding, and perhaps living arrangements. The contract may also state that if the dog doesn't work out for you, you will return him to the breeder. Not all breeders will offer, or require, such a contract, though. Mine didn't. But when she heard—secondhand, not from me—that I had lost a Shepherd I'd purchased from her nearly six years earlier to progressive epilepsy, she contacted me and insisted I come choose a puppy from her new litter. In effect, I got two outstanding dogs of good lines and wonderful temperament for the price of one. That's a good breeder.

It's also quite possible that a conscientious breeder who knows that everything possible has been done to produce good, sound, healthy puppies will take a different approach by guaranteeing the puppies "to the end of the drive," as one such breeder said. A bad attitude on her part? Not necessarily. When a breeder goes to such an extreme to put out

Keep dangerous items like electrical cords out of reach of your puppy.

good puppies, it's terribly frustrating to be told months later that a puppy has something wrong with him and the breeder knows it is not her fault.

Your breeder will provide you with an AKC registration application when you purchase your puppy. Be sure that the breeder has completed the appropriate sections of the form and signed it, and if the section you are to fill out looks confusing, the breeder can help you do it correctly. After the AKC receives your completed and signed registration application, your puppy will become part of America's largest registry of purebred dogs and when older will be eligible for the competitive events we spoke of earlier.

## BEFORE HE COMES HOME

Carefully choosing your breed was the first step. Finding your puppy was step two. Step three—arguably the most important—is preparing your home for your puppy.

Attention from children, other family members, and neighbors is the beginning of socialization, one of the most important parts of training your puppy. Training isn't just about "sit," "down," and "stay." It's about learning to trust and being a good canine citizen.

## Puppy-Proofing the Home and Yard

Before bringing your puppy home, ensure his safety by inspecting everything indoors and outside with an eye to what might harm him. By taking as much time as necessary to puppy-proof your home and yard, you protect your puppy from harm and you and your family from potential grief.

### Indoor Hazards

Starting indoors, check each room for items within a puppy's reach that could be chewed, pulled down, or ingested. If you have indoor plants, be sure that they aren't toxic to dogs. (The ASPCA's website lists plants, with photographs, that have been reported as having caused systemic or gastrointestinal effects in dogs.) Even if you are certain that your indoor plants aren't toxic to your puppy, you don't want them to give him a tummy ache or cause his death by chewing, so put them out of his reach. The same goes for family heirlooms, photo albums, shoes, and clothing. Because you can't—and shouldn't—watch your puppy every minute of the day, consider spraying a bitter apple spray on decorative or immovable items that he could get to. Keep the door closed to any room you want to be off limits to your puppy, or else secure the room with a baby gate. (See section "Supplies," later in this chapter.)

Not counting urination, your puppy has three strategies for damaging your belongings: his teeth, paws, and wagging tail. Tape or remove table runners or other hanging material, and put away objects on coffee tables and other low furniture. Of vital importance is that he not get to hazardous materials, so stow out of reach all cleaning and painting products, medications, and anything else that could be poisonous to your puppy. You will also want to secure phone wires and electric cords, which puppies often find particularly appealing to chew. You can wrap them in plastic sheathing or PVC tubing, or spray a deterrent on them such as a bitter apple spray. Training a dog not to tamper with anything plugged into a wall is time well spent.

When you have your children put their toys out of the puppy's reach, explain the importance of not leaving anything on either the floor or low furnishings that their puppy could choke on or swallow. But don't trust young children to remember all the "do's" and "don'ts" that come with safeguarding their puppy. Yes, he is their dog too. But you own all responsibility for his welfare.

If your puppy is one who likes to sink his teeth into wood, you will have little trouble training him not to do it. But you can't do everything, including teaching him what is yours and not his, all at one time. So consider using thick plastic sheeting or PVC tubing to cover chair and table legs and the edges of low wood tables. I must admit, though, that I've had many puppies but have never found tiny teeth marks in chair or table legs. There was the time, though, when an adult dog I adopted chewed a corner off the coffee table. She looked so cute with teakwood hanging from her mouth, I couldn't be upset. (Using carpenter glue to reattach the wood, followed by sanding and staining, will make a table attacked by a dog look almost as good as new.)

### Outdoor Hazards

Now let's look at the possible hazards in your garage and yard. First, if you mulch your garden, be aware that cocoa garden mulch is very toxic to dogs, who unfortunately like the flavor of those cocoa-bean hulls—which contain theobromide and theophylline, two neurotoxins for dogs. Put away chemicals and potential poisons, including fertilizers, insecticides, and of course paint products. Garden hoses, children's toys, and tools with plastic parts or sharp metal edges or points should be secured too. A dog can be injured by open-ended wire lying around. If you have a swimming pool, block access to it, just as you would with children. (When your dog is older, you may want to allow him in the pool with supervision. A dog can drown in a pool if he doesn't know where the steps are to get out or for some reason can't get to them.)

If your yard isn't fenced, of course the puppy will be on leash when he's outdoors. If it is fenced, very carefully check for potential escape routes or small openings into which he could

stick his head and get stuck. (Imagine the dreadful outcome this could have.) Puppies can squeeze through openings in a gate or fence, and they can squirrel through shallow open spaces between the fence and lawn. Speaking of squirrels, if you are outside with your dog off leash and not contained, all it takes is one squirrel running across the street with your pup giving chase for you to lose him. Keeping a dog on leash is keeping him alive and in one piece.

## Setting Up a Schedule

As with people, dogs are happier and have more confidence in themselves when they have a daily schedule to follow. Just as you wouldn't like waking up in the morning wondering when and if you will have a meal, get to use the bathroom, or get some exercise, your dog doesn't want to live with uncertainty either.

A child should never have the chief responsibility of caring for your GSD.

Things can't always be the same, though. Sometimes circumstances will cause a walk or dinner to be late. Weather conditions might prevent outdoor play. That's okay, as long as there's a legitimate reason and the dog isn't deprived of sustenance or a bathroom break long enough to cause suffering. But having a schedule for your dog that you will stick to as much as humanly possible will help him adjust to his new environment, give him self-confidence, and deepen his trust in you. What makes this daily regimen of meals, potty breaks, exercise, and grooming all the more wonderful is his being petted and praised for doing everything on the schedule. When he goes to the bathroom, licks his bowl clean, has his teeth brushed, or obeys a command, he knows that he's being good because you tell him so. He also knows that he's a smart dog who fits very well into this new family he's so lucky to have.

Whether it's just you and the puppy or this is to be a family dog, writing down a schedule will make things go more smoothly. Your family might even want to have a roundtable discussion on who should be responsible for certain chores: keeping the water bowl filled, brushing the dog's coat (and not leaving hair on the floor), putting away toys the pup is through playing with, taking him outside to potty, and cleaning up after him. An older child can post a schedule of tasks on the refrigerator or a bulletin board, and younger children can draw pictures of the tasks being done. But no matter how eager children might be to help, even older children, they cannot shoulder the responsibility of making certain that the dog has a proper diet. They may help with training but cannot assume the role of chief trainer. Nor should a child take the dog out on walks without an adult along. These tasks are too much responsibility for a child. They're for you to do.

## Supplies

Now that you have a schedule in mind, let's consider the supplies needed for your dog's health and welfare. There are many, and you will want to have those that are absolutely essential in your home before the puppy gets there. Shopping before bringing baby home also allows you time to find quality products at good prices. Having ready in advance all the supplies required also will ensure a smooth transition for your pup from his first home to his forever home. There will be less stress for you and more bonding time with your puppy. And by all means, feel free to ask your breeder for product recommendations. The breeder has owned and raised many puppies.

### Baby Gate

A baby gate, or dog-safety gate, has several uses. It will confine your puppy to a specific room in the home, block doorways so that he can't go where you don't want him to go, and can be used to restrain him from going up or down stairs—both stairs inside the house and deck stairs outside. (But don't leave a puppy outside on the deck without adult supervision, not even if the deck slats are too closely spaced for him to stick his head through.). To me a baby gate is an extremely useful tool for puppies and adult dogs. I've even used one to keep a senior canine citizen with failing health from taking stairs that could imperil his life. If you should decide that you don't want to crate your dog, a baby gate will be essential. But I wouldn't want to be without either crate or gate. There is a wide variety of gates for dogs on the market: freestanding, extendable, tall, not so tall—and made of metal, wood, plastic, or wood and wire.

## Collar

For a puppy's first collar, many fanciers choose a nylon flat-buckle style that is inexpensive, easily cleaned, and enlargeable as the puppy grows. My preference—because I'm a chronic worrier—is the quick-release collar, also called a breakaway collar, which is designed to prevent strangulation if the collar should catch on something. A breakaway collar is the only type that you can safely leave your puppy wearing when he is home alone, and it too can be adjusted for size. For a proper fit with either style, you should be able to insert two fingers between your puppy's collar and his neck. And remember that the puppy's neck will enlarge quickly, so check often to see whether the

collar needs to be widened. Later, when your dog is grown, you may choose to invest in a collar as handsome as he is. But no matter the dog's age, he should never be outside without his collar and identification tags.

## Crate

A crate is useful when introducing a dog to his new surroundings and also is an aid to housetraining. Most of all, it's a cozy home within a home where your dog is safe and secure when he has to be confined. Besides, a puppy needs his sleep and should not be interrupted by a child wanting to pick him up or play. Even when your puppy is awake, he can enjoy the comfort of his own "den." This also will be a safe place for him when you are out for a few hours—but not all day, as it wouldn't be fair to keep him cooped up for many hours. The crate must be large enough for him to stand up and turn around in with ease.

German Shepherd puppies grow fast, so you may want to forgo purchasing a puppy-sized crate and get one for an adult dog. If you do, put a barrier in the crate to block off part of it so that the pup won't divide his crate into half-bedroom, half-bathroom. With soft bedding and a favorite toy or two, it will indeed be his own snug den. Wire crates are preferred by many dog owners because they give the dog

For your puppy's first collar, consider a nylon flat-buckle style.

## Save Stuffed Toys

Cuddly stuffed toys can be as much cherished by a dog as they are by a child, but I wouldn't give one to a puppy, who would surely tear it open and perhaps swallow a piece of stuffing. A ripped-open stuffie may also expose a noisemaker that could be ingested. So save stuffies for when your dog is older, and even then prevent him from exposing a potentially dangerous noisemaker. You can remove it yourself and sew the stuffie back up, or save yourself the trouble and buy stuffies that don't go "moo" or "quack." (A stuffie injured in play should be "hospitalized" out of reach of your dog until you have time to restuff and sew it up. Use dental floss instead of thread; it holds up better.)

a good view of his surroundings. But plastic crates with cutouts for air circulation and a wire door are easier to clean as well as being more den-like. There also are soft-sided crates with zippered mesh doors and large storage pockets. These are easy to set up and carry and thus are popular for traveling, especially with show dogs.

I like a wire crate for Shepherds and to have it in the kitchen, where there is usually family activity. You may want to put a second crate in your bedroom while your dog is a puppy, and when he is older the crate can keep him safely confined when riding in the car. Both wire and plastic crates that are kept clean hold up very well and last many years. So purchasing two crates that can be used by a Shepherd in all life stages is not a frivolous investment. Buy a

dog bed that fits the crate or a cushy pad made for dog crates. Whatever you put in the crate should be durable and washable. Imitation sheepskin fits that bill, and once past the teething stage, your pup might appreciate a snuggly quilt. Don't put carpet made from long strings in the crate, as swallowed strings would create a dangerous situation.

### Dog Bed

If you don't have a crate in your bedroom (and I heartily recommend that you do, at least for a while), you will need a dog bed there. And a bed in the family room or wherever you sit watching television or reading in the evening would be much appreciated by your GSD. Any bed you buy should be well cushioned, large enough to allow him to stretch out his legs,

and easily washable. Dogs like to dig in a bed (I call it making the bed) before lying down, so get one that can withstand this treatment. As with the crate, buy a bed that your Shepherd can grow into. There's no point in purchasing one he'll use only for a few months unless you're pretty sure that when he's grown you will want to bring another puppy home.

## Food and Water Bowls

You'll need two large bowls: one for food and one for water. Stainless steel is preferred, as plastic can cause an allergic reaction in dogs, especially if the bowl gets scratched. Ceramic bowls have the advantage of being hard to tip over, but they can crack. Both plastic and ceramic bowls, when even slightly cracked, may harbor dangerous bacteria. Also, recent research has found that using raised feeders contributes to gastric volvulus distortion, or bloat, a usually fatal condition which we will discuss in Chapter 8. Be sure to wash your puppy's food bowl after each use and the water bowl at least once a day—and remember to fill it with fresh water every morning.

## General Grooming Supplies

To care for your Shepherd's thick double coat (fluffy underneath to keep him warm, longer and harsher on top to repel dirt and shed rain and snow), you will need two tools: a slicker brush for daily grooming and a shedding rake for twice a year when the fur is really flying. Another useful tool is the curry comb, which with its short rubber nubs helps remove dead hair from the outer coat. And you will want a flea comb for trapping fleas, which you then dunk in soapy water to suffocate the pests.

On a more pleasant note, you'll need a doggy toothbrush and yummy chicken- or beef-flavored doggy toothpaste. By getting your dog used to having his teeth brushed when he's a puppy, it will be a lifetime ritual that you both will enjoy. His enjoyment will come from that utterly delicious toothpaste. (I haven't met a dog who doesn't love it.) And your enjoyment will come from knowing that you're helping him to stay healthy and keep his teeth.

You'll also need a tearless dog shampoo for when you bathe your dog, usually two to four times a year or more if needed.

His nails must be trimmed every week or two, so buy doggy nail clippers, either the scissors style or the guillotine style, the easier to use of the two. Of even greater ease on both dog and human is a "Dremel-type" rotary grinder. The noise may make the puppy nervous at first, but giving him treats when you turn the grinder on and after each nail is trimmed should make him come to accept the grinder.

For ear cleaning, you may want to find out what your vet recommends. Pet supply stores usually carry a variety of ear-cleaning products, both dry and liquid.

To care for your GSD's double coat, you'll need a slicker brush for daily grooming.

Lastly, you'll need a pooper scooper for your yard and a continuous supply of plastic bags for outside your yard. Being a conscientious dog owner means never leaving your dog's feces where humans or dogs can step on them.

## Identification

Your GSD should never be without an ID tag with your name, address, and phone number—as well as his license tag if your city requires one—attached to his collar. But collars can be lost or removed, rendering ID tags useless. Microchips, however, are permanent, and microchipping is so commonly used now that most shelters and veterinary clinics are able to scan a lost dog to find where he belongs. The microchip is a tiny transmitter, about the size of a grain of rice, that is inserted by syringe under the skin over the dog's shoulders. It isn't painful at all and won't cause an allergic reaction. You'll be given a chip number that you can register into a lost-pet Internet database. This enables the finder of a lost pet to locate his owner. Another option is tattooing, which involves marking a permanent code on the belly or inside flank of your puppy. As with microchipping, the tattooed code is entered in a database. Your vet can advise you on whether to choose microchipping or tattooing.

## Leash

Your puppy's leash (also called a lead) should be 6 feet (2 m) long and made of nylon , cotton, hemp, or leather. Don't buy a vinyl leash, though, as it won't last as long as the other kinds or be as flexible. By purchasing a nylon collar and leash at the same store, you will be able to get them in the same color, which looks attractive. Some people like a braided leash; I prefer mine to be flat and smooth. Retractable leashes are very popular today, but they give the dog a lot of freedom and aren't suitable for walking and training your puppy. If you haven't put a leash on a dog in recent years, hold a few leashes by the loop on the end to determine what is comfortable for your hand.

## Toys

Dogs love toys and people love buying toys for their dogs. It's not only fun to watch them play, but puppies burn a lot of energy in play, and when your pup tires himself out and takes a nap, you'll get some rest too. Only three things will hold you back from buying every great-looking dog toy you see: your bank account, your awareness that not all dog toys on the market are safe for all dogs—and some aren't safe for any dog—and the realization that too many toys left lying around can become a bore, just as with children's toys.

Let's talk about safety, which should be your number-one concern. Toys made of durable rubber are safe for your Shepherd, but the product must state that the rubber is durable—which means your dog can't chew off pieces of rubber and swallow them. Rawhides are not safe for your puppy. Also, pass by dog toys with either plastic parts or dangling strings that can be torn off and swallowed.

Any toy or chew you give your dog should be too large to become lodged in his throat or swallowed, so make sure that your puppy doesn't outgrow his toys and chewies. Nylabone nylon chews of the right size for your pup are virtually indestructible, as are durable rubber toys. A ball of the right size is suitable and can be pushed around by your dog or carried in his mouth.

*Never* give your dog an empty container to play with, or he will look on other containers—including those that once contained toxins—as suitable toys. Of lesser importance, except to your budget and perhaps your sanity, is that old shoes are unsuitable as puppy toys because your dog can't differentiate between the worn-out shoe you gave him and the designer shoes for which you just spent a bundle. But when he's older and wiser, you may teach him to fetch your Manolo pumps—and to put his toys back in his toy box or basket when he's through using them.

## BRINGING PUPPY HOME

Try to choose a time when life is relatively calm to bring your puppy home. A good time *not* to bring him home, if possible, is during the holidays when you have cookies to bake, errands to run, and gifts to wrap. And while socialization is very important for your puppy, having guests coming and going when he is adjusting to this huge change in his life will be stressful to him as well as to you. Of course, if you are very low key about the holidays and typically breeze through the weeks between Thanksgiving and New Year's Eve as if you were on a solitudinous vacation, this would be a swell time to bring your puppy home.

If you can, have an adult relative or friend go with you when you pick up the dog at the breeder's, and have your friend be the driver. This way, you can hold the puppy on your lap on the drive home, wrapped in a blanket or towel if he's very young, or if the weather is

Try to choose a time when life is relatively calm to bring your puppy home.

chilly. In the future you will have him in a crate on car rides, at least until he's big enough to ride in the back seat wearing a harness, but not this trip. He needs the comfort of being gently held, which besides soothing him on this somewhat scary adventure will keep him from causing injury to himself, or heaven forbid, causing an accident (not the peeing kind).

You also want to prevent stomach upset, so ask your breeder to please not feed the puppy the day you bring him home. The breeder probably wasn't planning to, especially if you are picking him up early in the day (which would be the best time), as she too wants to prevent him from getting carsick. But ask just in case the breeder forgot. And before leaving the kennel, try to get the puppy to go to the bathroom. If he won't, consider staying a little longer so that you won't have to make a potty stop on the way home. If you do, however, don't use a highway rest stop, as such areas can be contaminated with organisms that cause dog diseases from which your puppy is not yet protected. For his safety's sake, drive a little farther to find a grassy area. And if he doesn't hold it and relieves himself in the car, you can honestly assure him that it's not important and he's a good puppy.

## Introductions

If children are waiting at home, be sure that they know in advance not to mob the puppy when he gets there. Of course they will be eager to welcome him, but too much attention—especially hands-on attention—may overwhelm him. Introductions should be low key, not noisy. By explaining this to your children before bringing the dog home, hopefully you won't have to tell them when he gets there, which might make them feel bad on what should be a happy occasion. If there are other pets at home, they should also be properly introduced to your puppy. But safety is key here. Don't let a cat near the puppy unless the puppy is in a safe place—your arms (not a child's) or in his crate with the door closed.

One introduction that should be very calming for your dog, who by now is a little stressed and definitely tuckered out, is the introduction to his crate—his secure place with a few puppy treats inside, perhaps a toy and soft bedding to snuggle up on for a much-needed snooze. While he dozes, you can relax by looking at this sweet new member of the family and thinking about the wonderful life you will give him.

## WHAT TO EXPECT THE FIRST FEW DAYS/WEEKS

Your puppy is going to need plenty of time to adjust to his new home, so if at all possible, try to be home with him the first few days. After all, everything is strange here. Where are his mother and littermates? He's looked all around and can't find them. He can't even smell them, and that really is frightening. On the other paw, there is so much exploring to do. And explore he will, along with having a few accidents in spite of your diligence in taking him outside after he wakes, eats, and plays. Speaking of indoors and outdoors—both have noises that are new to him, and some of the noises may seem scary. Don't commiserate if he runs from the vacuum cleaner or your blow-dryer, as that will reinforce his fear. Having small treats in your pockets at all times during this initiation stage will be helpful. Both puppies and older dogs lose their fears more quickly when they're rewarded for losing them. The dog, in his

Your puppy will need socialization to all kinds of people during his first few weeks with you.

puppy way of analyzing things, determines that if every time Mom waves that noisy thing at her head she tosses him a treat—then the noisy thing is his friend, not his enemy. Soon you won't have to give him edibles for his bravery. Words of praise and petting are treats too.

Most important these first weeks—other than bonding with his new family, learning that this place he is in is his true and forever home, and being housetrained—is exposing him to the vast and remarkably varied world. He needs socialization to all kinds of people—young and old, men and women, even different races if possible. The same with dogs. Introduce him to puppies, adult dogs, and different breeds. Take him on short walks and on car rides to places where he'll be welcome, such as pet supply stores. A visit to the veterinarian's office—not for him to be examined, but introduced to the staff and see how nice they are—would be beneficial. All of these interactions are part of a puppy's training. You're teaching him that the world is a good place. And within this period of adjustment, you would be wise to choose a puppy class in which to enroll him. We'll talk in detail about puppy kindergarten in Chapter 4.

## The First Few Nights

There is only one good place for your puppy to sleep at night, and it's in your bedroom and next to your bed. It's understandable for a child to want the puppy to sleep near her, but you will have to explain that the pup is going to need the bathroom in the middle of the night—not just once but two or three times—and you must be the one to take him outside. Besides, he may waken and cry for his littermates, and you will need to comfort him with your touch and soothing words. Because you both are already awake, this would be a

*Nighttime Tip*

The time when your puppy is most likely to miss his littermates is at night. Consider taking a towel with you when you go to pick him up at the breeder's. Have the breeder touch it to each of the puppies, or wrap each one in it for a few minutes. The scent of the puppies will remain on the towel and may be a comfort to your pup in the middle of the night.

good time to take him out to the bathroom. It isn't playtime, though. Carry him outside and put him where you want him to do his business, then praise him for doing it and carry him back up to bed. If he still needs nighttime potty breaks after the first week, you can put a leash on him and have him walk outside with you. But as before, don't play with him or let him roam in the yard, as this could lead to going potty after midnight becoming a habit.

Because he doesn't have other puppies to snuggle with, loosely wrap him in a soft towel when you put him in his crate or in a padded, uncovered laundry basket that he can't climb out of. This can be the towel with his littermates' scent on it or a clean one. Some people advise putting a plush toy in the crate, but I would be leery of this until I knew his chewing habits. Also, if he sleeps in a wicker basket, cover the wicker so that he can't chew on it. Have a spare crate pad or quilt in your bedroom, as he may have an accident in spite of your efforts to prevent it, and you will have to change his bedding. When you get up very early and tired in the morning to take him outside again, keep in mind that this too shall pass and that soon he will be sleeping through the night.

# CHAPTER 3

# CARE OF YOUR GERMAN SHEPHERD PUPPY

You were dedicated to giving your puppy quality care even before you brought him home. You created a safe environment for him and purchased the supplies needed for his comfort and well-being. Now it's time to choose a diet and feeding schedule to meet his needs and a veterinarian to help you keep him in good health, as well as to learn what health issues may crop up and how to deal with them. Care of your puppy also includes teaching him that grooming is one of life's deepest pleasures because it's something special that the two of you do together every day.

## FEEDING A PUPPY

Books can give only general guidelines for feeding your puppy, and we will do that here. But the best advice on what and how much to feed will come from your breeder and your veterinarian. Also, how much to feed depends on the brand of food you choose for your peppy newcomer. A few rules are across the board, though. Young puppies have fewer reserves of the nutrients they need than do mature dogs, and they are also at a point in life when nutritional deficiencies can cause lasting effects. That is why, in spite of

good arguments for home-cooking for your dog when he is older, it is best to feed your puppy a top-quality dry commercial dog food, preferably what he was fed by his breeder. Even Dr. Michael W. Fox, the syndicated columnist and author of many dog books—who offers a home-cooked recipe for dogs—advises us that "puppies should be fed commercial food that is complete and balanced; it will say so on the label. That way they will get the nutrients they need for growth."

Among the things to consider when choosing your puppy's diet is that by spending more on quality food you increase the likelihood of your dog's staying healthy. Because of his outstanding diet, there may even be fewer visits to the veterinary clinic between annual checkups. Something else to consider when choosing what to feed is that what your pup eats now will determine what he considers palatable when he's all grown up. Odors, textures, and even the temperature of what he's fed as a puppy will influence his likes later on. The times of day he's fed matter too. If your puppy's first meal of the day is before sunup, it wouldn't be fair to switch it to late morning when he's older. You don't have to feed him at the same times of day his entire life and certainly not as frequently as he's fed in puppyhood. But he will be happier if his schedule and diet don't change too dramatically as he gets older. If you loved a breakfast of hot cereal when you were a kid, I bet you still enjoy it now.

Your dog's table manners matter too, whether it's his dinner time or yours. Prevent food guarding—which is growling or snapping at anyone who dares come near his chow—by putting your fingers in your puppy's bowl for a few seconds while he's eating. Do this frequently, each time praising him for being a good boy and wishing him bon appetit. And as much as you and your family love the puppy, you must thwart your desire to offer him tidbits while you are eating. Otherwise he will grow up to be a beggar at the table.

## What to Feed a Puppy

After choosing a brand of top-quality commercial dog food for your puppy, forgo the puppy version kibble and purchase the

Among the things to consider when choosing your puppy's diet is that by spending more on quality food you increase the likelihood of having him stay healthy.

adult version, which is recommended by many breeders for several reasons. Foremost is research has shown that large-boned dogs who get too much of any single nutrient are more susceptible to bone, joint, and digestive problems. I checked two well-known brands that definitely are high quality, and in both brands the puppy food contained more crude protein and crude fat than did the adult version. Actually, adult food is suitable for most GSDs throughout their lifetimes, including the senior years. Even if you should find a very good puppy kibble with ingredients identical to the adult version, it will be more expensive. As my breeder put it, "Puppies need the larger kibble to chew, and why pay more for the same thing just because it's in a different form?"

## How Often to Feed

For a Shepherd eight or nine weeks old, it is generally advised that he be fed three meals a day, with this schedule continuing until he is six months old. However, if the pup is a little underweight, your breeder might suggest you give him an extra feeding for a short time to help him catch up. (You want him to be lean, not thin.) After he reaches the six-month mark, you can give him two feedings a day. He may even indicate when he's ready to go down to two feedings by not eating all of his lunch. Regarding how much he should eat, there is no single answer. There are guidelines, though, and these should be given by your breeder before you take your puppy home. As the months go on, consult with the breeder or with your vet about increases in the amount fed. (At the six-month mark, my Shepherds consumed six cups of food a day and were at an ideal weight. After that, they were fed considerably less, about four and a half cups a day. But this could be too much food for your dog.) Be sure to ask your vet when and by how much you should reduce the amount of food. In fact, you can periodically stop by the veterinarian clinic to have your puppy weighed. There will not be a charge for this, and as an added benefit, the brief visit will socialize your puppy to both people and pets.

## What Times of Day to Feed

The times of day when you'll feed your dog depend on your family's schedule. If you leave for work at seven in the morning—which hopefully you won't be doing the first two or three weeks after you get your puppy—or drive the kids to school at eight, the dog must be fed early enough for him to be taken outside to the bathroom before you leave. Even if you're going to be a stay-at-home mom to your lucky pup, don't wait for him to signal after eating that he needs the bathroom. As soon as he's through, pick him up and take him outdoors to his potty area. After he goes, reward him with praise and a very small treat. This is part

of his housetraining. And think how easy it is. Just by giving him a regular feeding schedule, you ensure regular elimination.

Some people advise free feeding for puppies and adult dogs as well. Free feeding—also called self feeding—means that you leave a constant supply of food for your dog so he

can eat whenever he wants and however much he wants. This method was tested on some German Shepherds with half the dogs being allowed to self feed. The amount the other dogs were fed in a given day was 75 percent of what the free feeders ate. The result of this experiment was that the free-fed group had more than twice as many dogs with hip dysplasia (a disorder we will talk about later in this chapter) as the group that had restricted rations. Although I know of responsible dog owners who free feed dogs of all ages, I strongly believe that this is not the way to feed a growing German Shepherd.

### Treats

The treats you give your puppy when training him aren't part of a feeding schedule, but they do have calories and should be counted as part of the pup's daily food allowance. They should also be nutritious and reasonably kind to the dog's teeth. No miniature marshmallows for your dog, please! Cut treats up into tiny pieces so that you can reward your pup often without overfeeding him. Besides being healthful and small, treats used during training should be soft so that your pup can chew and swallow them quickly. Crunchy treats are better for his teeth but won't do in a training session. My husband bakes crunchy biscuits for our dogs,

The treats you give your puppy should be counted as part of his daily food allowance.

but soft and small and nutritious commercial liver treats are a staple in our home. Morsels of cooked (but not fatty) chicken or beef and cheese are also good rewards. To find out how much food you're feeding while training your puppy in a given day, fill an 8-ounce measuring cup with tiny treats in the morning and see how much is left at puppy's bedtime. If he's getting a cup of treats a day, deduct this from his scheduled meals.

## GROOMING A PUPPY

Daily grooming of your puppy, beginning the day after he comes home and continuing throughout his life, will benefit him tremendously. Grooming is more than keeping a pet beautiful; it's keeping him healthy. And your grooming him cements your relationship as much as your being the keeper of his food bowl. In fact, you can instruct someone else what to put in your dog's food bowl, and it won't be any less delicious because you didn't do it. But no one can groom him exactly the way Mom or Dad does, and that's special.

### Bonding Time

Grooming requires touch, and your touching a puppy in ways that comfort and please him create deep emotional attachments between you both. This is called bonding. Indeed, research has shown that physical contact with your dog is as rewarding to him as your giving him his best-loved treats. Grooming can also reveal a problem that otherwise would have taken longer to discover. For instance, if your puppy shies away when you touch his head, this could signal an ear problem. The more you touch your puppy in a gentle, soothing way, the more he will appreciate your touch. Once the bond between you takes hold, your dog will know that you never mean to hurt him with your hands or a grooming

Grooming your puppy will help you bond with him and keep an eye on his overall health.

tool, but he will let you know if he's hurting somewhere by crying or moving away from your touch.

Another result of being gently handled during grooming sessions is that once your puppy is accustomed to your touch, he will be more receptive to handling by the rest of his family, family friends, and his vet—not to mention handlers and judges if he's destined for the show ring. There's just no end to the benefits of his acceptance of human touch.

But bonding does not mean being joined at the hip. Your puppy, after a day or two, should explore his home and yard with relative freedom—meaning that you are nearby but not shadowing him every minute. Still, if you're going to be absorbed in a project indoors or in the yard, you will want to know what the puppy is up to while you're slaving away. Consider purchasing an exercise pen, also

called an ex-pen, for such times. The equivalent of a baby's playpen, the ex-pen is collapsible and easy to carry from room to room or to set up outdoors. That way your pup can play with toys and snooze in his pen while you work. It's also a good tool to have if you prefer to housetrain your puppy without confining him to a crate.

## Health Check

By grooming your Shepherd daily you will come to know every part of his body; you'll know when there's a change anywhere. Our doctors advise us to be familiar with our own bodies and be alert for change, and it makes good sense to do this for our pets as well. Whether an eye, ear, or skin problem; a cut or sore or small tumor anywhere on his body; or inflammation of the gums—nothing will elude you. If there is sensitivity to touch anywhere but you don't feel a lump or skin problem, consult with your vet anyway. Depending on what you report, he or she may take a wait-and-see approach or want you to come in right away. During grooming you may detect a bad odor from the mouth or ears or a hot and dry nose—even tiny parasites that don't show on his coat. Here's a hint for detecting nasty critters on your perfect dog: blow gently on your puppy's tummy and brush the hair on his back and sides backward. If small dark specks scurry or hop away or something black that looks like dirt is on the skin, your pup probably has fleas. Ticks, which can be light or dark, will cling to the skin or walk slowly on the dog. If you do find critters on your dog, don't think for a second that it's your fault. Neither of these parasites, which we'll talk about in Chapter 8, indicate poor housekeeping.

## How to Get Your Puppy Used to Grooming

I confess to never having had a German Shepherd puppy who didn't enjoy being touched all over from day one. But some puppies do feel nervous about being handled, and those are the ones who most need to be oh-so-gently and happily touched all over. Make it a game. If your pup realizes that you're having fun, he will too. Go slowly and reward him with tiny treats for allowing you to touch his feet, knees, bottom, tummy, chest, muzzle, ears, chin, gums—the works. You touch his tail, he gets a treat. You touch the tip of his darling nose—another treat. However, if he doesn't like having his nose or toes or teeth touched, don't force it. Move on to a different body part, and when you come back to the feet, touch one toe for just a second or two, then treat him. Repeat the sequence with the next toe. Pretty soon you may find yourself saying, "This little piggy went

to market," with your puppy looking calm but eager for the next toe to be touched. After he has become used to your touching him all over, touching by the family comes next. But children should not do this unsupervised, as accidentally hurting the puppy would make the child feel terrible. Even worse, the puppy could become fearful of the child.

## Grooming Supplies

Your puppy is too young to require grooming with a shedding blade. Your slicker brush can be used for grooming his coat every day, or you can purchase a grooming tool that my Shepherd puppies always enjoyed and is effective on adult dogs too. Called a Zoom Groom, the "brush" removes loose hair without pulling on the fur. It has "fingers," or "nubs," or whatever you want to call them that reach through the coat to gently make contact with the dog's skin—just as you might enjoy doing with your fingers.

Once the puppy is used to having his teeth touched, begin brushing them daily. First, purchase toothpaste made for dogs, as your toothpaste gets frothy and probably would taste as bad to him as his toothpaste would to you. Besides, your toothpaste isn't meant to be swallowed, and dogs don't rinse and spit. Use a doggy toothbrush instead of a finger brush while he's very young, as your finger is larger than the toothbrush and his mouth is still small. His toothbrush probably is angled to be comfortable in his mouth and also has large bristles for large dogs at one end of the handle and small bristles at the other for puppies and small breeds. Using the smaller end of the brush, start gradually and of course be very gentle. Happily praise him while he's experiencing that yummy doggy toothpaste that probably would make you gag if it was in your mouth. It's better to start slowly, brushing just a few teeth and increasing the number as he grows used to this routine. Even though the toothpaste is a treat in itself, reward him with a tiny treat or two immediately following the brushing. Your dog's toothbrush should always have soft bristles that won't be harsh on his mouth and gums. When the bristles become worn down they become rougher, and it's time to get a new toothbrush.

At around four or five months, puppies start getting their permanent teeth. This period of "teething" can be painful. To ease the pain he will want to chew a lot—possibly on your hand and probably on furniture. Discourage this and try to help him in other ways. A washcloth or small towel that has been soaked in water, wrung out, and then rolled up and frozen may be a helpful chewy for when he hurts. You can purchase a chew toy specifically made for teething puppies. But it's possible that chewing on a teething toy will be painful. Don't give him any hard chew toys until he has all his adult teeth, and even then be mindful of what you buy. Read what the packaging says. Do research if you're not sure that the product is safe. Young teeth can fracture or break. Oh—one other thing. You probably won't be able to put any of his baby teeth under his pillow for the tooth fairy to find, as your puppy will probably swallow them all.

Speaking of purchases and grooming supplies, if you live in a rural area where

## Pet Insurance

If you are thinking of purchasing health insurance for your Shepherd, a good time to do it is when he's still a puppy. Dogs, like people, can get sick even when they eat well and exercise, and like us, they need routine checkups. Ask your vet and other dog owners to recommend insurance companies, then compare rates and find out what's covered and what isn't in the policies offered. If your dog has a preexisting condition, you don't want a policy that excludes it. Also find out whether the insurance covers illnesses that are associated with particular breeds. Most companies offer basic and upgraded plans. Look them over carefully before choosing your plan. If you have more than one pet (whether two or three dogs or a mix of dogs and cats), ask the insurer whether a multiple-pet discount is offered. Know what you're buying so that there will be less chance of your being disappointed in the company or policy you choose.

there is a possibility of your dog's coming into hostile contact with a skunk, you may want to be proactive and buy a commercial product for removing the nasty, foul odor that will envelop your poor puppy. These products are easy to find online and in pet supply stores. (It wouldn't hurt to read and memorize the instructions, then put the bottle on a shelf and hope you'll never have to use it.) Another way to remove skunk odor is by applying a mouthwash such as Listerine to the affected areas on your dog, then let it soak a few minutes before you rinse it off. You may have to repeat the steps once or twice. While cleaning a dog with any product that removes skunk odor, avoid getting it in his eyes, as it will sting. If the skunk sprays your dog in the face, use a washcloth or paper towels to very carefully apply the cleaning solution.

## HEALTH

Helping your puppy maintain good health requires teamwork—with the team consisting of you and your puppy's veterinarian.

### Finding a Vet

Just as important as providing your Shepherd with a good home environment and a healthful diet is providing him with quality medical care—both preventive and when he is ill. Don't wait until your puppy needs to see a veterinarian to find one for him. The ideal time to choose your dog's doctor is before you bring your pup home or very soon after. Your breeder can refer you to a vet, if the location is suitable, or else give you suggestions based on what she has heard about other veterinary clinics. Another source for finding a vet is your dog-loving friends or neighbors.

If you have several recommendations that all seem good, call each clinic and ask questions. What does a routine visit cost? Will another veterinarian be there to see your dog if his regular vet isn't available? Does the vet to whom you were recommended have a specialty? Vets often do, the same as medical doctors. Veterinarians also must take continuing education courses to keep up with new information and protocols and do this throughout their entire careers. Impressive, isn't it? I think of this when I move to another city or state, and it makes me feel more relaxed about finding a good vet for my dogs.

Questions to ask your potential veterinarian should include the

The ideal time to choose your dog's doctor is before you bring your pup home or very soon after.

protocol on vaccinations. And consider asking what the vet recommends for feeding your pup. Even if you've already decided with the help of your breeder on a food brand and schedule, a second opinion should be welcome. No matter what questions you ask, if the vet answers in "medicalese" that you can't quite understand, ask for an explanation in a way you can understand. The vet has probably had this happen many times and wishes she was better at explaining medical terms in an easy to understand way.

Keep in mind that the vet you decide on doesn't need to have other German Shepherds in the practice. She just has to like German Shepherds, be very good at what does, and take time to listen to your concerns and get to know your dog as an individual. That way, in an emergency situation, your Shepherd will have a doctor who knows him well and whom he already trusts. Speaking of emergency situations, they do not always happen during regular veterinary clinic hours. So along with finding a good veterinarian, you will want to find a good emergency clinic in your area. Your vet can advise you on this, as can your

breeder. And because you won't be using the emergency clinic on a regular basis, keep the address and phone number where you can see it in your home and in your car.

### The First Checkup

Your puppy's first checkup is a getting-to-know-you time. The doctor will ask you where you got your dog, if she doesn't already know, and while you two talk will be showing your dog—by voice and by touch—that she is kind and can be trusted. While at the clinic he will be weighed, and the vet will check his heart and lungs with a stethoscope. His eyes, ears, nose, mouth (including his teeth), skin, coat, feet, and nails also will be checked. His abdomen and groin area will be palpated, and the vet will feel along the length of his spine. Hopefully he won't mind any of this because you have already gotten him used to being touched all over. And I'd bet my dogs' next Frosty Paws that the doctor will reward your pup with treats for being such a good patient.

### Vaccinations

Vaccinations are a wonderful thing for humans and their pets, as they provide immunity against dangerous and often lethal diseases. But the subject of vaccinating dogs has become somewhat controversial, and for good reason. Vaccinosis is an acute autoimmune disease brought on by adverse reaction to a vaccine. It is because of vaccine-related diseases that concerned veterinarians have for some time been changing their protocols. They know that vaccines are necessary to protect our pets from certain diseases, but they also want to avoid overvaccinating and giving vaccines that may not be necessary for all dogs. (The difference between "necessary" and "not necessary" can be determined by the dog's lifestyle and environment.) Also, your vet may schedule

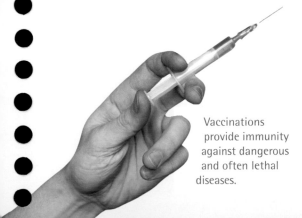

Vaccinations provide immunity against dangerous and often lethal diseases.

vaccines a couple of weeks apart to reduce the risk of soreness or a possible reaction. Our concerns about certain vaccinations are legitimate. Even so, we should be grateful that a single combination vaccine can ward off many devastating diseases to which our dogs are susceptible. Below is a list of dog diseases for which there are vaccines.

**Bordetella:** Bordetella, also called "kennel cough," causes a nagging, raspy cough but generally is not fatal. However, it is highly contagious, and quality boarding facilities will not accept dogs that aren't protected against bordetella. But even when protected against bordetella, a dog may still catch kennel cough. Fortunately, kennel cough usually isn't overly serious and can be treated with antibiotics.

**Coronavirus:** Canine coronavirus is a viral infection that affects the intestinal tract, causing very odorous diarrhea for about a week. Highly contagious but rarely fatal, coronavirus is not a disease your dog absolutely must be protected against. Find out how your vet feels about it. Some veterinarians recommend it only for show dogs and for others who on a regular basis come into contact with many other dogs.

**Distemper:** Canine distemper is a highly contagious viral disease that is fatal to most puppies. Adult dogs die of it too but have a better chance of survival. Even so, they are likely to be paralyzed by the disease and lose some or all of their hearing, vision, and sense of smell—not a good life for a dog. Symptoms of distemper include diarrhea, vomiting, pneumonia, and neurological problems. Your vet will administer a series of three or four

vaccinations to assure that your GSD will not be stricken by distemper.

**Hepatitis:** Infectious canine hepatitis is a viral disease that attacks the liver, lungs, kidneys, and spleen. Spread via the urine and eye secretions of affected dogs, it is characterized in mild cases by loss of appetite, depression, mild fever, and often a bluish cast in the cornea of the eye. In some dogs, especially puppies, the symptoms may include abdominal pain, diarrhea, vomiting, and swelling of the head and neck. Puppies usually receive a series of three shots for hepatitis—a disease that can result in sudden death.

**Leptospirosis:** Leptospirosis is a bacterial infection often spread through urine, especially the urine of rodents. It can damage a dog's liver and kidneys and in severe cases be fatal. Symptoms include vomiting, fever, and lethargy. In spite of this, many puppies get allergic reactions to the vaccine—with the reactions ranging in severity from mild to fatal. Hence, many veterinarians no longer vaccinate against leptospirosis routinely. Talk to your vet about it.

**Lyme Disease:** Lyme disease, which is spread by the deer tick, causes lethargy, loss of appetite, and often lameness. There is a vaccine for Lyme disease, but unfortunately it provides only short-term immunity and therefore annual revaccination is recommended. Many veterinarians believe that the Lyme vaccine may predispose a dog toward Lyme nephritis, a rare but severe complication of the disease. Because of this, the vaccine is controversial even in

## *Want to Know More?*

For more information on GSD health and wellness, see Chapter 8: German Shepherd Health and Wellness.

areas where the deer tick is common. A new vaccine for Lyme, recently released, may be a significant improvement. At the time of this writing, though, it is too soon for a full evaluation.

**Parainfluenza:** Canine parainfluenza, characterized by coughing and hence sometimes, like bordetella, called kennel cough, is an infection of the upper respiratory system. Spread via nasal and oral secretions of infected dogs, it is highly contagious. Puppies are usually given a series of three vaccinations for parainfluenza, and your vet may give them in combination with other vaccines.

**Parvovirus:** Canine parvovirus (CPV), called "parvo" for short, is also highly contagious, and puppies usually receive a series of three vaccinations for it. This is a viral disease that attacks the dog's heart muscle, intestinal tract, and white blood cells—causing him to suffer from vomiting, severe and foul-smelling diarrhea, depression, high fever, and loss of appetite. Puppies who survive parvo, which can be fatal within a few days of the initial symptoms, may have permanent heart

damage. An outbreak of parvo is hard to eradicate, as the virus spreads through contact with feces of already infected dogs and is transported from place to place by dog paws and the shoes and clothing of people.

**Rabies:** The rabies vaccine is mandatory for your dog, as it should be, because this viral infection attacks the nervous system and can be spread to any mammal, including humans. Worse, it is widespread in North America and is always fatal once symptoms appear. The rabies vaccine should not be given at the same time as other vaccinations.

The time not to vaccinate is when a dog is sick, injured, pregnant, or nursing. Also, many veterinarians and a majority of veterinary schools now recommend that vaccinations be repeated every three years rather than annually or every two years. The American Animal Hospital Association (AAHA), an international association of more than 36,000 veterinarians, recommends that you ask your vet about the efficacy and duration of recommended vaccines. Additionally, you will also need to check with your city or town.

Puppies are usually given a series of three vaccinations for parainfluenza.

## Puppy-Specific Illnesses

While your Shepherd puppy may grow into old age without experiencing any illnesses specific to his breed, you should know what these illnesses are and how to recognize them. So let's talk about illnesses, minor and severe, that are commonly found in GSD puppies.

### Carpal Subluxation Syndrome (CSS)

Frequently called down pasterns and also referred to as subluxated pastern/hyperextended hock syndrome, CSS is a condition that causes a dog to walk with his pasterns (the part of the leg between the elbows and feet) down almost to the wrist joint. This condition can be seen with or without the accompanying condition of downed (subluxated) hocks. It is most common in German Shepherd puppies but also is seen in several other large breeds, including Labrador Retrievers. Many knowledgeable fanciers think that downed pasterns in GSDs may be caused by a high-protein diet, while others feel that it is purely a hereditary matter. If you see your puppy walking on his pasterns instead of the pads of his feet, let your breeder know, as well as your veterinarian—either or both of whom may suggest a change of diet. And don't panic. My Charlie began walking on his front pasterns one day when he was a puppy, and a few weeks later he stopped doing it.

### Elbow Dysplasia

Elbow dysplasia, like hip dysplasia (see below), is a heritable disease with a high occurrence in large breeds such as the German Shepherd. Onset usually occurs between four and six months of age, with affected dogs becoming lame or having an abnormal gait characterized by excessive paddling (which looks like flipping) of the front feet. Range of motion

> ## *Multi-Dog Tip*
>
> As intelligent as GSDs are, an adult dog may not understand why he is fed just twice daily when the new pup is fed more often. Giving your grown-up dog a big tasty biscuit when the puppy has those extra meals will help remind him that he is still the love of your life.

in the elbow is decreased, and the dog may hold his elbows out or tucked in and perhaps stand with his feet rotated outward. According to the Orthopedic Foundation for Animals (OFA), at what age lameness will actually occur can't be predicted, and beginning signs may be subtle. Treatment for elbow dysplasia is often a combination of medical and surgical management. Weight control, exercise in moderation, and anti-inflammatory medications play an important role.

### Exocrine Pancreatic Insufficiency

Exocrine pancreatic insufficiency, also called EPI, is a medical condition in which the pancreas of the affected dog stops producing enough digestive enzymes to digest food normally in the small intestine. In the United States about 70% of dogs with EPI are German Shepherds, with the dog usually being between one and five years of age at the time of diagnosis. This is a serious condition because if your GSD can't digest his food, he can't absorb all the nutrients he needs. Typically, the exocrine functions of the pancreas malfunction in one of two ways. In acute pancreatitis, the pancreas becomes inflamed, causing the dog to vomit, lose his appetite, and become dehydrated. Other symptoms you may notice in a dog with EPI are a ravenous appetite, very smelly and soft stools, noisy sounds from the digestive tract, and excessive drinking of water. If your dog has these symptoms, take him to the vet's as soon as possible. EPI has the potential to be life threatening, but there is effective treatment, often involving the replacement of pancreatic enzymes and occasionally oral antibiotics. Treatment is a lifelong commitment, and your vet will counsel you in how to feed your dog a tasty meal that combats the EPI while keeping your boy happy. If your dog isn't severely affected, it may even be possible to regulate the condition just be feeding a low-fat, low-fiber diet and giving an over-the-counter enzyme supplement. EPI is serious, but many dogs with it live a relatively normal life that includes enjoying their food.

## Hip Dysplasia

Hip dysplasia, which was first diagnosed in 1935, is seen in many breeds but especially in large dogs, including the German Shepherd. Hip joints of dogs who develop dysplasia are normal at birth, and the age of onset is typically 4 to 12 months. Usually the dysplasia will occur in both legs, but it can occur in just one hip of the affected dog. Puppies may show pain in the hip, limp when walking, or walk with a swaying gait. When getting up, they experience difficulty in the hindquarters.

One way to erase this problem from the German Shepherd's profile is, in the words of my breeder, to "breed good hips to good hips to good hips." But hip dysplasia, although heritable, is not always genetically transmitted. My breeder and yours know all too well, and with much sadness, that how a Shepherd is raised plays a vital role in this major concern of all GSD lovers. Help prevent hip dysplasia

Elbow and hip dysplasia have a high occurrence in large breeds such as the GSD.

by not giving your dog too much exercise or overfeeding him when he's young. The last thing you want to do is feed a high-caloric diet to a growing Shepherd, as the rapid weight gain will place increased stress on his hips. Also, be wary of inappropriate exercise during your puppy's period of rapid bone growth. Take him on short walks, not long ones. He should not jump down from a height taller than he is at the shoulder, and there should be no strenuous exercise, which includes jogging, until he is at least 18 months old. Even then, don't exercise him to the point of exhaustion, and never ever force exercise.

As with elbow dysplasia, the age at which a dog with hip dysplasia will show clinical signs of lameness can't be predicted. Medical treatment includes restricting activity and giving medication prescribed by your vet. Swimming, or canine hydrotherapy (see Chapter 13) can improve muscle mass and joint flexibility without overstressing the hips. There is new research showing that minerals containing selenium can help in the prevention of hip dysplasia, but don't give your dog any supplement without discussing it first with your vet. Giving the wrong vitamins or minerals in an attempt to treat any disorder can make matters worse. Surgical interventions for hip dysplasia, including total hip replacement, depend on the dog's age and condition. Your vet may recommend a surgeon for consultation, or you can find a board-certified surgeon through the American College of Veterinary Surgeons (ACVS). Visit www.acvs.org, click on Animal Owners, and then click on Find a Surgeon in Your Area. The OFA offers a consoling note on its website, www.offa.org. Some dogs with hip dysplasia will play vigorously as if nothing is wrong.

## Panosteitis

Panosteitis, an acute shifting lameness of growing dogs, is also called "long bone disease" or "wandering lameness," and often just "growing pains" or "pano." It is self-limiting and typically eases with maturity, but it causes deep pain. Definitely a breed problem in North America, panosteitis is caused by excessive bone production on the long bones. It generally presents between 5 and 12 months of age. Treatment may include analgesics and anti-inflammatory medications to make the pet more comfortable until the problem runs its course. My Chapstick had pano and it went away without surgery.

### Soft Ears

All German Shepherds are born with floppy ears, and normally the ears begin to stand erect in the second or third month. But through an inherited recessive trait, some GSDs never develop the ear musculature required for this to happen. These floppy-eared dogs are also more prone to ear infections than a GSD with erect ears. A GSD with perennially soft ears will never win Best in Show, but he's your sweetheart—and those floppy ears may come to endear him to you all the more.

All German Shepherd Dogs are born with floppy ears.

## SPAYING/NEUTERING

There are many good reasons why you should spay or neuter a puppy at the age-appropriate time, but only one valid reason why you shouldn't: he or she is destined for the show ring. You may have heard that neutering makes a male dog effeminate. Not so. That's ridiculous. He will still be a guy, and both you and he will know it. But an unneutered male can become more aggressive, especially with other male dogs, and even in his own home. He also is more likely to mark indoors, which you certainly don't want. The truth is that keeping him intact will make training him to be a good boy at home and everywhere else a much more difficult task. An equally unwanted result of not neutering your pup is that he may try to get loose to roam the neighborhood,

which can result in dog fights, being hit by a car, eating garbage or hazardous chemicals, or even being stolen. Another safety factor is that neutering is removal of the testicles, and a dog without testicles can't get testicular cancer. A neutered dog does remain at risk for prostate cancer, but this is a very rare occurrence in neutered dogs.

Spaying your female GSD is equally important, as by doing so you reduce her chances of getting breast or ovarian cancer, or a uterine disease. She also won't be at risk for impregnation by whatever male dog happens to make sexual contact with her when she's in heat.

So you see that by spaying or neutering your Shepherd you'll have done the responsible thing for your dog and your neighborhood while making life easier for yourself.

# CHAPTER 4

# TRAINING YOUR GERMAN SHEPHERD PUPPY

Training your GSD while he's a puppy is a must if he is to have the quality of life you committed to giving him when you told the breeder, "I want this dog." Your puppy is always learning, and what he learns is up to you. If you don't teach him while he's very young to go potty outdoors and walk nicely on leash, you will have trained him that peeing indoors and pulling as hard as he's able to on leash are not real issues. Then, when the time comes that you do try to teach him good manners, he will be confused and resistant—and rightly so. But teaching him the basics of good behavior now will make him receptive to learning even more behavior-enhancing skills as he gets older. A trained dog is a happy dog. He knows what he should and should not do and is spared the frustrations of uncertainty and frequent reprimands. His bond with his family isn't frayed at the edges by his misbehavior and the scoldings that ensue when he misbehaves. Moreover, a dog as smart as the German Shepherd knows when he's away from home whether he is liked and admired or not liked and feared. Which of these two societal options do you want for your dog? Right! So let's get started on making him a pleasure to

know and an ambassador for his breed. And remember that you get what you train for.

## INTRODUCTION TO TRAINING

Training your puppy is essential to his well-being, and the time you put into it, which will be considerable, should be rewarding and fun for you both. To make it fun, all you need are treats and what I call the three Ps: praise, petting, and patience.

### Why Is Training Important?

Training is important because without it your puppy and you will have problems that over time will grow bigger and more difficult to deal with. You simply won't be happy with an untrained or minimally trained German Shepherd. If your puppy is between 8 and 16 weeks old, now is the ideal time for training to begin, as it is the most impressionable time of his life. Everything that happens, good or bad, makes an impression on him. Don't waste a day of this receptive period, during which he soaks up everything he's taught—either purposely or unintentionally. His training begins the day you bring him home, when you show him where to potty and where he will eat and sleep. From then on, most of his training will take place at home, as what he is taught in class must be practiced a number of times a day between classes. And that's good, because every training session gives your puppy physical exercise, mental stimulation, and the comfort and fun of being with you—all while growing more confident in himself. You train him; he wins. That's a positive idea on which to build!

## The Importance of Positive Training

Not so many years ago, the philosophy of dog training included harsh methods with the purpose of showing the dog quickly and forevermore who was boss. Some methods were designed to mimic how a puppy's mother would have administered discipline, such as grabbing the scruff of the errant dog's neck firmly but without causing pain. Another way to correct an errant puppy was the "alpha roll" or "knock down, rollover" in which the trainer rolled or flipped the dog onto his back and held him in place with one hand on his throat and the other hand on his stomach. When the pup averted his eyes from the person holding him in place and relaxed his body, he was released. Methods such as this are not meant to hurt, but they can hurt if not performed correctly—and in addition they can make him fearful.

The alpha roll almost disappeared from use but unfortunately has made a comeback and is popular with certain trainers once again. In the relationship between human and dog, of course the human must be top dog. That is for the dog's benefit. But for us to be top dog, we must train our pups to obey a variety of commands, from not moving when we don't want them to (which can save a dog's life), to

*By the Numbers*

Between two and three months of age, a GSD puppy should begin learning his daily schedule of eating, eliminating, being groomed, and going to bed at night. He will also quickly learn where his belongings are kept and where he is expected to go potty. Your job, after teaching him the "where and when" of life is to keep him on schedule and make sure that his belongings and bathroom are kept clean and safe for him.

walking nicely on leash in all circumstances—which keeps us from being pulled off our feet and makes our dogs good citizens.

Today we do this by training with positive reinforcement—meaning that the focus is on what we want the dog to do, not what we don't want him to do. We train our dogs by consistency of method in order not to drive them nuts and by being patient in order to show that we have confidence in them. Our tools, besides consistency and patience, are delicious treats, generous praise, and our loving touch. From the moment you meet your puppy until the end of his life, never use your hands to punish, only to praise. You'll like yourself better if you do this. If your Shepherd doesn't obey a command you've taught him, he doesn't get rewarded—but he doesn't get scolded either. Keeping training sessions short, easy, and fun is also part of positive reinforcement. If he enjoyed working on the *sit* command today, he'll look forward to working on it again tomorrow.

When training your puppy, try not to vary the way you communicate with him. Use the same words and hand signals for each command he learns so that he won't get confused. Also avoid using your puppy's name in combination with correction words such as "no" or "wrong," as his name shouldn't be said in an angry or scolding tone. And while training your puppy, also teach young children what is permissible and not permissible in training him. Make sure that they understand that the puppy is not to be punished or shouted at for doing something wrong. He shouldn't be forced onto his back or in any other position he doesn't want to be in. Also explain that teasing the puppy by holding a toy or treat out of reach to get him to jump up is harmful to his growing bones. It

can also result in excessive barking—a difficult habit to break, as I know from experience with another breed. Children don't like being teased and should be able to understand that animals don't like it either. When explained briefly and in simple terms, they understand health hazards too.

Training is forever. Long after your puppy has learned to sit on command, he will associate sitting with being rewarded. So if he suddenly sits and looks up at you expectantly, and you don't have treats in your pocket, reward him with praise and petting. Your voice and the touch of your hand will always be appreciated. As a matter of fact, your love and praise are what he lives for.

Always remember that you get what you train for with your GSD puppy.

### Clicker Training

Another sound your dog will love hearing, should you decide to use clicker training as your method of positive reinforcement, will be the distinctive click of a small device that's easy to hold in your hand and will fit in your pocket. With clicker training, you click at the very moment your dog does what you want him to do, and you immediately follow through with a treat. You also teach verbal and hand signals so that when your puppy is trained to obey your commands you can stop using the clicker and communicate with him using just your voice and/or hand signals. If you clicker train, there are rules that must be followed for the method to work. Paramount is that the puppy must be treated every time you click, even when you click accidentally, which will happen now and then. You also

Training is important because without it your puppy and you will have problems that over time will grow bigger and more difficult to deal with.

must remember to click just once when your dog does what he's supposed to do, as multiple clicks for one required action will undermine the method's premise of one click, one treat. Keep training sessions short, five minutes at most, as you would if training a puppy by another method. And to make certain that your pup doesn't lose faith in the clicker, instruct children not to play with it. Even if they're in their bedroom with the door closed, the puppy will hear the click and be very upset that he isn't getting treats.

In lieu of the clicker, you can also use a marker word, such as "Yes!" to mark the desired behavior. It's just that the clicker can sometimes be more precise. Excellent books have been written about clicker training, both the principles of the method and how to do it. You probably can find one or two at your library. However, not everyone loves the clicker. So if you give it a try but don't care for it, you can be just as successful training with positive reinforcement minus the click. Clicker training is an option, not a requirement.

## HOW TO FIND A TRAINER

Three good ways to find a great trainer in your area are to ask your breeder and your veterinarian for recommendations, search the Association of Pet Dog Trainers (APDT) website at www.apdt. com, or check the list of regional GSD clubs at www.gsdca.org to see whether there's one in your area that offers training. If given my druthers, I would select an all-breed puppy kindergarten for the advantage of socializing my pup to a variety of breeds. On the other hand, a class given by a Shepherd fancier for Shepherd puppies only would be very tempting. So if both were within reasonable driving distance, I might sign up for the all-breed class and when it ended sign up for the other.

Additional ways to find a trainer are to ask neighbors or friends with well-trained dogs where their puppies were trained, to look online for puppy training classes in or near your town, or check your phonebook. (I checked mine and found several classes from which to choose.) A good boarding kennel is also likely to know of training classes in the area. As an aside: some people believe that driving distance is the least important consideration in choosing an obedience class for a dog of any age, and there certainly is validity to this. But as someone who drove two and a half hours each way for a Shepherd to earn his Canine Good Citizen certificate and later took him to obedience and agility classes just 20 minutes from home, I can truthfully say that distance matters. It just doesn't matter as much as the quality of training. If your local pet supply store offers puppy training classes by a skilled trainer—lucky you!

## What to Ask

Whether there's just one puppy training class (also called puppy kindergarten or puppy preschool) in your city or yours has the good fortune of having several trainers to choose from, ask questions before signing up. Also, observe the class environment to make sure that it's clean and has a groomed potty area and whether classes are held indoors or outside. The trainer may have a brochure giving her credentials and a thorough outline of her training methods and what she requires of you before your pup joins the class. If not, you need to know these things. Inquire about her credentials and accreditation and how long she's been training. What are her methods? Feel her out on whether she believes totally in using positive reinforcement or believes that punitive methods are acceptable under certain circumstances. (If it's the latter, thank her for her time and cross her off your list.) And finally, ask the trainer her opinion of German Shepherd Dogs. If she acknowledges that they can be overprotective of their family or aloof toward strangers, that's an acceptable answer because they can be the former and usually are the latter. But the answer should also include positive characteristics of the breed—of which there are many. Her gushing that GSDs are just *so* beautiful and she loves seeing them in dog

## *Chapstick and the Alpha Roll*

I must confess that many years ago when I had a typically rambunctious and stubborn Shepherd puppy, I took the advice of a seasoned dog trainer and corrected the pup with an alpha roll so that she would understand who was in charge. After rolling her onto her back and kneeling with my hands placed gently on her throat and tummy, I looked her in the eye—waiting for her to acknowledge my dominance by looking away. But she looked at me with such a quizzical expression that I burst out laughing. Then, lying on the floor nuzzling her, I resolved to never treat a dog so foolishly again. Chapstick became an exquisitely trained dog through positive training.

shows is not a good answer, but she still may be a good trainer. If you are comfortable with her credentials and the class environment and sense that she is a true dog lover, and she says that German Shepherds are fast learners and highly trainable or that they are good with children and someday she hopes to own one—you have found your trainer.

## SOCIALIZATION

Socialization is teaching your dog to be comfortable with people and pets and situations both at home and in the wider world. It's not enough for him to be calm when he goes to see his veterinarian or when your best friend comes to visit. He must quickly come to understand that there's nothing scary about being walked on leash past other dogs walking on leash and nothing scary about the plumber who is knocking around under your kitchen sink. Everything the puppy becomes accustomed to after leaving his breeder and his birth family adds to his socialization.

Don't worry that your puppy will be stressed outside the cocoon of his own home. A study conducted by Dr. Michael W. Fox showed that putting puppies in mildly stressful situations during their first five weeks of life actually develops dogs who are better at learning and in competitive situations. Not only are they better able to handle stress and learn more quickly, but they are more outgoing than puppies who have not been subjected to mild stresses. Also, while your puppy's personality will change in little ways throughout his life, it will be pretty well set by the time he is four

Socialization is teaching your dog to be comfortable with people and pets and situations both at home and in the wider world.

months old. So don't waste time. Get him socialized as much as you can while he's very young, especially to dogs and people. But don't compromise his safety. If for good reason there's a lack of socialization after you bring him home, problems that may arise because of that lack usually can be corrected with the help of a competent trainer who understands the situation.

I brought my Charlie home at eight weeks of age when there was a very severe outbreak of parvovirus in our area. Both his breeder and vet rightly advised that Charlie be kept home for a few weeks. This my husband and I did, feeling that our adult female Shepherd would help socialize Charlie. And I invited many friends to the house to meet him. But the friends who visited either didn't have dogs or had dogs who for one reason or another were not suitable for socialization with a young puppy. As soon as our vet gave the all clear, I enrolled Charlie in a puppy kindergarten with a highly recommended trainer. It was summer. Classes were held outdoors. I parked the car and began walking Charlie toward the training area. To my utter dismay, he snarled and barked menacingly at the other puppies while pulling on leash so he could get to them quickly and rip their guts out.

Or so I thought, but I was wrong. Charlie's confinement to home when he should have been meeting lots of dogs had resulted in fear aggression. The trainer instantly realized what the problem was. He had me hand him Charlie's leash, then said, "Okay, tough guy, let's go," and started walking toward the other puppies. Charlie pulled back while shivering in such desperate fear that I wanted to take him home and protect him the rest of his life. Instead, I enrolled him in the trainer's puppy day care and kindergarten, held at his home. The first day, Charlie made a little progress

Give your puppy the chance to have a variety of different experiences.

by not showing aggression when walked on leash away from the other four pups, who were off leash during play periods. The second day he made more progress. On day four, when I drove up the trainer's driveway to get Charlie, five puppies were at the gate standing on their hind legs—and Charlie was shoulder to shoulder between two of his new friends. With GSDs, socialization is imperative. Even if started late, a good trainer can make it happen.

## How to Socialize

A good way to begin socializing your dog to people is to ask a dog-loving friend to meet you and your dog outdoors, either on your lawn or your friend's. Either way, your puppy will be on leash. To dissuade him from jumping up to greet your friend, ask him or her to kneel down in front of the puppy and casually reach out a hand to pet him. If you know that he especially likes being petted on the head or resting his chin on your hand, let your friend know this. And of course you will provide the friend with a few yummy training treats for use in rewarding and for letting her pet the new canine friend. If he sits while forming this new friendship, tell him "Good sit," and reward him for that too. Repeat this easy method of socialization by asking your other friends, relatives, and neighbors of both sexes and various ages to come meet your dog.

You can use the same method to socialize your pup to other dogs by asking friends and neighbors who have well-behaved dogs to meet you (one at a time, of course) and your puppy outdoors. Have the friend instruct her dog to sit while you and your dog walk past them. Then reward your puppy with treats and praise. If you don't have any nearby friends who own dogs, you may find that other dog owners you meet while on walks will be delighted to help train your puppy to be comfortable with other dogs. But socialize him only to polite dogs who would not try to dominate a puppy.

Socializing your GSD to children is also vitally important, and here too you don't want your puppy subjected to rough play or angry behavior. One incident of a child's pulling your dog's ears or tail, even though not meaning to hurt him, can make him fearful of all children. This would be a shame, especially since Shepherds seem to have an innate affection for children—one of the reasons they are highly desirable as family companions. Teach children who will interact with your puppy not to rush up to any dog, to keep their hands away from a dog's face, to pet very gently without pressing on the dog, and to never disturb a sleeping dog.

## Training Tidbit

While housetraining your puppy, avoid feeding him canned food, as it has a high water content that will put extra pressure on his bladder. Also, the sodium nitrate that often is used in canned dog food to enhance the color can act as a diuretic, making your puppy need to urinate more frequently.

Now some words of caution regarding socialization. You may have a kitten or grown cat who likes dogs, and your puppy may instinctively want to play with the feline family member. But don't be quick to assume that the two are safe together, because you cannot know for sure—not after a week, a month, or a year. Socializing a dog of any age to a cat must be undertaken with great caution so that neither animal is injured, and the caution should continue after they've become great friends.

Also be aware that parks and other places where any dog is welcome may harbor organisms that cause contagious diseases that are particularly dangerous to puppies, even after a puppy has had his initial shots. Don't overshelter your puppy from a virus that's going around, as I did my Charlie, but don't put him at unnecessary risk either. There will be plenty of time later on for you and your well-socialized dog to explore together all of the beautiful parks in your vicinity.

## CRATE TRAINING

Crate training is teaching your dog to accept and come to enjoy his own cozy place when he's home alone or you can't supervise him or when he shouldn't be running around or playing hard—such as after a meal when he needs to rest and digest his food. You don't have to feel any guilt or qualms about crating your puppy as long as he's not left in the crate for an unreasonable length of time. Crate training is an aid to housetraining, but crating him longer than his small puppy bladder can "hold it," about two hours, would be counterproductive. And when he's older, leaving him crated more than four hours wouldn't be fair. But when your puppy is home alone and crated, you don't have to worry that he might hurt himself tearing through the house or chewing something that could be a danger to him. When he's mature and you know his habits and can be confident that he won't get into trouble when left alone, don't ditch the crate. Just remove the door if you like and let him keep his comfy place with the snuggly crate mat.

## How to Crate Train

Teach your puppy to go into his crate without your putting him in it by tossing a treat in and saying "Crate," or "Kennel" or "Kennel up." (Choose one and have the whole family stick with it so that the puppy won't get confused.) When he goes in to get the treat, praise him lavishly and give him another treat. If he whines when you close the crate door, ignore the whining (yes, this is hard to do) but treat and praise him as soon as he becomes quiet. It's best to take him outside to potty before crating him so that you'll know when he whines that it's not from needing the bathroom. And never crate your pup to punish him, as then it would not be a wonderful place where only good things happen.

Your puppy may instantly take to his crate, especially if it's next to your bed or where the family gathers the most, but if he doesn't he will in time. Put treats or a special toy into the crate when he's not looking and you have no intention of crating him. He'll make the happy discovery that rewards sometimes show up in his crate when he doesn't have to be in it. But some dogs come to love their crates except when being crated means being home alone. (Your puppy will soon be able to tell when you're leaving, even if you try to keep it secret.) If he won't go into the crate because he thinks that if he refuses to you'll stay home or he'll get to go with you, don't repeat the command. Just pick him up and put him into the crate. Then praise and treat him. Always be casual about leaving. No goodbyes are necessary. And be just as casual on your return. Although you love each other madly, your puppy's being reunited with

Housetraining is a matter of getting your pup outdoors to do his business before he does it indoors.

A well-trained GSD puppy is a pleasure to live with.

you should never be a big deal, as this would reinforce his feeling of anxiety on your leaving.

## HOUSETRAINING

Philosophically, one could argue that housetraining is teaching your dog that life isn't fair. After all, here he is in a warm and pleasant building with one or more small rooms where his family and their guests go potty. Yet he must go outdoors to relieve himself, even on a cold and windy night. But let's be logical instead of philosophical. Housetraining is necessary so that the house won't smell bad and so that people won't slip and fall on urine or poop and be laid up in bed where they can't earn a living or go to school—let alone feed, groom, train, play with, and walk the puppy. And housetraining—even though it can't be done overnight or in just two

or three days—isn't difficult to do and really isn't hard on the dog.

Basically, housetraining is a matter of getting the pup outdoors to do his business before he does it indoors. Your puppy will need to go many times a day: after waking from sleep, eating or playing, and before bedtime. Take him to where you would like him to relieve himself and tell him "Go potty" or whatever command you choose. ("Hurry up" is popular.) Praise him while he goes, and treat him when he's finished. The command should be brief but more than one word and must be used by everyone in the family. Be diligent in training your pup, but realize that if there's an accident—and there *will* be—it's not his fault and he should not be scolded for it. Also, be sure to remove all traces of odor from the site, or he will relieve himself there again, and this time it won't be an accident. That is because his puppy logic will tell him that you came to your senses and have given him an indoor potty area. Why else would it smell like one? And his sense of smell is far greater than yours, so don't rely on regular cleaning solutions. Pet supply stores carry special products that neutralize odors so that even a German Shepherd Dog can't smell them. Besides removing attracting pheromones and destroying odors to prevent the dog's re-soiling, the product will discourage the growth of bacteria and germs. It can also be used for cleaning carpeting or flooring after a dog vomits.

## How to Housetrain

With the exception of his first potty outing of the day, when getting him out to the yard must be done quickly, you will want to have your puppy on leash when you take him outside to go potty. On leash he can be directed to his potty area without being distracted by the wonders of his new yard. But early in the morning carry him through the house and out the door to his bathroom so that there won't be an accident. After he has been praised and treated for doing his business, take him inside and feed him, then crate or baby gate him while you have your breakfast—perhaps gazing at him and thinking how adorable he looks asleep with a full belly. His post-breakfast snooze should last about a half-hour, after which you might give him some playtime before taking him out to go potty again.

Having a crate for your puppy may speed up housetraining significantly, as he won't want to soil his crate and will try his best to "hold it." But if no one can come home to take him outside after he's been crated for awhile, you will need to paper train him as well as crate train him. To do this, confine him to an uncarpeted but not dark room such as the kitchen, laundry room, or a windowed bathroom. Cover the floor with newspapers and have his crate, water bowl, and toys in a corner of the room. When you come home, remove the soiled newspapers and clean up thoroughly—including checking the puppy's paws to make sure they're clean. After moving the crate back to where it's usually kept, resume crate training. If paper training must be done daily, you can reduce the area covered by papers a little at a time as the pup selects an area of the room for his indoor potty place.

If your puppy sleeps in a crate or basket in your bedroom at night, and he's kept warm so he won't wake up shivering in the middle of the night (puppies always need to go when they wake from sleep), training will progress at a quicker pace. But count on having it take a month or two before he's trained. Then you'll be pleasantly surprised if housetraining takes just a couple of weeks.

Puppies give you clues that they need to go. If you see your pup sniffing the floor while turning in circles, get him outside. Try to remember to keep treats in your pocket,

## Multi-Dog Tip

An adult dog can be your training helper when practicing basic commands in your home. Addressing the mature dog by name, command him to come and then sit—and treat him when he obeys each command. The puppy, wanting some yummies too, may play copycat and eagerly come to you and sit. Praise and treat both dogs, with an extra loving pat for your demo student.

because you don't want to miss an opportunity to treat him for doing his business outside, even when you virtually have to fly out the door with him in your arms to make it happen. Of course, if you don't have a fenced yard, you can't fly out the door until you've put him on leash. Safety *always* comes first. That includes keeping your puppy's potty area clean and safe. Try to pick up feces each time he goes, and be sure that it's done at least once daily. If your yard fills with snow in winter, shovel a walking path and a "poop station" for his comfort. To protect him from slipping on ice, which could injure him or make him fearful of the yard in winter, use a pet-safe ice melt product.

Another thing to be aware of while housetraining your pup is that if he always eliminates in his own yard, he may not want to potty anywhere else. Highly trainable dogs often train themselves, and once they're convinced that the only good place to "go" is at home, it's hard to change that attitude. I learned this from a friend whose Labrador Retriever decided there was no place like home for going potty, and therefore she was not going to do it anywhere else—not even when she was vacationing hundreds of miles from home. My friend got a great deal of exercise walking her dog on that trip—but not much sleep.

## BASIC OBEDIENCE COMMANDS

The commands that every puppy should learn are *come*, *down*, *sit*, and walk nicely on leash. The latter isn't really a command but a learned behavior, which is why it has a longer name.

Teach the *come* command as soon as your puppy has settled in and is comfortable with his collar and leash.

## *Want to Know More?*

To teach your dog the *down-stay* and *sit-stay*, see Chapter 9: German Shepherd Training.

For your puppy's safety—and yours—it's essential.

## Come

The command *come*, also referred to as the recall, is what you teach your dog to keep him from chasing after another animal, running into the street where he can be hit by a car, or making you chase after him in his yard when you're already late for his vet appointment. Teach *come* as soon as your puppy has settled in and is comfortable with his collar and leash. As with all basic obedience commands, you will want to teach *come* with treats in hand and a smile on your face. Sound excited and happy when giving the command, which is how your puppy should feel each time he comes to you. This means that no matter what occurs before you call him to you—whether he chewed a hole in the sofa or dug up your favorite pansies—if you tell him to come and he does, he gets praised, treated, and lovingly petted for being a good boy. What he did before obeying your command has been totally forgotten. In fact, anytime your dog comes to you, even if you're busy doing something and weren't thinking about him at all, show him you're happy he wanted to be near you. It is an honor to be loved by a dog.

### How to Teach It

1. With your puppy on leash, walk a little away from him, then turn and kneel to face him.
2. Tuck the end of the lead securely under your knee so that your hands will be free to reward and pet him when he comes to you. He should be able to see that you have a treat in your hand, or you can be holding a food-scented toy he will like.
3. Call the puppy's name to get his attention, and when he looks at you, say "Fido, come!"
4. If he starts toward you before you have a chance to give the *come* command, give it anyway. When he gets to you, welcome him with open arms and a happy, "Good *come!*" Then treat him. What a smart dog he is!

After your puppy is used to obeying the *come* command while on his regular leash, you can make a longer leash by buying nylon cord and a brass or metal bolt snap. Affix the bolt snap to one end of the nylon cord, then attach it to the metal ring on your pup's collar. Now you can train him to come to you from a greater distance. Ultimately he will learn to obey the *come* command when he's not on leash.

## Down

Teaching *down* is a tool for getting your puppy to rest when you feel he has had enough exercise or is being too rowdy. When he has learned both *down* and *stay*, the combined commands will come in handy for other reasons, including having him be polite when you have guests. Although you and I find it difficult to understand, not everyone who comes to our homes wants social contact with our dogs. And when you need your dog to be out of the way so that you can get some work done, it's very pleasant to say the *down* command and have him immediately lie down near you, then say the *stay* command and have him not move from where he is. *Down* instills self-control in a dog, but for the command to function it must mean just one thing: lie down. If you or your children command "down" when the dog jumps on someone or is on a piece of furniture that's off limits to him, he'll be confused. One of the commands to teach later is *off*, meaning, "Get down from there" or "No jumping! You'll rip Mommy's hose!"

## How to Teach It

1. For your puppy's comfort, teach *down* indoors on a carpeted floor or outside on nice soft grass.
2. You may start with your puppy standing or sitting. Either way, hold a treat in front of his nose and let him sniff it, then slowly lower your hand toward the floor and slide the treat away from his nose while saying "Down."
3. His head will follow the treat, and as it does the rest of him should wiggle to the floor until he's completely down.
4. The second his belly touches the ground, treat and praise him. (If you're clicker training, click and treat him.) As he gets more proficient at *down*, you won't have to hold the treat in front of his nose, and you'll be able to have him stay down a bit longer before treating him. Being a submissive action, *down* is easier to teach when your Shepherd is very young. Be sure to always reward him while he's still in the *down* position, not after he gets to his feet.

## Sit

*Sit*, like *come* and *stay*, can be a life-saving command. If you have your dog in a *sit-stay* or a *down-stay* and he's trained so well that you can trust him not to get to his feet until you release him from the command, he is not going to put himself in a dangerous position or snitch a bite of the baby's cookie. Teach your Shepherd, when he's a little older, to sit while you're preparing his meal, before coming indoors on a rainy day (so that you can wipe

his feet off first), and before crossing a street while you're on a walk.

## How to Teach It

1. With your puppy standing in front of you, hold a treat right over his nose and slowly lift the treat up and over his head.
2. To keep his eye on the treat, the puppy will sit—at which second you will give the command to sit. (If you hold the treat too high above his head, though, he might jump up to get it. To prevent this, be careful to move the treat over but *close* to his head.)
3. As soon as your pup's tush touches ground, say "Good sit!" and treat him.

This is an easy and fun lesson that can be

The *sit* is one of the easiest commands to teach a dog.

practiced a number of times a day. If during any *sit* session your puppy stands up before you treat him, withhold the treat and have him sit again. He'll catch on quickly, and soon you'll be showing off your puppy-training skills by having him perform *sit* when friends drop by.

## Walk Nicely on Leash

The reason we teach puppies to walk nicely on leash is so that we won't be pulled off our feet and dragged down the street when they are older. Seriously, you are not in control of your German Shepherd if he won't walk politely at your side. And if he isn't under your control when the two of you are out and about together, he's in danger. It's quite okay for your puppy to walk nicely on a loose leash instead of in a strict *heel*, which we will talk about in Chapter 9. But as your dog grows older, stronger, and protective of you, teaching him to heel will be a necessity.

### How to Teach It

1. With treats in hand and your dog's leash attached to a flat buckle collar, begin your walk

2. Soon something will attract your puppy's attention, and he'll pull on the leash. Your response will be to stop in your tracks—the "no forward progress" approach. Because you're not moving, he can't go forward.

3. It may take a few seconds, but he'll stop pulling and will look at you, at which moment you praise (or click) and treat him.

4. Continue your walk and repeat the "no forward progress" ploy until your puppy understands that pulling on leash means that he'll have to stop walking, but walking nicely on leash will win him rewards.

5. Remember while training your pup to walk nicely on leash that the distance you walk should not be long. At this tender age, the amount of exercise he requires is not great, and too much is a liability. But teaching him to walk nicely on leash now will help make him a wonderful walking partner in the years to come.

## PUPPY KINDERGARTEN

Even if you have owned many dogs and have wide experience in training puppies, I urge you to give your GSD pup the benefits of puppy kindergarten. The socialization he'll receive—with both humans and dogs—is well worth the class fee and your time. You are almost certain to learn things you didn't know, and the puppy you are training now is not mentally or emotionally identical to any puppy you have trained before.

When you have located a puppy kindergarten via the ways we discussed early in this chapter, ask the first trainer you call whether you may observe a training session. If the answer is that you may not observe a class before signing up, this is not the trainer you want for your puppy, so call another. However, it isn't unreasonable for the trainer to charge a small fee for observing a single session. This keeps people from coming to class to learn what they can with no intention of ever paying for training sessions. When observing a class, turn off your cell phone and sit quietly so as not to distract the trainer, puppies, or the pups' owners. But do take notice of the class size. The trainer may be excellent but with a very large class may be unable to give every dog a lot of attention.

An extra benefit of enrolling your pup in puppy kindergarten is that your social life might expand to include other German Shepherd Dog lovers. This could result in your GSD having other GSDs for friends throughout his life. Now, that's a lucky pup!

PART II

ADULTHOOD

# CHAPTER 5

# FINDING YOUR GERMAN SHEPHERD ADULT

As someone who has adopted a five-week-old pound puppy and four dogs between three and five years of age from a breed rescue, I know that there is equal joy in bringing either a puppy or adult dog into your home. But the emotional rewards of adding either a German Shepherd puppy or adult to your family must be weighed against other factors. Unless you already have your heart set on purchasing a puppy or adopting an adult, it's a difficult choice and one to which you should give much thought. Of course, you could start by adopting an adult Shepherd—two years of age or older—and down the road purchasing a puppy. Or vice versa. Yes, it's still a tough choice. But by weighing the reasons for getting a puppy or adult dog, taking a clear look at your lifestyle, and considering the needs of a puppy versus an adult, you will make the right choice. And the road will still be there, leading to your having another Shepherd—puppy or adult—if you so desire. I'm betting you will.

## WHY ADOPTING AN ADULT IS A GOOD IDEA

One hardly knows where to begin listing the advantages of adopting an adult dog. A two-year-old Shepherd may still have a lot of puppy in him, but he won't have a puppy's small bladder that needs to be emptied several times a night after you've gone to bed and many times a day while you're at work. A three-year-old male Shepherd may still have lots of puppy in him, but he's past his "teenage" stage of trying to convince other male dogs that he's big and bad and they'd better not mess with him. The adult Shepherd you adopt from a rescue group or shelter will most likely have had obedience training, from either his former owner or the shelter or rescue volunteers. Keep in mind that it takes a German Shepherd Dog one and a half to three years to reach emotional maturity, and ask yourself whether you'll be comfortable waiting that long.

## *Want to Know More?*

If your heart is set on acquiring a GSD puppy, see Chapter 2: Finding and Prepping for Your German Shepherd Puppy for more information.

The adult Shepherd you adopt from a rescue group or shelter will most likely have had obedience training, from either his former owner or the shelter or rescue volunteers.

There's more to the big Shepherd versus little Shepherd picture. Most dogs adopted from rescues and shelters have been spayed or neutered; not so the puppy you get from a breeder. Shelter and rescue Shepherds definitely have been screened for temperament problems. They've also had a thorough veterinary exam, so you will know whether there are health issues and if there are what is required to treat them. Puppies are wonderful but can tire you out, and while you're resting they may chew a hole in the sofa. Consider, too, that bringing a German Shepherd puppy into your home and not providing him with obedience training would be unconscionable.

People who know that you plan to bring a GSD into your life may urge you to adopt an adult Shepherd because by doing so you will save a life, whereas one needn't worry about a puppy from a respectable breeder, as the pup will be snatched up by someone else. As an animal shelter volunteer going on 11 years now, I don't agree with this thinking. An adult dog adopted out of pity may live happily ever after in his new home. Or he may find himself back in the shelter because as an adult he already has a distinct personality and habits that aren't what the adopter wanted. These habits may not be noticeable while he's without a home. A three-year-old dog I adopted was meek and mild at the rescue. Today I call her my wild child. Moreover, who is to say that the Shepherd puppy you didn't purchase because you felt obligated to adopt an older dog won't wind up in a GSD rescue or a shelter? The adult dog in need of a family once was a puppy whose breeder believed that he was being sent to a wonderful home where he would live out his days.

Weigh the advantages and disadvantages to your family of getting a puppy as opposed to an adult Shepherd. Then follow your heart.

## ADOPTION OPTIONS

Breeders very rarely have adult dogs in need of a home, so the places to look for your adult Shepherd are animal shelters and GSD rescues. Let's take a look at both options.

### Rescues

A rescue organization differs from animal shelters in one or more ways. Shelters always have a physical location for the care and housing of animals, while a rescue may have a specific location but is more likely to house unhomed pets in the homes of volunteers until the pets are adopted. Essentially, this is foster care, with the animal receiving training from his foster family. At the time of this writing, I found 27 German Shepherd Dog rescue groups by visiting the American Kennel Club's (AKC) website, www.akc.org, clicking on "clubs," and on that page clicking "breed rescue groups." Another resource is the American German Shepherd Rescue Association (AGSRA), a fundraising group with programs for protecting GSDs from suffering homelessness, cruelty,

neglect, or misuse. AGSRA lists 44 states and Washington D.C. in its directory of rescue groups at www.agsra.com.

If you have children less than ten years of age, the rescue group you contact may suggest that you not adopt a Shepherd who wasn't raised with young children. The same consideration should be made if you have a cat. While a GSD may be known as cat friendly or cat neutral, or may have adored the kitty in his former home, that was a different cat, and the rescue group will want to assure *your* cat's safety with the dog you adopt. After all, the Shepherd is a herding breed and does possess a prey drive (although you wouldn't have known it from a couple of my Shepherds). One thing the rescue group will not consider is adopting out a dog to be kept primarily outdoors. A GSD cannot thrive in such circumstances. Much stronger than his prey drive is his need to be with and protect his people.

A GSD rescue exists for the sole purpose of rescuing, rehabilitating, and rehoming German Shepherds. Typically an incoming Shepherd will be temperament tested and then assessed in a foster home. If intact, incoming dogs are spayed or neutered. They are given vaccinations if needed and checked for heartworm and other internal parasites—as is done in an animal shelter. They may also be microchipped. If not fully housetrained, this is worked on. So too is teaching the dog any basic obedience commands he doesn't already know.

### Meet and Greets

One way to meet adoptable GSDs is to go to German Shepherd meet and greets, which often are held at local pet supply stores. Besides swooning over the beautiful Shepherds, you'll meet dedicated rescue volunteers who love answering questions about their breed. The American Kennel Club has "Meet the Breed" booths at most of its shows. You can meet German Shepherd breeders who can help you find the dog of your dreams.

One of the many GSD rescue websites I visited proclaimed the group's pride in its less than 5 percent return rate. They should be proud, both of their organization and of the breed they love. Rescues, like shelters, charge an adoption fee, which helps offset costs incurred from fostering, veterinary expenses, and microchipping, if that is part of the rescue's program. While some rescues will adopt out of their area, or even out of state, most will not. Likewise, a few rescues will take in mixed breeds, but most confine their operation to purebred Shepherds. This isn't because they don't care about the mixes; it's because they are a small group of dedicated German Shepherd Dog lovers with limited resources.

Volunteering for a GSD rescue is a wonderful way to become familiar with the breed and make friends with Shepherd lovers. Until you have become Shepherd savvy enough to volunteer solo, you can gain experience by assisting volunteers in grooming, walking,

Animal shelters are facilities that house homeless animals who were abandoned, lost, or surrendered by their owners.

transporting, and introducing dogs to prospective adopters. Foster families are always needed, and some rescues allow volunteers to "foster to adopt." A rescue might also teach you to conduct home visits in which aspects of a prospective home and family are assessed so that the right dog goes to the right home.

## Shelters

Animal shelters are facilities that house homeless animals who were abandoned, lost, or surrendered by their owners for a variety of mostly acceptable reasons. Among these reasons are unpredictable forces of nature such as owner illness or death in the family. Job loss and other causes of financial straits put many animals in shelters—a reminder to us all that animal ownership is expensive and love won't buy kibble or veterinary care. A beloved GSD whose family must relocate to rental housing that won't accept large dogs may find himself in a shelter, his owners sobbing while saying their goodbyes. Worse is an owner who doesn't have the time or the desire to give the Shepherd proper training, socialization, and adequate exercise—but not surrendering the dog until frustration with his unfulfilling life has caused behavioral problems such as excessive barking. There are other heartless reasons for surrendering a pet. I'm thinking of the aging dog who lost his hunting skills and of those who came to the shelter because the new puppy in their family didn't like him. The bottom line, though, is that the owners of these dogs did not put them out on the street or drop them off in the woods. They brought them to a safe place, gave the receiving staff information on the dog's health, behavior, training, former lifestyle, and what their favorite toys are—and perhaps made a small donation to the shelter. So one tries not to condemn but to be grateful.

There are several types of animal shelters. Some take in a variety of animals, from dogs, cats, and birds to small and furry critters, such as ferrets and rats, while others specialize in one or more species. A no-kill shelter won't euthanize an adoptable animal, which raises the shelter's esteem in the community. However, a no-kill shelter, large or small, is likely to be selective, as opposed to the open-admission shelter (also called open-door shelter) that accepts any pet, excluding those that won't physically fit in the facility, such as a horse or cow. In addition, an open-admission shelter does not have a waiting list. My shelter, which has five campuses, is open-admission. It explains in detail when an animal has an ongoing or recurrent illness and perhaps isn't likely to live long, or why for any other reason this animal requires an "exceptional owner." An exceptional owner is one who can and will commit to giving the animal the extra care he needs, be it extra grooming or training, a special diet, or medication and frequent health exams. And the exceptional owner always steps up to the adoption counter—not out of pity but because sickness doesn't define a pet, and this is the right one for him or her.

Records for the past two years at my shelter show GSDs coming in mostly as strays. Otherwise, they were surrendered generally because of a family move, inadequate facilities (usually meaning the owner felt that she didn't have adequate housing or containment for the dog), the owner couldn't afford to keep the dog, and landlord issues. How a GSD fares in the shelter depends on his history, temperament, and socialization—the same as any other breed. Other than a puppy, any dog who goes from home life into a shelter must deal with the huge change of unfamiliar surroundings and people, plus a new schedule for being fed, groomed, and exercised.

## Multi-Dog Tip

Ideally, a dog who already shares your home will be introduced to the new dog at the shelter or rescue. This is a neutral territory where they can sniff each other and hopefully enjoy a walk together. By the end of this first meeting, they may be fast friends.

Some shelters provide dogs to local law enforcement agencies and service dog organizations.

Surprisingly, given their attachment to family and property, German Shepherds acclimate as well as any other dog who comes to a shelter. Some Shepherds need more tender loving care, and more time to adjust. Others adapt quickly. But they all adapt.

The German Shepherd you meet in a shelter may be very friendly, but it's just as likely that he'll seem uninterested in having company. If the latter is the case, it could be that he arrived at the shelter intact and is now recovering from surgery. Otherwise, separation from his family and home, which basically is all he held dear, may have left him bewildered and depressed. Whatever the reason for his lethargy, accept his ignoring your presence, say a few kind words to him, and if you're interested, talk to the shelter staff about him. If he's not recovering from surgery, they may let you go inside the kennel and sit next to him on the floor, stroking him gently. Later, he may be up for a walk on the grounds with you and a shelter volunteer. Don't feel that visiting with a shelter dog gets his hopes up and makes him feel more dejected when you leave. Whether you adopt him or not, you gave comfort. That's a lot.

Some shelters provide dogs to local law enforcement agencies and service dog organizations without fee. The agency checks

## Training Tidbit

If you fall in love with an adult Shepherd but don't like his name, just change it. The dog won't mind and will quickly respond to the new name if you address him by it consistently. In fact, the name you don't like may not have been his real name. Strays without ID tags arrive at shelters every day of the year. Shelter personnel must assign them names but don't have time to ruminate daily over monikers for 6 stray dogs and 12 stray cats. It's also easier for the staff if there's only one Jake and one Julie in the kennels or cattery. Believe me, there are some strange names on cage cards, dreamed up by the shelter staff or the animal's former owner. But if a stray Shepherd comes to the shelter wearing a collar with ID tags giving his name as MudPaws, MudPaws it will remain within the allotted time the shelter keeps a dog on "hold" before putting him on the adoption floor—and probably until he is adopted. If you are the lucky adopter, you may celebrate the occasion by changing "MudPaws" to "Mike."

the shelter's website or phones the shelter when looking for a candidate. I watched as a police officer visited a German Shepherd at my shelter. Anyone could see it was a match made in heaven—or rather, in a shelter kennel.

You may be surprised at the price the shelter charges for an adult Shepherd, but it's minimal compared to what you would pay for a well-bred Shepherd puppy. And animal shelters are nonprofits. Large or small, the shelter costs a lot of money to run, and it usually can't afford to hire all of the personnel needed. If you get your Shepherd from a shelter, consider volunteering there after your new family member has settled in. Donating just a few hours of your time a week can make a big difference. Volunteer opportunities offered at my shelter and many others include dog walking, dog or cat grooming, helping

customers find the right pet for their family, fostering animals not yet ready for adoption, and keeping those who are ready comfortable and happy while waiting to be adopted. (Contrary to what you may have heard, shelter animals in a caring environment can be very happy.) My shelter has an Oh Behave Program in which volunteers prepare dogs for adoption by training them to sit before going through doors, walk nicely on leash, and perform other polite behaviors. More ways for volunteers to lend a hand include helping with fundraisers to support the shelter's programs, assisting the veterinary services staff, and becoming an animal ambassador by taking their own pets to nursing homes, hospitals, and other facilities where people with disabilities can be cheered by the touch or smile of a dog.

# CHAPTER 6

# GERMAN SHEPHERD GROOMING NEEDS

Grooming your German Shepherd will give you quality time together while keeping him looking like the proud and noble breed that he is. It also will help you detect possible health problems early on, not after they've become advanced. You will come to know every part of your dog's body, so you'll know when there's a change anywhere. Eye, ear, or skin problems; tumors; inflammation of the gums, and any other abnormalities will not elude you if you brush your dog's coat and teeth regularly and bathe him a few times a year. Nor will a nail become abnormally long and need to be shortened under general anesthesia (I thought anesthesia was just for dental problems!) if you keep his nails trimmed. So try not to think of grooming as a chore but as a multifaceted opportunity. And never get angry at your dog or show impatience while grooming him. He has a good memory and won't forget that he was scolded for jumping out of the tub during a bath. Rather, if he jumps out of the bath and shakes water all over you and the walls, laugh it off and put him back in. Many years from now you will remember the incident fondly.

## BRUSHING

Your German Shepherd's double coat—short and downy next to the skin but longer with coarse guard hairs on the outside—should be brushed regularly for his health and comfort, but also, and not insignificantly, for the cleanliness of your home and car. You don't want fur flying in your face when merging on the Interstate. Brushing a Shepherd three or four times a week is adequate. But if you brush him every day, which you can do in just a few minutes, you will greatly reduce the time you'll spend on brushing over the course of a year. Guard hairs, the long and usually stiff outer hair that protects the underfur in certain animals, are shed all year round, while the coat is blown just twice yearly—with the entire undercoat coming out in clumps over a period of about two weeks. A *lot* of hair comes out. Depending on your dog, it can fill several garbage bags. You'll know when your dog is starting to

## Want to Know More?

For more information on GSD skin problems, see Chapter 8: German Shepherd Health and Wellness.

Your GSD's double coat should be brushed regularly for his health and comfort.

blow his coat by the small clumps of hair that begin to fall from him.

While it's okay to brush your dog's coat several times a week instead of every day, don't even consider brushing it just a few times a month. Regular grooming of a GSD's coat is essential to keep the woolly undercoat from matting. Matting isn't just unsightly; it can result in skin problems such as bald spots, hot spots (a localized skin inflammation medically known as pyotraumatic dermatitis), and rashes. Besides removing loose hair, a daily brushing of your Shepherd's coat will help distribute natural oils that keep his coat lustrous. If you begin a routine of brushing him at the same time every day, this will become as natural to you as feeding him and will be a ritual he looks forward to.

## What You'll Need

You will want a slicker brush with short, bent wire teeth for daily grooming and a shedding blade, which is U-shaped and held together by a handle, for when your dog blows his coat. The shedding blade, which was used on horses before it became a tool for grooming dogs and cats, looks a little ominous but is actually a gentle tool for stripping and collecting dead hair before it is shed. Use the blade looped for working on small areas, such as the shoulders and tail, and open the loop at the blade's handle to create a straight blade for working on the back and sides of your dog. Other grooming products to consider, of which there are many, include the Love Glove Grooming Mitt and the Dog Zoom Groom. The Love Glove fastens to your hand with a Velcro strap and removes dead hair while you massage the dog. It also removes hair from furniture. The Zoom Groom, as described in Chapter 3, has rubber "fingers" that collect loose hair from the coat, whether dry or wet. (I use this for shampooing my dogs.) Both products are inexpensive. An ordinary lint roller with sticky tape will remove dog hair from anywhere you don't want it, including your clothes, but you will have to purchase refills for the roller.

Another option is to treat yourself to a grooming table. Although mostly seen at dog shows, these folding tables with nonskid surfaces are helpful at home too, especially if you're prone to backaches. The dog may stand or lie down on the table while you groom his coat or trim his nails. You can also buy a grooming arm, which looks like an inverted "L" with a hangman's noose on the end. Actually, it's a comfortable loop that slips over your dog's head to keep him from turning or lowering it to see what you're doing—or just to give you a kiss. I see two problems with using a grooming table, however. First, how does someone with low back issues comfortably lift a grown German Shepherd onto and off a table? (There are hydraulic tables on the market, but they're expensive.) Second, if you use a grooming arm, you may not under any circumstances move away from the table while your dog is on it. Not if the baby cries. Not if something's burning on the stove. Because if the dog were to jump down, that loop really would be a hangman's noose. However, there are people with low back issues who use a table to protect their backs while grooming. One breeder in particular has taught her dogs to go from a chair to the table. Once trained, they don't need a grooming arm. German Shepherd Dogs lead the blind, work with the police, and find people in rubble from earthquakes—you can teach them to stand on a table!

Whatever tools you use, make brushing your dog pleasurable for both of you, but also take it seriously. Just as dental disease is the result of not brushing a dog's teeth, not brushing his coat on a regular basis—which optimally means daily—will probably result in problems. Plus frequent brushing lets you know whether there's a scrape or cut on his skin. Dogs can be very stoical and keep minor wounds to themselves. Grooming the coat may also reveal fleas, mites, or ticks. This is something you want to know now, not next week.

## How to Do It

- Weather permitting, take your dog outside to be brushed. Otherwise, brush him indoors in an area that's easy to clean. You don't want to brush him near your beautiful wool throw or embroidered sofa pillows.
- While holding your Shepherd by his collar, have him stand to be brushed. (Eventually you won't have to do this, as he will know to stand and not walk away.)
- For routine brushing, use your slicker to brush every part of your dog's body except his face, ears, belly, genitals, anus, and feet. Be firm but gentle, and be especially gentle while brushing the stomach area and legs. You may choose to use a comb on the legs, chest, and tail where there's soft, feathery hair.

- Trim any long hair between the toes with scissors that have a blunt end. Doing this helps prevent small grass seeds, sticky cottonwood seeds, and any other foreign matter from lodging in the paws.
- When your dog begins to blow his coat twice a year, use your shedding blade instead of the slicker to brush him. Be especially gentle using a shedding blade on the stomach and lower legs. Any part of the body that doesn't have a double coat doesn't require brushing with a shedding blade.
- Finish by smoothing the coat with a clean dry chamois cloth, or with a hound mitt with short bristles on one side. This will make the coat extra shiny while wiping loose flakes of skin from the surface.

- Any time you brush your dog, be on the lookout for lumps, cuts, or sores. Sensitivity to touch anywhere on your GSD's body means that something is amiss.

## BATHING

As with brushing, bathing your GSD is necessary for keeping his skin and coat healthy, but it's something you probably won't need to do more than four times a year. That is, unless your GSD has had a joyful romp in the mud, rolled in something obnoxious, had a quarrel with a skunk, or for no apparent reason just smells "doggy." Then he will need a bath even if he had one recently. But for the mostly indoor dog who doesn't get muddy or stinky and who doesn't have a skin condition that

A bath to celebrate each new season should suffice for your GSD.

Never use shampoo made for humans, not even a baby shampoo, as it will irritate your dog's skin. If your dog has dry skin, which usually happens in winter, bathing him with a doggy shampoo that has oatmeal as a main ingredient will be soothing and will provide added moisture. Another aid in helping the skin retain moisture is rubbing or spraying the coat with an oil-free humectant, a substance that promotes retention of moisture. Ideally, the shampoo and cream rinse you purchase will contain the vitamins, oat proteins, and other ingredients needed for keeping your dog's skin healthy, but your vet may also recommend adding a fatty acid supplement to his diet.

After the bath, when your Shepherd is clean from head to toe, you may pat yourself on the back for doing a good job bathing him and keeping him calm. You'll probably notice, after you open the bathroom door and set him free, that he's extra frisky. Whether this friskiness is from relief that the bath is over or because being clean feels so good is something we'll never know for sure.

under a veterinarian's advice requires more frequent bathing, a bath to celebrate each new season will suffice. Your dog probably will be as glad of this as you are, because most dogs don't look forward to getting in the bathtub or shower. Because of this almost universal reluctance, don't give the *come* command at bath time, as *come* should be reserved for things your dog likes. Just take him by the collar, or put his leash on if necessary, and cheerfully praise and treat him twice—once for coming with you and once when he's in the bathroom and you have the door shut so that he can't get out.

Your staying cheerful and confident while bathing your dog is important, so if possible have a second person present when you give your dog his first bath in your home. This should be someone who loves dogs, but it must not be a young child. If the person with you has experience bathing a large dog, that's all the better. It's unlikely that your dog will try to escape from the tub or shower stall, but if he does, an extra pair of hands and a second upbeat voice would be a big help.

## What You'll Need

Use any good-quality puppy or doggy shampoo, followed by a doggy conditioner.

## How to Do It

- Line the bathroom floor with towels to keep it dry. There may be splashing, so put away anything that you don't want to get wet. If you have a shower curtain, pull it to the end of the tub, opposite the faucet, so it won't get in your way.
- You will be standing next to the bathtub or shower stall the whole time your dog is in it, so before you put him in there make sure everything you need is within reach. This includes a washcloth for his face, cotton balls for his ears, shampoo, a dog scrubber (if you choose to use one), cream rinse, and towels for drying him.
- Whether bathing your Shepherd in a bathtub

or shower stall, put a nonskid mat on the tub or shower floor to prevent his slipping and falling. One small slip can make him more nervous than he already is.

- Also adjust the water temperature before getting your dog wet. It should be warm but not hot. You don't want to burn his toes.
- Put a little baby oil on two cotton balls, then gently put them in your dog's ears. Don't push hard on the cotton balls. Your dog may shake them out while he's being bathed, but if you're careful you won't get water in his ears, or at least not very much.
- Wet your dog down by using a shower hose attachment (an ordinary one will do fine, or you can buy one made for bathing dogs). Otherwise, use a large plastic measuring cup with a handle to wet him all over before applying shampoo.
- Wipe the face gently with a wet cloth.
- Apply shampoo all over the dog except his face, beginning with the top of his head. Give special attention to the areas under his legs and tail.
- Using your hands or a rubber Zoom Groom, rub the shampoo through his coat.
- Rinse your dog using the hose attachment or measuring cup. Begin with the head after gently tipping it back so soap won't get into his eyes.

- Rinse the rest of his body but without lifting his paws from the nonskid mat.
- Do a second rinse, again protecting the eyes and not lifting the paws.
- As soon as you turn the water off, begin drying your dog with towels. Keep him in the tub or shower stall until you've dried at least his head, back, and sides. The more you dry him while he's in the tub, the better, as his natural instinct is to get dry, and (with apologies to Jerry Lee Lewis) there will be a whole lot of shaking going on!
- Take him out of the tub. Continue drying him with towels, and with a damp towel gently wipe the inside of his ears. After drying him all over with towels, you may use a blow dryer on the lowest setting. This is especially advisable if it's cold outside. But be sure that the blower is only warm, not hot, before aiming it at your dog's coat.
- When he's dry, brush him lightly to remove any dead hair that has been left in his coat.

## EAR CARE

Ear care is necessary for preventing excess wax or debris from accumulating in the ear, causing discomfort or an infection. There's also the possibility of your dog's having ear mites. This is mostly seen in cats, not dogs, but that's not a guarantee that your dog won't get these nasty pests. So anytime you see your dog scratching in or around his ears, look for reddish-brown or black spots. These spots indicate the presence of mites, which must be dealt with by your veterinarian. A vet visit is also required any time your GSD has a discharge or bad odor from an ear or a buildup of debris. Fortunately, Shepherds aren't prone to ear infections, as dogs with upright ears tend not to be. But it can happen, so be aware of any change in the ears.

## By the Numbers

You'll help your Shepherd keep his teeth by brushing them seven days a week. And it's amazing how quickly you can brush 42 teeth and do a good job.

## What You'll Need

Various ear cleansers are on the market for routine cleaning. They include pre-moistened small wipes or pads for removing dirt and wax on the outer ear to prevent it from getting into the ear canal, and liquid solutions for topical use within the ears. But don't stock the liquid before there's a problem. Of all the dogs I've had, only one required a special ear cleanser.

## How to Do It

- Inspect your Shepherd's ears once a week while brushing him unless he has a history of ear problems. That would call for daily inspection.
- When cleaning the ears, check for wax, odor, crusty or scaly deposits, inflammation, and grass seeds or awns. (See Chapter 11.) But don't probe deeply or you may push wax or foreign objects farther in.
- Clean wax deposits from the ears by gently wiping with warm olive oil on a cotton ball or with a commercial product made for dogs.
- If your dog tilts his head to one side, scratches his ears, or rubs his head on the ground repeatedly, schedule an appointment with his vet.
- If the underside of the ear is very hairy, you may trim it to avoid a buildup of dirt.

## EYE CARE

Eye care is another part of grooming you do to prevent your dog from getting an infection. On a regular basis, look carefully at his eyes to see whether anything is amiss. Signs of a potentially serious eye problem include redness, swelling, a thick mucus discharge, itchiness (evidenced by his rubbing the affected eye), and squinting. A little mucus in the corners of the eyes is nothing to be concerned about, but if it builds up it will

Use a cotton ball, not a cotton swab, to remove excess wax or debris from the ear.

create a breeding ground for bacteria. To keep this from happening, gently wipe mucus away with a clean moist washcloth. Eye care for your German Shepherd also includes protecting his eyes from injury. Soap and chemicals can seriously damage your dog's eye tissues, so be careful when bathing him not to get any product you use into his eyes. You'll know that his eyes are healthy if they are moist and clear and he isn't bothering them with his paws. But if anything seems different or strange, take him to the vet. You love looking into those beautiful eyes and want them to stay healthy throughout your dog's lifetime.

## How to Do It

- When grooming your dog, position yourself in good light so that you can look closely at his eyes.
- Conjunctivitis, the most common infection of the eye, is also the easiest to detect. Symptoms include redness around the eye and a yellow or greenish discharge. Don't try to treat this or any other eye problem yourself. Take him to the vet.
- When giving your dog a bath, keep the shampoo and conditioner out of his eyes.

On a regular basis, look carefully at your GSD's eyes to see whether anything is amiss.

Because eye care for your German Shepherd includes protecting his eyes from injury, don't let your dog stick his head out the window when he's in the car. The possibility of permanent damage from a bug or debris hitting him in the eye isn't worth the risk.

## NAIL TRIMMING

Most dogs don't relish having their nails trimmed, and some would tell you, if they could, that between a bath and nail trimming they would take the bath. But keeping your dog's nails at a comfortable, healthy length is an essential part of grooming. It's best to schedule nail trimming on your calendar so that you won't forget to do it, but anytime you hear your Shepherd's nails clicking against the floor is trimming time. Use a guillotine-style nail clipper (they're shaped like pliers) or a grinding tool. Guillotine-style clippers—which can't slip and injure your dog, as human nail clippers can—are available at any pet supply store, as are grinding tools. I prefer a corded electric grinder because it's more powerful than battery-operated grinders, and I don't have to worry about the battery dying while I'm still trimming. But a battery-operated grinder has the advantage of being more mobile.

Because the Shepherd's nails are black on the outside, you won't be able to see the pink nail bed, also called the "quick." This is the part of the nail that contains blood vessels and nerves, and you want to avoid cutting into it. If you're not sure, or if your dog hasn't had his nails clipped in quite a while, you can ask your vet exactly where to begin trimming. With frequent trimming—twice a week if necessary but more likely once a week—the quick will recede more and more, allowing you to cut the nails shorter each time. But you must always take special care not to cut into the quick, which will cause pain and bleeding. Trim only tiny amounts at a time. In the event of accidentally cutting into the quick, keep styptic powder (or flour or cornstarch) within arm's reach to stanch the bleeding. You do this by dipping the nail into the styptic powder and applying pressure until the bleeding stops. What you don't want to do is act upset about this very small accident or you'll give your dog more reason to not like having his nails groomed.

If your dog still has his dewclaws, they need trimming too. These are the nails about a third of the way up the forelegs in what are known as vestigial toes. They are inherited from the mother and are found in many species. Dewclaws don't serve any function and are removed from show Shepherds when they're a few days old. My breeder explained that

this is done to prevent a puppy from getting a dewclaw caught on something and having it partially or totally torn from the leg.

Nail trimming really isn't hard to do, but if you're not sure you want to try it—or the thought of possibly cutting into the quick gives you the willies—it can be done at your veterinarian's clinic or a dog grooming salon. To trim your GSD's nails at home, it's best to have another adult there to help keep him still and to cheerfully administer very small treats during the clipping or grinding process. If you trim the nails with your dog standing facing the refrigerator, you can smear peanut butter on the door for him to lick while you trim. If he's lying on his side and you have a friend with you, the friend can feed him treats while you work.

## How to Do It

- Have your dog stand or lie on his side, whichever makes him more comfortable. If he's standing, bend each foot backward so that you can see the underside of the nail.
- Hold the clipper or grinder in one hand and with your other hand push gently on the paw pad to make the nail you are going to trim expand outward.
- If using a clipper, cut very thin slices of the nail, about 1/16th of an inch (.159 cm), especially if it's excessively long. That way you clip just the hooked end of the nail and don't risk cutting the quick. If using a grinder, grind no longer than three seconds, then go on to the next nail.
- After all of the nails have been trimmed, check to see whether there are any rough edges. If there are, use an emery board to smooth them. Then give more treats. It's possible that your dog will actually look forward to nail trimming because of all the rewards he gets. (I'm not making this up. I currently have two dogs who come running to have their nails trimmed. It's all about the treats.)

## DENTAL CARE

Dogs get dental problems just as we do, so brushing your Shepherd's teeth is an essential part of his care. A dog whose teeth are kept clean from an early age has a head start on avoiding dental problems in his later years. But it's never too late to make dental care part of his grooming routine, and brushing his teeth at home will mean fewer cleanings by a veterinarian. This will save your dog the discomfort and danger of anesthesia and will save you money. Also, and of great importance, reducing the chances of periodontal disease reduces the chances of diseases of the heart, kidneys, and liver—any of which can result from neglecting his teeth. But even when a

dog is spared the most serious ramifications of dental neglect, he will almost certainly suffer from gingivitis (inflammation of the gums) and resultant tooth loss. This is because food particles can stick to the gum line until they harbor bacteria, which in turn will form plaque. Plaque presents as a raised patch and becomes tartar. The end result of this incrustation? Gingivitis, an infection of the gums. What comes next is dental care under anesthesia. All because we didn't bother to brush our dog's teeth. Hard dog biscuits given as snacks and chew toys such as Nylabones, used under supervision, are also helpful but won't take the place of brushing. Nothing will. So let's get out the doggy toothbrush and toothpaste and keep our dogs healthy.

## What You'll Need

In addition to dog toothbrushes and finger brushes, which were discussed in Chapter

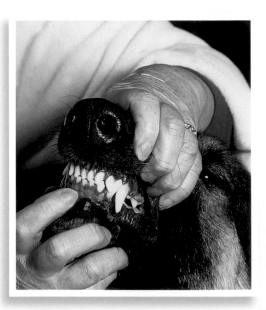

Dogs get dental problems just as we do.

3, you have the option of cleaning your dog's teeth with either a dental sponge or dental pads. Both are small and disposable, and the sponge has a flexible handle. While a toothbrush or finger brush is better at preventing tartar buildup, a dental sponge or pad is useful in introducing routine home dental care to an adult dog who never before experienced it. Whichever tool you decide on, if your dog didn't grow up with regular teeth brushing, your first step is to have him taste the delicious doggy toothpaste. Let him lick some from your finger, then praise and treat him for licking the toothpaste. (Of course, if he doesn't like the flavor you chose, you'll have to try another. I would start with chicken, which seems to please most canine palates.) Once he is enjoying the toothpaste, you can use your finger to rub a little on his front canines (the big teeth in the front of his mouth). After this, let him lick toothpaste off the toothbrush. Throughout these steps, you will praise him, and if you're so inclined you will give him a treat after each step. I don't do this, though, as all my dogs have loved their toothpaste.

Now that your Shepherd is used to having a cleaning device and toothpaste in his mouth, it's time to actually brush his teeth. Throughout the process, you will want to talk to him in a happy voice. You'll also need to reload the toothbrush with paste, especially if your dog is grown and has all 42 of his choppers. (I reload three times to ensure adequate paste for brushing the upper and lower teeth on both sides of the mouth and in the center.) However, if your dog is new to brushing, you may want to brush just a few teeth at first and slowly build up to the full mouth. Either way, you needn't brush the inside surface of the teeth unless you wish to, as your dog pretty much takes care of that with the movement of his tongue. In fact, while you're brushing the

Regular dental care is an essential part of grooming.

front of his teeth and cheerfully talking to him, his tongue will be going a mile a minute on the back surfaces.

## How to Do It

- Put a generous amount of doggy toothpaste on the toothbrush, finger brush, sponge, or pad you are using to brush your dog's teeth.
- Stand facing your Shepherd with him facing you. He may sit or stand, whichever he is more comfortable doing.
- Lifting the upper lip gently and placing the brush at about a 45-degree angle to the gum line, slowly move the brush up and down, not sideways, until you have brushed all of the upper teeth. You may start at the back of the mouth or wherever else you choose. But by starting at the back on one side and working your way around (like a train coming around the track), you won't miss any of the teeth.
- Reload the brush if necessary, then very gently pull back on the corner of the dog's lip to insert the brush so that you can clean the bottom teeth. Start with the lower molars and work your way around.
- Be alert when brushing your dog's teeth

# How to Find a Professional Groomer

As important as grooming is, some perfectly wonderful people simply aren't comfortable bathing their dog, trimming his nails, or digging in for some really serious brushing when the dog's coat has become matted or is about to blow. If you are in this category, hold your head up high and take your Shepherd to a professional groomer for those parts of grooming. It's enough that you help your dog stay healthy and comfortable by brushing his teeth and coat routinely and making certain that his ears and eyes are free of problems.

Your veterinarian, breeder, or trainer may know of a capable groomer to refer you to. In fact, some vet clinics, doggy day care businesses, and even animal shelters offer grooming services by licensed professional groomers. In choosing a groomer, your dog's health, hygiene, and comfort come before cost and convenience. Visit the grooming salon you're considering before taking your dog there–whether the salon is at a commercial location, in a mobile unit that comes to your home, at a shelter, or in a portion of the groomer's residence. The salon should smell clean and not have gobs of hair on the floor; if the dog is to be caged for any amount of time, the salon should have clean cages large enough for a GSD to be comfortable in. Also ask what products will be used on your dog and whether you may bring a product of your choice—perhaps a shampoo that your vet recommends. Many commercial salons, such as those at pet supply stores, have windows for viewing, but not all do. If you would like to watch your dog being groomed, ask whether this will be allowed. There may be good reasons for a groomer to not want owners to observe their dogs being groomed, but you'll feel more confident in the groomer if you're told why.

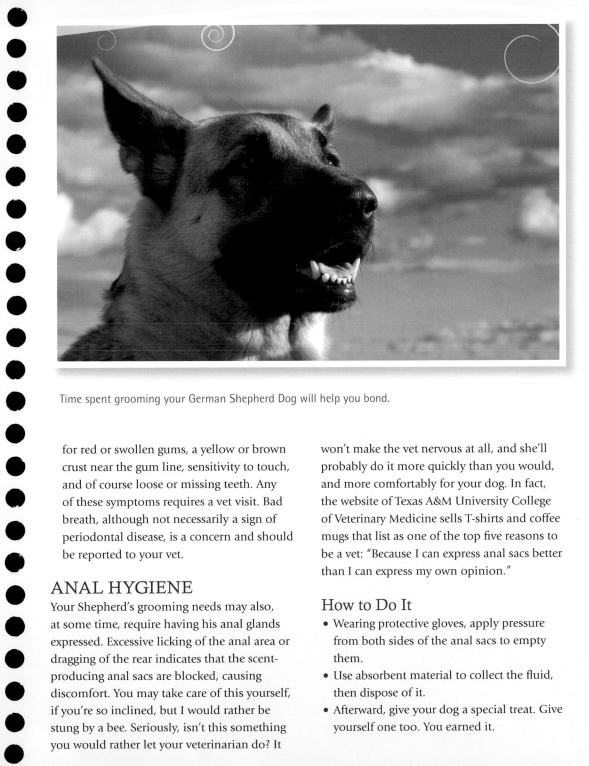

Time spent grooming your German Shepherd Dog will help you bond.

for red or swollen gums, a yellow or brown crust near the gum line, sensitivity to touch, and of course loose or missing teeth. Any of these symptoms requires a vet visit. Bad breath, although not necessarily a sign of periodontal disease, is a concern and should be reported to your vet.

## ANAL HYGIENE

Your Shepherd's grooming needs may also, at some time, require having his anal glands expressed. Excessive licking of the anal area or dragging of the rear indicates that the scent-producing anal sacs are blocked, causing discomfort. You may take care of this yourself, if you're so inclined, but I would rather be stung by a bee. Seriously, isn't this something you would rather let your veterinarian do? It

won't make the vet nervous at all, and she'll probably do it more quickly than you would, and more comfortably for your dog. In fact, the website of Texas A&M University College of Veterinary Medicine sells T-shirts and coffee mugs that list as one of the top five reasons to be a vet: "Because I can express anal sacs better than I can express my own opinion."

### How to Do It

- Wearing protective gloves, apply pressure from both sides of the anal sacs to empty them.
- Use absorbent material to collect the fluid, then dispose of it.
- Afterward, give your dog a special treat. Give yourself one too. You earned it.

# CHAPTER 7

# GERMAN SHEPHERD NUTRITIONAL NEEDS

Your German Shepherd's ordinary, everyday meals—eaten in just a few minutes from a bowl unceremoniously plunked on the floor—are to him what dining at a five-star restaurant or relishing a ball-park hotdog is to you. I think of a dog at his bowl as a dog experiencing heaven on earth while doing a job and doing it well. Nothing should interfere with this job—not children wanting his attention and not another dog wanting to get at his food. It's our job to make mealtime peaceful and pleasant for our pups while ensuring that what we put in the bowl is as nutritional as it is tasty. Because nutritional needs vary from dog to dog, according to lifestyle, health, and age, we're fortunate to have a wide selection of top-quality commercial foods and home-cooked recipes from which to choose. If we wish, we can feed raw, after learning how to do it properly. And in many parts of the country, pet supply stores and entrepreneurial businesses offer home delivery of dog food or people food suitable for dogs. Whether nationwide or local, virtually all businesses that sell dog food have websites on which they list the ingredients in every product offered. They also provide customer reviews. So all we need do is open our eyes to the possibilities, make our choices, and then fill the bowl with delicious, nutritious food. And no hotdogs, please, except for very small pieces used in training.

## WHY IS GOOD NUTRITION SO ESSENTIAL?

For your adult GSD to be healthy and have a good chance of reaching old age still feeling like a youngster, he absolutely must be fed a balanced diet appropriate to his activity level and unique Shepherd needs. When it comes to eating, dogs are like people. They require clean fresh water and a balanced diet to provide the right amount of carbohydrates, fat, protein, vitamins, and minerals. And it has to be appealing, or they won't eat it unless they're starving. So start by feeding a high-quality commercial kibble, preferably but not necessarily organic, and formulated for active adult dogs. To this tasty food, add one or more home-cooked recipes, making certain that they too provide the nutrients your dog needs. It really is a good idea to feed a wide variety of foods, including some that are crunchy to ward off dental problems. Conversely, a really bad idea is to buy cheap kibble and "balance" this non-nutritious food with table scraps that

# Obesity

Obesity is as serious a medical problem in dogs as it is in humans. There's no avoiding the dangers of being overweight, which include stress on the dog's heart, kidneys, lungs, liver, and joints. As if that weren't enough, obesity will make your Shepherd significantly more at risk for complications of surgery, should it be required, and excess weight makes a dog more prone to injuries requiring surgery. Obesity also causes respiratory problems in hot weather and leads to diabetes mellitus. It can worsen osteoarthritis (also called degenerative joint disease), which large-breed dogs are prone to.

So what causes this sad situation? Well, being sedentary, for one. Our dogs need and thrive on exercise. They don't need to run like the wind; vigorous walking and joyful games of fetch will do very well. Nor do they need to be fed table scraps or have constant access to food. They do need us to monitor their weight. Your vet will weigh your dog at each visit. Between

visits, check for increased fat by lightly sliding your hands over his sides. If you can't count your dog's ribs, he's eating too much. Fortunately, cutting down on the amount of food he eats won't be unpleasant for him if it's done gradually. Put a little less food in his bowl and break his treats in half. Just this, plus more exercise (but not strenuous exercise if he's overweight) will soon show progress. Don't rush it, and keep your vet involved. You can't undo obesity in a week or two. But you can safely bring your dog back to a healthy weight through good nutrition provided in the right amount.

probably are loaded with carbs. Just as a poor diet makes us grow fat while it whittles away at our health, the same goes for dogs. So choose wisely. Read the ingredients of any dog food product you buy. Read nonprejudicial reviews. Consult your breeder or a canine nutritionist if you're still not sure. And be glad that you and your dog live in a time when many manufacturers in the pet-food industry are putting out products of genuine quality.

When reading dog food labels, keep in mind that they serve the dual purpose of telling us what's in the bag, can, or box and convincing us to purchase the product. By law, though, five pieces of information must be on the label. They are: guaranteed analysis (including a "life stage" claim), nutritional adequacy statement, ingredients, feeding guidelines, and the manufacturer's name and address. But many words and phrases found on labels have no standard definition or regulatory meaning and thus are of no significance. These words include "senior," "premium," "natural," "improves doggy breath," and "recommended by veterinarians." (You have to wonder how much food is sold based on that last soothing but meaningless assurance.) The words "beef dog food" or "chicken for dogs" mean that the product contains at least 70 percent of beef or chicken. The percentage of beef or chicken

drops to a minimum of 25 percent when "platter" or "dinner" is part of the description, and the word "formula," as in "dog formula with beef," brings the minimum percentage to 3 percent. Add the word "flavor," as in "chicken flavored," and the meat in the product is virtually nil. Some words, such as "animal byproducts," put people off a particular food, just as "recommended by veterinarians" can clinch a sale. However, the protein quality of byproducts—which may contain heads, feet, viscera, and other body parts that don't stimulate most people's appetite—are sometimes better than protein from muscle meat, which does not put people off unless they're vegans. To learn more about pet food labels, visit www.fda.gov/cvm, the website of the U.S. Food and Drug Administration's (FDA) Center for Veterinary Medicine.

## THE BUILDING BLOCKS OF NUTRITION

Basic to a dog's diet are carbohydrates, lipids (fats and oils), proteins, vitamins, minerals, and water. Those are the building blocks of nutrition. Too much or too little of any of them may harm your dog. So will getting them from the wrong sources. Fortunately, our dogs are far more likely to eat well than were their distant ancestors. It wasn't until World War II

Your GSD must be fed a balanced diet appropriate to his activity level and unique needs.

Carbohydrates supply your German Shepherd with energy.

had ended that many American dog owners began feeding commercially prepared food instead of a hodgepodge of table scraps to their dogs, without knowing what was and what wasn't good for them. But at war's end, more people were able to afford the luxury of prepared foods, so the pet food industry began to grow and profit. Undeniably, there are advantages to feeding good-quality commercial food to your dog. If carefully chosen, a bowl of kibble will provide your Shepherd with a complete and balanced meal. So will a diet of home-cooked or raw foods, if carefully chosen, but they require a good deal of your time. If you feel torn between these options, you can feed your dog all three. My dogs' daily menu includes a carefully chosen kibble, Dr. Michael W. Fox's Homemade Natural Dietary Supplement for Dogs (http://www.twobitdog.com/DrFox/Dr-Fox-Homemade-Dog-Food), crunchy biscuits (commercial and home baked) for snacks, and small amounts of fresh fruit and veggies. They also get the occasional raw shank bone. But don't pat me on the back for any of this, as hubby does all of the home cooking and baking for our pups.

## Carbohydrates

Carbohydrates, which come from grains, sugars, fruits, and vegetables, supply energy and assist with digestion and regulation of body temperature. As a source of energy, carbs are less expensive than proteins or fats, so many dog foods contain more carbohydrates than our dogs need. A balanced diet will have about 50 percent carbohydrates. And while most dog foods have corn, soy, rice, potato, or wheat as their primary carbohydrates, a top-quality brand may not include corn or soy at all. Don't purchase any food for your Shepherd that includes the cheap feed known as "filler." It contributes very little nutritional value or none at all.

## Fats

Fats, besides being a concentrated source of energy, contribute to a dog's coat, skin, connective tissue, and kidney health. They also provide a vehicle for fat-soluble vitamins. Your dog, knowing none of this, loves fats for the same reason you and I do: they make food taste better. But go easy. Fats fed in excess cause obesity, especially if the dog isn't getting lots of exercise. And too much fat in the diet can bring on pancreatitis, a severe inflammation of the pancreas—an organ that aids in digestion of food. GSDs are prone to pancreatitis, which occurs in both puppies and adult dogs. Never feed fat trimmings from any kind of meat or poultry to your Shepherd or to any other dog, for that matter.

## Proteins

Proteins are organic compounds made of long chains of 20 or more different chemicals known as amino acids. Among their many vital functions, they form enzymes that metabolize food into energy. Does this make you dizzy? It does me. But all we need to remember is that good sources of protein without too much fat are required for a dog's growth and maintenance and that too much protein can harm a dog's kidneys and possibly affect his temperament. Proteins from meat and meat byproducts are more complete and easier for a dog to digest than proteins from plant sources. So when reading the list of ingredients in a commercial dog food, note whether or not meat products are near the top of the list. If the first ingredient is chicken, fish, lamb, bison, turkey, or beef, that's good. Otherwise, "animal-based protein" or "animal byproducts" should be near the top of the list.

## Minerals

Minerals are any of the inorganic elements, such as calcium, iron, potassium, and sodium, that are essential to the body's functioning properly. Fluid balance, bone formation, muscle metabolism, and the nervous system all depend on minerals, which are listed on

Fats contribute to a dog's healthy coat and skin.

## *Want to Know More?*

For more information on Cushing's disease, see Chapter 13: Care of Your German Shepherd Senior.

dog food labels. Sodium is usually listed as sodium chloride, which is salt. While almost never deficient in a dog's diet, too much of it has been linked to hypertension. Too little potassium can cause heart and kidney lesions and weakening of muscles. Muscle weakness can also be caused by magnesium deficiency. And so it goes; minerals play a vital role in the health of our dogs. On food labels, the word "chelated" before the name of a mineral is a good thing, and the words "chelated organic" before the mineral is very good. Veterinarians specializing in nutrition will tell you that organic chelated minerals are better assimilated than inorganic minerals.

## Vitamins

Vitamins are organic substances needed in small quantities to help regulate body processes and protect the dog from environmental toxins. Found in minute amounts in natural foodstuffs or else produced synthetically, vitamins break down nutrients such as carbohydrates, proteins, and fats so that your dog's body can employ them for normal metabolism. They also improve the quality of life for your dog by helping with digestion, muscle and bone growth, and keeping his skin and coat healthy. They can't be added haphazardly to a diet, though, as they must be given in proper amounts and scientifically determined ratios. There is also danger in giving too much of some vitamins. Water-soluble vitamins are excreted from the body if they are not put to use, but fat-soluble vitamins are stored in fatty tissue and can build up to the point of toxicity. One example is vitamin A, a fat-soluble vitamin that in excess can lead to bone disease. Your kibble probably has a number of vitamins listed in the ingredients. They're all there for a purpose and in the proper ratio for your dog's health.

## Water

Water, the clear liquid that on cloudy days descends in the form of rain and adds to our planet's creeks, streams, lakes, and oceans, is a major constituent of all living matter. We can't live without it. Nor can our animal friends. And the water in your Shepherd's bowl should always be as fresh and clean as the water in the glass from which you drink. Dogs dehydrate

Commercial food is purchased ready to eat and comes in a bag, box, or can.

easily, and dehydration harms kidneys and other organs. Both warm weather and exercise increase the body's need for water, so check often to make sure that your pup's bowl isn't empty. If you're going to be out together on a long walk or car ride on a warm day, take along a bottle of water and a bowl or portable pet canteen for him to drink from. You should never restrict water except on the advice of your veterinarian. And call your vet if your dog suddenly is drinking excessive amounts of water. This behavior, called polydipsia, can be caused by a urinary tract infection or something else that is easily treatable. But it may be a symptom of serious problems such as liver or kidney disease, diabetes, or Cushing's disease.

## WHAT TO FEED

There is not just one all-purpose, wholesome, health-boosting, and canine-tested delicious diet for your GSD or any other dog breed. Even if there were, your Shepherd would be better off having some variety in what he's fed. All dog lovers I know are dedicated to their dogs' health and well-being. Yet some feed an entirely commercial diet, some home cook for their dogs, and others feed raw. Many combine two or all three of these options to good effect. I've had dogs live long and healthy lives on mostly commercial food, usually kibble, or kibble and canned if they were fussy. But that was before dog owners had access to carefully formulated home-cooked and raw doggy diets—each of which has special benefits (as does a great brand of kibble). And by teaching your dog early on that variety is the spice of life, rather than giving him the same food every single day, you prevent his being emotionally or physically upset if his brand is cancelled or illness requires him to go on a special diet. Imagine what might happen if there was a

power outage lasting two whole days and all your dog's refrigerated and frozen home-cooked food—his staple of several years—had to be discarded. You'd be forced to buy commercial food. Your dog would be forced to eat it or else go hungry until you could cook for him again. And you both might wind up in counseling. All right; this is extreme. But so is making your dog dependent on one kind of food when there is no need to do this.

### Commercial Food

Commercial food is purchased ready to eat and comes in a bag, box, or can. It is mostly sold at pet supply stores, grocery stores, and online but is also offered by some veterinary clinics and even boarding kennels. With pet food now a multi-billion-dollar industry in the United States, there is an astounding number of commercial dog foods from which to choose. Among them are huge differences in quality. Many brands will provide your dog with the balanced nutrition he needs, especially if you choose dry food or a raw diet—the latter being relatively new to the pet-food industry. All you have to do, when feeding commercial food, is make sure that the brand you buy meets your dog's nutritional needs and also make sure that he doesn't get fed more or less food than he needs. When purchasing any dog food, even a box of treats, don't forget to check the expiration date. Make sure, too, that dry-food bags aren't torn anywhere and that cans aren't dented. If a can leaves the store in good condition but becomes dented before you get it into your home, it's still good but must be eaten soon. Whatever commercial food you buy—dry, canned, or semi-moist, etc.—the label should state that the food meets the guidelines of the American Association of Feed Control Officials (AAFCO), the governing body for all animal feed products. The Center for Veterinary Medicine (CVM), a branch of the U.S. Food and Drug Administration (FDA), works with AAFCO in identifying feed ingredients.

## Dry Food

A high-quality dry dog food—which we all know as kibble—costs less and is more convenient than semi-moist and canned foods. Kibble also aids in dental health by scraping tartar from the dog's teeth while it's being chewed. Another bonus of high-quality kibble is that it can promote smaller and firmer stools. But not all dogs like dry food, even when it's moistened with water. And seeing your Shepherd sniff at his bowl and then walk dejectedly away will make you feel dejected too. If this happens, try adding small quantities of people food to the kibble as flavor enhancements. Some safe and beneficial choices include fish (sardines are a favorite), poultry, beef, vegetables (but not onions or garlic), cooked brown rice or oatmeal, unflavored nonfat yogurt, and low-fat or nonfat

cottage cheese. Milk should not be added, as most dogs don't tolerate it well. In addition to or instead of people food, you can mix in some good-quality canned food. The downside of adding water or soft food to kibble is that it reduces the kibble's tartar-scraping benefit. But if you brush your dog's teeth faithfully, this won't be a problem.

When feeding kibble, maintain its quality and flavor by transferring it from the large bag it came in to a large airtight container or several small containers. The small ones will easily fit in your pantry and be easier to scoop from with a measuring cup. Be sure to give any container you store kibble in a thorough washing when it's empty. This will prevent residual fat from turning rancid and contaminating the new kibble you pour in.

Should your dog suddenly lose interest in the kibble he greatly enjoyed before or have loose stools where before they were firm, check with the manufacturer to see whether the formula had been changed. I was perplexed when one of my dogs turned her nose up at kibble she used to love. The company had

When a dog has a poor appetite because of illness or old age, his vet may put him on a diet of canned food.

altered the ingredients but didn't mention this on the packaging, only on its website, which to me seemed deceptive and insulting to the customers.

## Semi-Moist Food

While dry food consists of about 10 percent water, semi-moist dog food contains up to 40 percent. This really isn't a good value or a good choice for your German Shepherd. He may like the soft kibble-like chunks, but they'll stick to his teeth and undermine your efforts toward dental health. Moreover, most brands of semi-moist dog food contain dyes as well as preservatives that may include significant amounts of sugar. If you do choose to buy semi-moist food, consider purchasing a brand with organic and all-natural ingredients. These factors make a significant difference

## Canned Food

Canned dog food doesn't deliver as much nutrition as kibble, because a whopping 75 percent or more of what's in the can is water. A can that's labeled "stew" or "with gravy," may be 88 percent water. Premium brands have better ingredients, so if you're going to mix canned food in with the dry, buy premium. I confess that a premium canned food made with slow-cooked whole chicken wings, chicken liver, fruit, and veggies tempted me to buy it. My dogs loved it, and even though the product is 81 percent water, I continue to buy it now and then. My reasoning? The ingredients are wholesome—and life is short. But this is a special treat in our house, not everyday fare. But when a dog has a poor appetite because of illness or old age, his vet may put him on a diet of canned food. Always keep canned food refrigerated after it has been opened, and discard it if it's not used by the time designated on the can—usually two days.

## Noncommercial Foods

Noncommercial dog foods are what you lovingly prepare in your kitchen, usually with your pooch lying within sniffing range of the delectable aromas that waft through the air. It is interesting that in spite of the plethora of prepared dog foods now available, more and more people are choosing to forgo the convenience of commercial foods and instead feed a homemade diet. In creating a noncommercial diet for your German Shepherd, you have a choice between feeding him cooked or raw food. Either will allow you to control the ingredients and provide excellent quality, but there are disadvantages as well as advantages to both.

### Home-Cooked Food

A home-cooked diet is lip-smacking delicious to most dogs, and many people who cook for their dog see improvement in his coat, weight, and vitality. But it takes time and energy—not to mention research—to successfully feed your dog home-cooked meals. You can save time by cooking large batches and freezing the food in daily portions. But of far greater importance than saving time is knowing what is safe to

Home-cooked diets allow you to control the ingredients you're feeding your dog.

feed and what isn't. There are a number of well-reviewed books on home cooking for dogs, so consider buying a couple to help you decide what's best for your Shepherd. For one thing, you need to know how much of each vitamin and mineral is required for his needs to be met—as well as what can harm him. Many foods and beverages that are safe for you and me can make our dogs mildly or very dangerously ill. Giving your Shepherd sugary foods not only can lead to dental problems and obesity but also puts him at greater risk for diabetes mellitus. And xylitol, a sugar substitute found in many foods, including baked goods, can cause liver failure in a dog. (If you think that your dog may have eaten something containing xylitol, call your vet.) Garlic is safe in small amounts, which is why it's found in many dog recipes, but onions are not safe, nor are fat trimmings, raw eggs, or raw fish. Liver in large amounts can cause vitamin A toxicity, and human vitamin supplements containing iron are unsafe too—as are grapes, raisins, mushrooms, chocolate, and macadamia nuts. Dairy products should be left out of your dog's diet unless they are lactose free. (A small dollop of plain nonfat yogurt may be beneficial to your dog's digestion.) Cooked bones of any kind can splinter and are very dangerous. Caffeine poisoning isn't as common as chocolate poisoning, but don't let your dog sip from your tea or coffee or cola. And alcohol poisoning, which can occur from just a small amount of beer, can cause a dog to lapse into a coma and die. Don't leave peaches or plums lying around in the house or outside under a tree, as a pit from either can obstruct your dog's digestive tract.

### Raw Diets

BARF, a well-known acronym among dog lovers, stands for a diet consisting of Biologically Appropriate Raw Food. It is also called Bones and Raw Food and has become a hot topic, with many knowledgeable people praising it. Others condemn it. The diet is made up mostly of vegetables and meat, including bones. Some veterinarians think highly of BARF as long as the people feeding it know what they're doing. Other veterinarians see it as irresponsibly dangerous because of the possibility of *E.coli* (short for *Escherichia coli*) getting into the food. The truth is two-sided: BARF can harm your dog, and BARF really is nutritionally superior. But do research before feeding raw, and consult with your vet. Books have been written giving both sides of the argument. Some foods that are safe for dogs when cooked are not safe served raw. For instance, frequent feedings of raw fish can result in a thiamine (vitamin B1) deficiency and cause seizures. Raw eggs contain an enzyme that decreases absorption of biotin (vitamin H, or B7) and may bring on problems of the skin and coat. Even worse, raw eggs may contain salmonella. Great care must be taken in handling raw foods. Utensils and work spaces must be thoroughly sanitized for your family's health. Another caveat is that feeding raw can be messy and time consuming. And you may need more freezer space than you have now, as you'll be storing bones, meat, and vegetables.

Commercially prepared raw dog food has safety instructions on the packaging, as well as information about the general amount of time it will take for the food to defrost in the refrigerator. Instructions for thawing the food in microwave ovens are included, with a reminder of the importance of not letting the meat temperature get so high that a bone might cook and harden. Either way that you feed raw—commercially prepared or prepared at home—it must be done with your family's and dog's safety in mind. But if you choose to do it, and are scrupulously careful, your GSD will have cleaner teeth and probably healthier skin and coat and firmer stools.

## Prescription Diets

If your dog has food allergies, an illness, weight issue, or behavior problems, your veterinarian may prescribe a commercial food formulated by canine nutritionists to help with the specific problem. Although a prescription diet won't cure a serious illness, such as cancer or diabetes, it might possibly help slow the progression. Among the many prescription diets available are those for skin, bladder, kidney, heart, liver, joint, or digestive health. These foods are sold at veterinary clinics or through a prescription from a veterinarian.

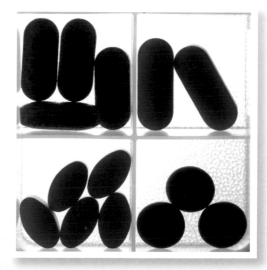

Supplements are a controversial topic that should be discussed with your vet.

## Supplements

Giving dogs supplements is a controversial topic and one you should research and discuss with your veterinarian before administering them. If your German Shepherd eats a high-quality diet, he probably doesn't need supplements. However, some medical conditions can be helped by supplements. Omega-3 and omega-6 fatty acids are important for allergic dogs, for example, but if the dog's diet provides plenty of omega-6 fatty acids, your veterinarian may suggest that you give only the omega-3s. Omega-3 fatty acids can also help reduce inflammation in arthritic dogs.

If you notice when out in the yard with your Shepherd that he's eating dirt, a behavior called pica, he may have a nutritional deficiency. Not necessarily, though, as pica can also be a sign of anemia, diabetes, or even cancer, so this must be discussed with your vet. If it is a deficiency, you can give your dog a daily multimineral and multivitamin capsule made for humans. Wrap it in peanut butter or cream cheese, or else crush it to put in his food. It's all right for a dog to eat a little soil if he has a fondness for it, but not more than a teaspoon or two a day. Probiotics, which you can buy at health stores, may improve his digestion and absorption of nutrients.

For excessive gas—the kind that can clear a room—you can give your dog a digestive enzyme marketed for dogs. It won't necessarily eliminate frequent flatulence, but it will help. Other remedies to try include eliminating soy from the diet and giving a small daily dollop of plain nonfat yogurt.

Be aware that human supplements may have ingredients your dog doesn't need (he manufactures his own vitamin C, which we do not) and other contents that may harm him. Too much iron, for example, can damage the lining of his digestive system and is toxic to his liver and kidneys. If you give your adult or senior dog a multivitamin made for humans, it should not have iron in it. And cutting the supplement in half will probably give him all that he needs of each component.

## Treats

Treats—the bits of food you give your dog between meals—add to his love of life and are an essential tool for training. They can be commercially made for dogs or just be pieces of people food, as when the two of you share a hot dog off the grill on a summer day. But choose healthy, kind-to-the-teeth treats for your German Shepherd, at least 90 percent of the time, and have him earn them by obeying a command 99 percent of the time. Linking treats to commands reaffirms that you're in charge, reinforces what he has already been trained to do, and gives him opportunities to show off how smart he is. Well-trained dogs almost always seem to take pleasure in performing commands with other people watching. And your guests probably would rather watch your GSD perform *come, sit, down,* and *stay* than listen to your child's first attempt at Mozart on the piano. Treats shouldn't be fattening or sugary, and they don't have to be expensive—just healthful. My dogs sit and perform tricks for a piece of kibble. But treating with peanut butter wrapped in a baby spinach leaf makes me as happy as it makes them.

Treats add to your dog's love of life and are an essential tool for training.

## Bones

Bones that you give your dog are treats too, except that unlike the others, they don't disappear in a flash. They also help reduce the risk of dental problems by controlling tartar buildup and scraping away plaque. The bones your dog gnaws on can be either real bones or toys that resemble the real ones and perform the same teeth-cleaning function. Know what you're getting with either type, though, as the wrong type of bone can do harm. If you choose to give the real McCoy, Dr. Fox recommends "no bones of any kind except raw beef shank bones, at least 2 inches (5 cm) long, scalded to kill off surface bacteria." Even though these bones are safe for your dog to gnaw, it's best not to leave him alone with a bone for very long. A really aggressive chewer can break off a chunk. For this reason, many people forgo real bones and buy synthetic ones instead. One good substitute for a real bone is a Nylabone with dental nubs to help control tartar and durable ends for powerful chewers such as your Shepherd. Make sure that all chew toys you give your Shepherd are designed for strong chewers.

## HOW OFTEN TO FEED AN ADULT DOG

Some knowledgeable GSD lovers advise that you feed a Shepherd who is older than 18 months but not past 9 years once or twice a day. Call me an old softy, but I believe that feeding any dog just once a day diminishes his quality of life. I don't want to eat just once a day; you probably don't either, and I can't imagine that any dog would. Other than the sheer pleasure our dogs get from eating, there is a major health factor on the side of two meals a day. It's called gastric dilatation volvulus, or bloat. (See Chapter 8.) The German Shepherd is a deep-chested dog and is prone to bloat. Wolfing down one very large daily meal will increase the risk of his getting this often fatal condition, and the risk will occur every single day. Plunk that bowl down on the floor twice a day, not because your dog must be fed twice daily but because you love him.

## When to Feed

What times of day you should feed your dog depends on your schedule. A dog should not be exercised the first hour after eating, because this will strongly increase the risk of bloat. So if you want to walk your dog in the morning, do that first and then feed him. Unless you are home during the day, which gives you the option of a mid- or late afternoon second feeding, the second meal should be in the evening. As with the morning meal, exercise him first or wait an hour or so after he's eaten and walk him then. Be sure that children understand that the dog is not to play fetch or have any other exercise the first hour after eating.

# CHAPTER 8

# GERMAN SHEPHERD HEALTH AND WELLNESS

Doing all that you can to keep your dog healthy is a responsibility you accepted the day you brought him home from the breeder, shelter, or German Shepherd Dog rescue. One of the best ways to fulfill this responsibility—or more appropriately, this privilege—is through preventive medicine. You do this by taking your dog for annual checkups, adhering to a vaccination schedule, and taking him to the vet when a problem surfaces rather than waiting until the problem becomes serious. By doing just these three things, you will have a trusted veterinarian who knows your Shepherd's medical and behavior history. That's an asset you'll be grateful for should your dog ever need treatment for a major concern.

## THE ANNUAL VET EXAM

At your Shepherd's annual veterinary visit, he will be examined from head to tail—literally. The vet will check his eyes, ears, nose, mouth (including teeth and gums), skin, coat, feet, and nails. Using a stethoscope, she will check his heart and lungs. The vet also will feel along the length of his spine and ribs and palpate his abdomen and groin area. At this visit and all other times your dog sees his vet, he will stand on a scale to be weighed. This part of the exam should never be skipped, as weight gain and unexplained weight loss can be the first signs of disease. The annual vet exam also offers you the opportunity to mention any concerns you might have. Don't hold back. Your vet doesn't have time for idle chitchat but wants to hear about real concerns you might have. And as in everything else that's important, there are no stupid questions.

## PARASITES

Parasites are tiny animals that at some point in their life cycle depend on a host for sustenance, and unfortunately that host may be your dog. Not all parasites are harmful, but the ones described in this section are.

### Internal Parasites

Internal parasites that are found in dogs range from harmless to deadly. Here are some that you and your vet will want to guard your Shepherd against.

#### Heartworm

Heartworms (*Dirofilaria immitis*) spend their adult life in the right side of the heart and the large blood vessels connecting the heart to the lungs of dogs and some other animals but rarely humans. Heartworm disease, found throughout the United States, is spread by mosquitoes carrying the worm's larvae. The damage it does is gradual, with the end result being congestive heart failure. Unfortunately, most dogs don't show signs of the disease early on. Some may have loss of appetite and weight and be listless. Another possible symptom is a dry cough. Heartworm is detected by a yearly blood test and if caught early can be treated, but the treatment is very hard on the dog. Your vet will have you give your dog a monthly preventive, which is safe, easy, inexpensive, and provides complete protection from the disease. What the medication does is interrupt heartworm development before adult worms reach the lungs and cause severe damage.

## Hookworm

Hookworms (*Ancylostoma* and *Uncinaria*) are common intestinal parasites of dogs and cats. Most infestations are in puppies and kittens, but older animals are at risk too. Hookworms attach themselves to the intestinal wall and feed on the animal's blood, causing severe anemia and digestive disorders. Symptoms may include paleness of gums, weakness, vomiting, diarrhea, and black, tarry stools. Diagnosed by examination of a stool specimen, hookworms don't need to be a concern for you, as your Shepherd's monthly heartworm preventive will also prevent hookworms.

At your Shepherd's annual veterinary visit, he will be examined from head to tail.

## Roundworm

Roundworms, often called "ascarids," look like strings of spaghetti and are the most common digestive-tract parasite in dogs and cats as well as humans. Roundworms infest the small intestine, causing malnourishment and sometimes anemia and pneumonia. A mama dog infested at any time in her life can transmit these worms to her puppies, during either gestation or nursing. A dog with a mild infestation may not show symptoms of disease except having the spaghetti-like strings show up in his feces. But with a severe infestation, there may be a thin, dull coat, a potbellied appearance, coughing, vomiting, diarrhea, or constipation. Roundworm is treated by deworming. But, as with hookworm, it can be controlled by giving a heartworm preventive. Even with the preventive, your vet will want to do an annual fecal exam, called a fecal flotation test.

## Tapeworm

Tapeworms, common in adult dogs, are flat worms having a head and neck plus a number of segments. Usually the head has suckers or muscular grooves by which the tapeworm attaches itself to the animal's intestine. The adult worm can be up to 20 inches (51 cm) long, and if that isn't disgusting enough, the many segments are full of eggs. The muscular sac wiggles around spreading tapeworm eggs, which are eaten by fleas. The dog eats the flea, and the cycle repeats itself. (You may see a rice-like segment in your dog's stool.) The only prevention is diligence in keeping your Shepherd free of fleas—much harder to do in a warm climate than a cold one. The only effective safe tapeworm medications are prescription dewormers available from your veterinarian.

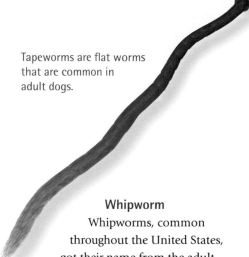

Tapeworms are flat worms that are common in adult dogs.

## Whipworm

Whipworms, common throughout the United States, got their name from the adult worm's whip-like shape. Living in the dog's (or cat's) large intestine and cecum (a pouch that receives waste material from the small intestine), the worms are 2 to 3 inches (5 to 7.5 cm) long, very thin, and rarely seen in the infested animal's feces. Your Shepherd becomes infected by ingesting food or water contaminated with whipworm eggs. An infection is diagnosed by a veterinarian's finding eggs in the feces. In a serious case, there can be bleeding into the intestine, resulting in anemia. Your vet will prescribe a common dewormer. Treatments may need to be repeated for several months.

## External Parasites

External parasites are those that remain mostly outside the dog's body while feeding.

### Fleas

Wingless insects with mouthparts adapted for piercing skin and sucking blood, fleas live off the blood of dogs, other mammals, and birds. Their ability to jump approximately 200 times their body length makes the flea one of the best jumpers on the planet and gives us more reason to despise them. Fleas can be a year-round problem in warm climates, but in cold climates they're usually seen only during the warm months. If while examining your dog you find shiny black specks the size of coal dust on your dog and they turn reddish brown on a piece of wet paper, they are flea droppings of digested blood. Use a flea comb to catch fleas, then quickly dunk the comb in a bowl of soapsudsy warm water or rubbing alcohol to drown them. Fleas get into carpets, rugs, and bedding (yours and your dog's), so if there are fleas in the house, machine wash and dry all bedding, and vacuum with a vengeance. Covering your dog's favorite sleeping areas and upholstered furniture with cotton sheets and rolling the sheets up to be laundered in hot water once a week during flea season will prevent flea larvae from hiding and maturing. Sprinkling borax on carpets and furnishings also may help. Let the borax sit for several hours, then vacuum thoroughly. If the infestation is serious, talk to your vet before taking action with a pesticide bomb or using topical products to kill the fleas.

## Mites

Ear mites, scientifically known as *Otodectes*, are in the arachnid group, as are spiders. An infestation of ear mites can present as a dark brown or black waxy discharge. Itching is intense and causes shaking of the head and scratching at the ears. The ear needs to be cleaned of debris, then treated with an agent designed to kill mites. If your dog curls up

### *Want to Know More?*

For more information on ear mites, see Chapter 6: German Shepherd Grooming Needs.

with his tail in contact with the ear, you may want to treat the tail as well. An untreated infestation of ear mites could possibly cause hearing loss.

## Ringworm

Actually caused by a fungus rather than a worm, the condition known as ringworm grows on the skin, causing hair loss and itching. The classic symptom is a small round lesion that's devoid of hair and may have scaly skin in the center. Diagnosis is made by examining the skin using a black light. Ringworm is contagious and can spread to humans. Don't try to treat this yourself. If you see even a very small bald spot on your Shepherd's body, take him to the vet immediately. Medication will be prescribed.

## Ticks

Ticks transmit the widest variety of pathogens of all bloodsucking arthropods, making them far nastier than fleas. Of the deadly diseases that ticks inflict on animals and humans, the one most people are familiar with is Lyme disease. But the other diseases are just as serious, and some can lie dormant for years before causing illness. Ehrlichiosis, for instance, can remain dormant for up to seven years before showing symptoms. Ticks are crawlers, not jumpers. In warm or hot weather, they wait on tall grasses and other plant matter for their food source to brush against them, then transfer from plant to animal. Check your dog and yourself for ticks after any outing to somewhere that ticks may be encountered.

## BREED-SPECIFIC HEALTH ISSUES

Unfortunately, the list of health issues to which German Shepherd Dogs are prone is long. However, that can be said of other

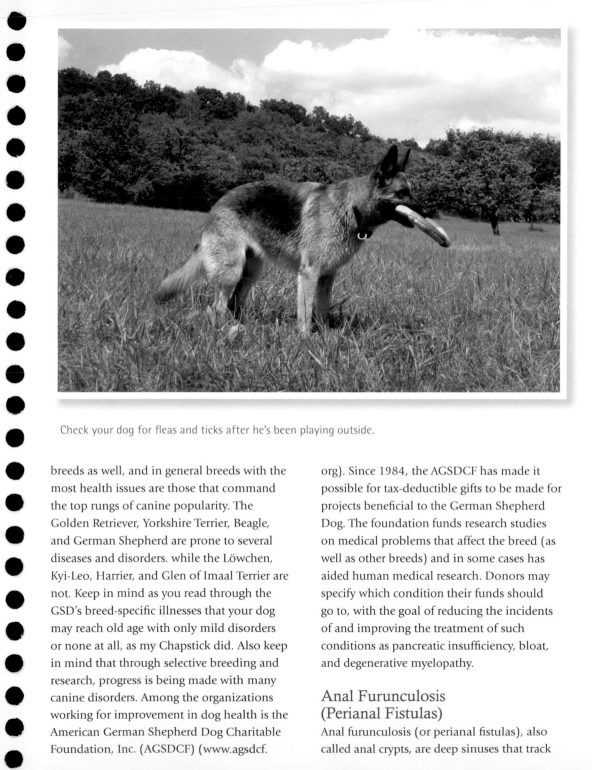

Check your dog for fleas and ticks after he's been playing outside.

breeds as well, and in general breeds with the most health issues are those that command the top rungs of canine popularity. The Golden Retriever, Yorkshire Terrier, Beagle, and German Shepherd are prone to several diseases and disorders. while the Löwchen, Kyi-Leo, Harrier, and Glen of Imaal Terrier are not. Keep in mind as you read through the GSD's breed-specific illnesses that your dog may reach old age with only mild disorders or none at all, as my Chapstick did. Also keep in mind that through selective breeding and research, progress is being made with many canine disorders. Among the organizations working for improvement in dog health is the American German Shepherd Dog Charitable Foundation, Inc. (AGSDCF) (www.agsdcf.

org). Since 1984, the AGSDCF has made it possible for tax-deductible gifts to be made for projects beneficial to the German Shepherd Dog. The foundation funds research studies on medical problems that affect the breed (as well as other breeds) and in some cases has aided human medical research. Donors may specify which condition their funds should go to, with the goal of reducing the incidents of and improving the treatment of such conditions as pancreatic insufficiency, bloat, and degenerative myelopathy.

## Anal Furunculosis (Perianal Fistulas)

Anal furunculosis (or perianal fistulas), also called anal crypts, are deep sinuses that track

## How to Remove a Tick

To remove an attached tick, grasp it with tweezers or a tick remover as close to where it's attached as you can, then slowly pull it straight out. Don't twist as you pull or the mouth parts will stay buried in the skin and can cause infection. Put the tick in alcohol or flush it down the toilet. Ticks are hard to kill and live for years, so don't throw one in the trash unless you're certain that it's dead. Your veterinarian can recommend a flea and tick preventive that you apply topically between your dog's shoulder blades. This preparation kills ticks before they have a chance to transmit disease. Use it only as directed by your vet.

through the skin, sometimes with flat open areas of ulceration. They are usually confined to the skin around the anus, but in severe cases may spread and run down the inside of the rear legs. They really aren't fistulas, as they remain in the skin and don't open into other organs. Fortunately, the anal sacs, rectum, and colon aren't affected by the disease, which occurs almost exclusively in the German Shepherd and German Shepherd mixes.

Anal furunculosis generally presents between the ages of three and eight. It affects both sexes, and the cause is unknown. Because these skin lesions are irritating, the first sign noticed may be the dog's licking and biting at the affected region. If there is pain, the dog may also be reluctant to relieve himself and not want his rear end or tail touched. Diagnosis is confirmed by ruling out other causes for the lesions. Depending on severity, treatment is with drugs, surgery, or both.

## Chronic Degenerative Radiculomyelopathy (CDRM)

Chronic degenerative radiculomyelopathy (CDRM) occurs almost exclusively in the older German Shepherd Dog, and as such is sometimes referred to as German Shepherd myelopathy. A dog with CDRM gradually loses the use of his hind legs, which frustrates the dog and often brings on depression. The cause

of CDRM is unknown, but the underlying disease is degeneration of the white matter in the spinal cord. Diagnosis is based on clinical signs and the absence of any other cause. At this time there is no known treatment or cure, and the disease progresses until the dog can't rise or walk on his hind limbs. The front legs, however, aren't affected, and a canine cart can provide mobility. Exercise for the duration of the dog's life is important, and walking and swimming help both with muscle tone and in keeping the dog's spirits up. It may take as long as a half year or so for paralysis to set in, or else it can happen over a couple of months. When the disease progresses for a longer than usual period, the dog may lose urinary and bowel continence, and weakness may develop in the front limbs. The one saving grace of myelopathy is that it is not a painful disease.

## Epilepsy

Epilepsy, a disorder of recurring seizures brought on by uncontrolled electrical activity in the brain, occurs in all breeds, large and small. But among those having a higher tendency to develop epilepsy is the GSD. Seizures can be caused by many and far-ranging conditions—from congenital defects or toxins or certain medications. "Grand mal seizures" cause severe muscle contractions throughout the body, while "petit mal" seizures are less severe and affect just a few muscle groups. If your dog appears to have epilepsy, your vet will perform a physical and neurologic exam with laboratory tests and perhaps X-rays. If a cause can't be found and the dog had his first seizure between six months and five years, the diagnosis will be idiopathic or primary epilepsy. Treatment is by medication, most commonly phenobarbital. No medication can cure epilepsy, but it may decrease the frequency, severity, and duration of seizures. If a dog has prolonged seizures, injectable drugs such as Valium are sometimes administered. Severe and long seizures are a medical emergency and can be fatal.

## Gastric Dilatation Volvulus

Gastric Dilatation Volvulus (GDV), commonly called bloat, or stomach torsion, causes a dog's stomach to fill with air and become twisted to the point that he may go into shock and die. There is a long list of breeds—large dogs with deep and narrow chests—that are susceptible to bloat, and the German Shepherd is one. It's mostly seen in dogs ages five and up. Dogs with a first-degree relative who suffered from bloat and those who wolf their food are additionally at risk. Recent research has found that eating from a raised feeder also increases the risk

The most frequently seen symptom is dry heaves (mostly unsuccessful attempts to vomit), with the second being an enlarged abdomen. If either symptom occurs, seek professional help immediately. If it's after hours, take your Shepherd to the nearest animal emergency hospital—phoning first if possible so that they can be prepared. Even

German Shepherd Dogs are especially prone to bloat; the best prevention is to restrict exercise before and after feeding.

if the stomach hasn't yet rotated, GDV is always life-threatening. Surgical intervention is frequently required but not always. An exploratory procedure may result in the surgeon's being able to perform what's called "gastropexy" to prevent subsequent episodes of bloat. The best prevention against bloat is to restrict exercise before and after eating—especially after. There should be no exercise for the first hour after a meal and no strenuous exercise for at least two hours.

A healthy diet and exercise will keep your GSD in good working condition.

## Hemangiosarcoma

Hemangiosarcoma, a cancer of the circulatory system (organs and tissues involved in circulating blood and lymph through the body), is seen more frequently in German Shepherd Dogs than in any other breed. Usually occurring as a tumor on the spleen or heart, in time it causes internal bleeding. Symptoms may include extreme thirst, gums becoming white, disorientation, collapse, and shock. There are no screening tests for hemangiosarcoma, and no hereditary component has been found. Sadly, most dogs succumb either to internal bleeding that can't be stopped or to cancer that has spread to other organs. I lost an older dog who was not a Shepherd to hemangiosarcoma. I mention this only to say that my dog seemed well and happy, and he had a good appetite until the morning he woke extremely ill. X-rays proved the worst, yet my dog did not suffer more than a few hours.

## Inflammatory Bowel Disease (IBD)

Inflammatory bowel disease (IBD)—not to be confused with Irritable Bowel Syndrome (IBS)—is a condition in which inflammatory cells infiltrate the stomach or intestine, or both. It is mostly characterized by cells invading the wall of the intestine as the body's reaction to an insult or injury. Possible causes are many and include a reaction to certain drugs, food additives, parasites, and psychological factors affecting your dog. IBD isn't curable but can be controlled by the proper diet and medications and careful monitoring by the veterinarian and owner. Diets low in fat are generally better tolerated in dogs with IBD. Carbohydrates low in gluten may also be helpful, so your vet may have you remove wheat, oats, rye, and barley from your Shepherd's diet. Home cooking may be tried if you make sure that the diet is balanced.

## Lick Granuloma

Acral lick dermatitis (also called lick granuloma) is a condition caused by excessive licking. Any dog can get lick granuloma, but it's most common in large-breed dogs such as the German Shepherd. Usually occurring when the dog is middle aged, lick granulomas almost always are located on the front of the wrist area or just above the paw of the rear leg.

Symptoms, in addition to chronic licking of the feet or legs, include hair loss and irritated skin that looks thickened. Often there will be ulceration and oozing at the center. For treatment, your vet may prescribe medication and have you apply a bad-tasting liquid to the affected area. The vet will probably want your dog to wear an Elizabethan collar—a head cover that's also called a cone or E-collar— to prevent further licking. And if there's a psychological cause behind the problem, she may also prescribe an antidepressant medication.

## Lumbosacral Stenosis (Cauda Equina Syndrome)

Lumbosacral stenosis goes by many other names, with cauda equina syndrome (CES) being most frequently used. Common in large-breed dogs, especially German Shepherds,

it is a neural condition that causes low back pain. Lameness, wobbliness, dragging a foot, and difficulty getting up from the floor are symptoms. Sometimes congenital but more often acquired later in life, the condition usually occurs between three and seven years of age. It is treated surgically or nonsurgically depending on a number of factors, including severity of the condition and overall health.

## Pannus (Chronic Superficial Keratitis)

Pannus, or chronic superficial keratitis, is a disorder of the immune system that affects a dog's eyes. It is often called German Shepherd Dog keratitis because the disease is found predominantly in German Shepherds and only rarely affects other breeds. With pannus, essentially the immune system decides that the eye is foreign tissue and attacks it. At this time, no one is really sure what causes pannus. Early symptoms are redness and sensitivity, and sunlight may worsen the condition. If your dog's eyes look red or he rubs them continually, take him to the vet. Pannus is treated with cortisone drops or injections of cortisone under the outer surface of the eye. As yet there is no cure, but the disease can usually be controlled without discomfort to the dog or loss of vision.

## Von Willebrand's Disease (vWD)

Von Willebrand's disease is an inherited bleeding disorder found in people and dogs, but among dogs a higher than normal incidence is found in the German Shepherd. What causes vWD is a lack of, or reduction of, the von Willebrand factor—which plays an essential role in the blood-clotting process. Often the disease goes undiagnosed until the dog is age three or older. It's quite common, with usually mild symptoms, and most dogs with vWD have only occasional bleeding episodes. There can be nose bleeds, blood in the stool, hematomas, and bleeding from the gums. Intermittent limping can signal bleeding into the joints. If the dog's gums tend to bleed, a diet of soft foods is in order. Before giving any over-the-counter medication to a dog with vWD, consult your vet. If a dog with vWD needs surgery, his vet will take special precautions to minimize bleeding. This is a serious condition because if untreated, excessive bleeding can lead to anemia, shock, and death. But the dog whose family and vet provide the supervision and care he needs can live contentedly for many years.

## GENERIC HEALTH ISSUES

The few health problems listed below range from easy to difficult to treat, but they all require veterinary care.

### Allergies

Allergies are disorders of the immune system that can be mild or serious. We and our canine family members can develop allergies to any number of things found in foods, household products, plants, or the air we breathe. Allergic inhalant dermatitis, or atopy, is a reaction to something inhaled, such as pollen, dust mites, mold, or feathers. It's even possible for human dander to cause a reaction in dogs, just as their dander can react in us. Flea saliva is a common cause of allergic reaction. There are more than 15 different antigens in a flea's saliva, each one capable of causing a dog to have an allergic response, so it's no wonder that flea bite allergies and flea bite dermatitis are problems for our dogs. And studies show that dogs with flea allergies may have inhalant dermatitis, which compounds the problem. Hence, allergy testing should be done before a specific therapy is prescribed—especially if the problem doesn't appear to be seasonal and doesn't respond to traditional treatment, which includes giving antihistamines. Not all veterinarians—even good ones—are comfortable testing for allergies or offering hypo-sensitizing treatments. You can ask for a referral to a veterinary dermatologist or look for one online. Intradermal skin testing is the most common method used by veterinary dermatologists to find the root of the problem,

but other methods are used as well. If your Shepherd is suffering from allergies, he can harm himself by licking, chewing, and scratching his skin. Your vet may prescribe medication to make him more comfortable and will likely have him wear an Elizabethan collar to keep him from bothering his skin. Treat your dog after putting the E-collar on him, and remove it for walks, potty breaks, and feeding. Other things you can do to help include using hypoallergenic detergents for your dog's bedding and hypoallergenic shampoo for bathing him. Use only stainless steel bowls for his food and water.

### Cancer

Malignant and invasive growths, or tumors, unfortunately are as common in dogs as in humans. The many cancers that dogs get include lymphosarcoma (lymphoma), osteosarcoma (bone cancer), mammary gland tumors (mostly in females who were not spayed early in life), testicular tumors (most common in intact older males), and mast cell tumors. (Mast cells are part of the body's immune system and normally occur in the skin and other tissues.) Symptoms vary with the cancer, and treatment, as in humans, can include surgery, radiation therapy, and chemotherapy. Again, as with humans, complementary and alternative medicine (CAM) is also being used to treat cancer in animals. (See section "Alternative Therapies.")

## Ear Infections

The medical name for inflammation of the outer ear canal is otitis externa, and about 20 percent of the dog population is affected by this disease. Because many things can be at the root of ear infections, there are many different symptoms: shaking the head or tilting it to one side, scratching or rubbing, odor, discharge, redness or swelling, and of course, pain. Even depression can indicate an ear disease. The problem can be hereditary or caused by an immune condition or a foreign body such as plant awns (see Chapter 11), or any of several other possibilities, including a tumor.

Treatment for ear infection depends on what caused the infection and on whether there are secondary conditions. Your vet may prescribe antibiotics for a bacterial infection,

or antifungals for a yeast infection. If a hormonal problem or allergy is the root cause, treating the whole dog, not just his ears, will be necessary. In many instances, food allergies are linked to ear problems. Or the condition can be caused by ear mites, as discussed earlier. No matter what you think may have caused the problem, if you think that your dog has an ear infection, call your vet. A holistic vet may recommend essential oils to help with chronic ear infections.

## Eye Infections

Eye infections, which may be contagious, are medical conditions resulting from viral, bacterial, allergenic, or other microbial agents. So too can be any disease that causes the eyes to become dry. Although not necessarily serious, an eye infection may bring on complications if not treated. Symptoms include excessive discharge or blinking, pawing or scratching at the eye, or red and inflamed eyes. Although an eye infection may not be cured quickly, treatment, which depends on the cause, is effective. This may include eye

About 20 percent of the dog population is affected by otitis externa, an inflammation of the outer ear canal.

drops (over the counter or prescription), oral medication, or an "eye scrub," which fortunately isn't nearly as harsh as it sounds. Don't use over-the-counter drops except on the advice of your vet—after she has examined your Shepherd's eyes.

## ALTERNATIVE THERAPIES

As in traditional medicine, alternative medicine includes a number of fields in which a vet may specialize. Alternative care for both humans and animals has been a growing phenomenon in Western countries for decades, while in the East it has been around for thousands of years. Health care from a holistic veterinarian may include alternative, complementary, or integrative medicine options and will rely on drugs and surgical intervention only when no other alternative is available. Terms used for conventional medicine used in combination with alternative therapies are "holistic care," "complementary medicine," or "integrative medicine." Holistic health care and medicine put the emphasis on prevention of disease for general well-being and good health. Becoming ever more popular among a growing number of people—for both their pets and themselves—holistic medicine involves looking at the whole animal, or person, when determining how best to prevent, diagnose, and treat diseases. If you decide to choose a holistic practitioner, be sure to get referrals and see only licensed professionals— the same as you would do in choosing a traditional veterinarian. Be aware, too, that as with traditional medications, herbs and supplements can have side effects.

### Acupuncture

Acupuncture involves sticking very small needles into specific points in the body to improve energy flow; it is the main treatment

Acupuncture involves sticking very small needles into specific points in the body to improve energy flow.

of a quarter of the world's population. It has been used in China for thousands of years, and the first book on acupuncture was written in China around 200 B.C. It took a long time for acupuncture to come to America, but today in the United States there are 16 schools of acupuncture, medical and nursing schools that teach the practice, and about 8,000 acupuncturists. Acupuncture is used in veterinary care to treat specific conditions while strengthening the body's immune system. Visit the American Academy of Veterinary Acupuncture (AAVA) at www.aava.org for more information.

### Chiropractic

Chiropractic is used to treat many conditions and can, through hands-on adjustments, identify and correct misaligned or fixated vertebrae—the series of small bones that form the spine. A dog who is especially active—in everyday play as well as in sports—may at

The goal of herbal therapy is to boost the immune system by helping the body heal itself.

times need spine alignment and will benefit from having a veterinarian who practices chiropractic. For more information, visit the American Veterinary Chiropractic Association (AVCA) at www.animalchiropractic.org.

## Herbal

The goal of herbal therapy is to boost the immune system by helping the body heal itself. Herbalists in the Chinese tradition customize a blend of herbs to promote well-being or balance in the body. In the Western (or European) tradition, a specific herb is used to treat a specific ailment. Consult with your Shepherd's regular veterinarian before starting your dog on herbal therapy. For more information, visit the Veterinary Botanical Medical Association (VBMA) at www.vbma.org.

## Homeopathy

Dating back to Hippocrates, homeopathy works on the principle of "Similia Similibus Curentur," meaning "like cures like." Homeopathic remedies are made from substances that in large doses can cause illness. But they are administered in diluted and minute doses to effect a cure. For more information, visit the American Holistic Veterinary Medical Association (AHVMA) at www.ahvma.org.

## Physical Therapy (PT)/TTouch

Physical therapy (PT), also called physical rehabilitation, can help animals recover from injuries, surgery, or chronic pain—just as it does for humans. Joint mobility and overall agility can be improved by doggy PT. And while sprains, arthritis, and hip and elbow dysplasia can't be cured by PT, the pain and stiffness these disorders cause can be reduced. Sometimes doggy PT is used to prevent problems before they can happen, as when a dog participates in a rigorous sport. PT should be performed on a dog only by a professional therapist specializing in the treatment of animals. In fact, only a licensed PT or licensed physical therapist assistant (PTA) working under the supervision of a PT is permitted by law to perform PT. It's also important that the therapist work closely with your dog's veterinarian.

A widely used and highly regarded form of physical therapy is the Tellington Touch method, developed by Linda Tellington-Jones. TTouch, as it is often called, is actually a behavioral therapy in which touch, manipulation, and guiding an animal through movement exercises works on emotional and health issues. TTouch isn't massage or acupressure but a calming way to keep an animal focused. A wide variety of behavioral problems, from barking to separation anxiety, can be helped by this method. Tellington Touch instructors can be found throughout the country. In fact, the official TTouch website (www.ttouch.com) claims that there are more than 1,000 practitioners in 27 countries on 6 continents.

## EMERGENCY CARE

First aid is giving basic medical care to your dog at home or wherever he was injured before you can get him to a veterinarian. Or in a mild situation, it's what you do for the dog before you phone the vet and find out how to care for the dog yourself because the problem isn't serious. And what a relief that is. But when it is serious, transporting your dog requires special handling to minimize the risk of further injury or worsening pain. Your Shepherd has a good amount of fur, so placing him on a rigid board, such as plywood, for the trip to the vet will not make him more uncomfortable and may be helpful. And a blanket or large towel can serve as a stretcher to get him into the car. It would be helpful if someone were with you to help lift him into the car. And whoever can go with you to the clinic can help keep your dog as comfortable and calm as possible. Always call ahead, if possible, as letting the clinic or hospital know why you're coming will let them be prepared before you get there.

If you don't already have a book on first aid for dogs at home, it's a good idea to get one. Read it before you need it, and anytime you go on a trip or camping with your dog, take the book with you. If a pet first-aid course is available in your area, this too would be a wise way to spend some time. There are two first-aid measures you definitely should learn to perform on your dog: cardiopulmonary resuscitation (CPR), compression of the chest in an attempt to supply blood to the brain and all around the body, as well as deliver oxygen to the brain and body (which is imperative for survival). The second: artificial respiration, sometimes called "mouth to mouth," is the process of breathing or blowing into the lungs of an unconscious person or animal to keep up the proper oxygen levels to the brain and other vital parts of the body. When CPR is successful, the person or animal may come around, and a life may have been saved. Your book on first aid for dogs will give instructions (complete with illustrations) on how to perform these procedures on your Shepherd. This is a book you really can't afford to be without.

### Bites

Dogs may be bitten by insects or other animals. With the former, owners usually become aware of the bites or stings long after they have happened. Usually a large swelling of the muzzle is noticed with no particular evidence

You may have to muzzle your dog in an emergency situation to prevent him from biting you, however unintentionally.

of pain. Or else there can be hives or welts—an allergic reaction to the bite or sting. As first aid, you may administer Benadryl or an equivalent product. But if there is no fever and the dog acts normally (even though abnormal in appearance), treatment usually isn't necessary, other than pulling out the stinger if you are able to see it. Swelling caused by a sting should go away in about 48 hours. With spider bites, however, swelling may last for days or weeks—sometimes being accompanied by sloughing of the tissue where the dog was bitten.

If your Shepherd receives multiple stings from bees, wasps, or hornets, take him to the vet. Any severe allergic reaction, which could be difficulty breathing, vomiting, diarrhea, or shock and collapse, indicates an emergency. If your dog has collapsed, you may need help lifting him into the car. When my Chapstick swallowed a bee and collapsed in shock, I phoned the clinic and two vet techs were waiting outside for us when we arrived. Corticosteroids were given, and Chappie was fine.

Should your dog be bitten by another dog, or any other animal, there may be damage to muscles and other tissues. Even a small wound from a bite can be contaminated with bacteria and prone to infection. Flush a bite wound with water or hydrogen peroxide. Bandage the wound as best you can. Then take your dog to the vet or emergency clinic. Even the most minor bite will probably require an oral antibiotic.

## Bleeding

Bleeding, the process of losing blood or having blood flow, is frightening to see in your dog. The important thing is to stay as calm as possible to stop the bleeding by applying a pressure dressing. To do this, place several pieces of clean gauze over the wound and bandage it snugly. If you see swelling below the dressing, the bandage is too tight and must

be loosened or removed. When bandaging, avoid using anything elasticized. If you don't have bandages available, place a pad or even your hand on the wound and press firmly. For bleeding that is only minor, you may flush the wound using Betadine, chlorhexidine, or clean water. Keep flushing until any grime or foreign material is gone, then apply an antiseptic ointment and cover the wound with a bandage. Bleeding that won't stop with direct pressure is an emergency requiring veterinary care as soon as possible. The same goes for bleeding into the eye. Internal bleeding, a severe problem, is deceptive in that no blood shows unless it flows from the dog's nose or mouth. Anytime your dog shows symptoms such as rapid or shallow breathing, pale gums, fainting, or a weak pulse, assume there is internal bleeding and seek help immediately. Do the same if your dog is hit by a car. Even if the accident is so minimal that he can walk afterward, he must be examined.

## Broken Bones or Other Injuries

A break in the bone or cartilage is usually referred to as a fracture and usually is the result of trauma, such as falling or being hit by a vehicle. A broken bone can be very painful, so your reaction will be to want to reduce the trauma as much as possible before getting the dog to the vet clinic. But don't attempt to stabilize fractures yourself. What you can do, if bone fragments are visible, is to use clean bandage material or a towel to cover the area until your dog is in the care of his vet. Cleanliness of any injury that breaks a dog's skin is very important in preventing further harm. Prevent harm to yourself, too, by not putting your hand in the dog's mouth if he's conscious. No matter how much your dog loves you, if he's in pain, frightened, or disoriented, he may bite without even thinking about it. If you have a muzzle, gently slip it on him and keep him warm with a blanket or your coat or jacket while transporting him to the vet.

## Burns and Scalds

Burns are injuries to tissues caused by heat, friction, electricity, radiation, or chemicals, while scalds are burns caused by hot liquid or steam. If your dog becomes burned or scalded, don't try to treat the injury with a topical solution. Use only cold water, or cover the affected area with clean wet towels, then call your vet. Severe or extensive burns or scalds are an emergency, as fluid loss and decreased blood flow can make the dog go into shock.

Frostbite results from prolonged exposure to freezing or subfreezing temperatures

Be cautious of over-exercising your GSD on a hot day—even if it's in water.

## Frostbite

Frostbite results from exposure to freezing or subfreezing temperatures and most commonly affects the tips of the ears, the tail, the scrotum, and the feet—especially the toes. If tissue actually freezes, it will die. Frostbitten tissue may appear pale or gray in color, and the area will be cold to the touch and hard. If you think that your dog has frostbite, warm the affected area rapidly with warm but not hot water. Don't use dry heat (as from a heating pad or hair dryer), and don't massage the area. Call your vet or the emergency clinic, as your dog must be examined as soon as possible.

## Heatstroke

Heatstroke (hyperthermia) is a life-threatening condition caused by prolonged exposure to the sun on a hot day or being in an enclosed area that is overly warm and poorly ventilated. Dogs don't sweat when they're hot, as we do. Instead, they pant, and hard panting on a hot day is cause for alarm. To cool an overheated dog before taking him to the vet, the American Kennel Club (AKC) recommends offering a small amount of water to drink, ice chips to lick, Pedialyte to restore electrolytes, hosing him down with cool water, applying an ice pack to the groin area, and rubbing alcohol on the paw pads. If you're not certain that your dog is in danger, assume that he is and take action because if he does have heatstroke you must act swiftly. Cool him down first, as best you can, then take him to the vet. And never exercise your Shepherd outdoors on a hot day or leave him in the car with the windows partially open, even on an only slightly warm day. The temperature inside the car will far exceed the temperature outside.

## Poisoning

Poisoning destroys or impairs life; unfortunately, the list of substances that are toxic to dogs is long, with many of them being in our homes, garages, and gardens. (See Chapters 2 and 7.) But even substances used on a dog's skin to keep him in good health—such as a tick and flea preventive or a solution for cleaning surface wounds—can be poisonous if ingested. In addition to keeping anything toxic to your dog out of his reach, it's important to recognize signs of poisoning. They include drooling, vomiting, loss of bowel control, trembling, weakness, uncontrolled muscle spasms, seizures (which may be misdiagnosed as epilepsy), collapse, and coma. Sometimes vomiting must be induced to prevent death, as when a dog has ingested oral rodenticides.

If you suspect that your dog has been poisoned, call your vet immediately, even if

## Training Tidbit

One way to prevent a disaster from happening to your Shepherd is to keep him from running free. Train him to come on command and to stay when you tell him to. A dog who is allowed to roam is far more likely to be hit by a car, injured in a fight, or poisoned than one who isn't.

your dog has not begun exhibiting symptoms. With some toxins, such as antifreeze, one small lick can cause kidney damage. Common pain relievers such as aspirin or ibuprofin can harm your dog too and should not be given except on the advice of your vet. If there is paint, motor oil, tar, or a petroleum product on your dog's coat, don't try to remove it with paint remover or detergents. Wear protective gloves while rubbing liquid paraffin or vegetable oil into the coat, then bathe the dog well with warm water and baby shampoo. Rubbing in flour can help absorb the poison. For help identifying plants dangerous to dogs, visit the websites of the Humane Society of the United States (HSUS) and the American Society for Prevention of Cruelty to Animals (ASPCA).

# CHAPTER 9

# GERMAN SHEPHERD TRAINING

The pleasures you'll derive from continuing your Shepherd's education are many. One is that with apologies to no one you will have control over another living being. We're not able to control our family and friends, nor should we want to. But not having control over a canine member of the family is negligence. We don't control our adult dogs by use of force, though, and never punitively. It's all done through the bond we have built with the dog, and we do it in ways that make him feel confident in himself and comfortable in the world beyond his home. I have restrained from mentioning the GSD's high intelligence in the last five chapters. Now it's time to bring it up again. The Shepherd needs to have his mind exercised as much as his body. If this isn't done, he'll be unhappy and frustrated for reasons he doesn't understand. It is somewhat like putting a college-bound A-student back in second grade. Don't do it. Keep training your Shepherd. Let him use his intelligence to develop new skills throughout his life. You'll always be glad you did.

I'm happy to say that I have never met an untrained adult GSD, but if I were to meet one, I would wish mightily that the Shepherd could go to a new home. At the animal shelter I do meet Shepherds with only a little training. They may sit or lie down on command. That's a start but doesn't come near what every Shepherd deserves: to be taught to *remain* sitting, lying down, or standing until released from the command; to walk in lock-step with his owner when told—not allowing any diversion to break this action we call heeling. Mastering these intermediate commands will make your Shepherd feel good about himself. You'll feel good too, as each of these commands will contribute to your dog's safety and your enjoyment of living with him. It's a win-win situation. Even the neighbors win.

## Want to Know More?

For a refresher on basic obedience commands, see Chapter 4: Training Your German Shepherd Puppy.

# INTERMEDIATE OBEDIENCE COMMANDS

You may teach intermediate commands at home, but do consider enrolling your Shepherd in an intermediate obedience class. There he will meet new dogs of many breeds, which will reinforce and add to his socialization. The importance of socialization for an adult Shepherd is almost on a par with health maintenance. Additionally, the group setting will add distractions while your dog is learning, and intermediate skills are *about* the dog's obeying commands in spite of distractions. In fact, you can't really know that your dog understands and accepts *sit-stay* or *heel* until you see him do it around other dogs who may not be obeying the command.

In addition to teaching your dog to obey verbal commands, you will teach him hand signals that complement the spoken word. Each of these discreet movements will be a pleasure to perform and see your dog respond to, as hand signals more than verbal signals reveal the depth of your partnership. I always enjoyed walking into a room where my Charlie was or finding him in the fenced yard and very lightly touching my hand to the side of my left leg. Charlie would immediately come to stand at my side, knowing that we were going somewhere together. Hand signals are also valuable and sometimes essential when communicating with an older dog who is hard of hearing.

Remember to always be positive when training your adult Shepherd, just as you would be if he were a puppy. Your tools for positive training through all life stages are treats, praise, and petting. That your dog isn't learning at the pace you expected or at the pace your other dog or dogs learned doesn't indicate a lack of intelligence. Try never to sound exasperated while training, and use your hands only to praise, not punish or force him to obey. When he doesn't obey he doesn't get rewarded—but he doesn't get scolded either. If every training session is short, easy, and fun, your dog will look forward to the next session. What treats to use depends on your Shepherd's palate. You may reward a dog who thrills easily with his regular kibble, which is nutritious and kind to his teeth and gums, but for the GSD gourmet you must up the ante. Tiny dog biscuits, pieces of hot dog (zap them

Small pieces of cut-up apple make a great reward when your GSD does something right.

in the microwave to make them less greasy), cheese, cereal, small pieces of apple, raw carrots, or green beans are all enjoyed by most dogs. Once in a while end a training session by "jackpotting" your dog (as my favorite trainer called it). A handful of treats at the end of a session tells the dog he's a star student.

And finally, before beginning a session at home or in class, it's a good idea to give your dog a short walk. You don't want to tire him out, but letting him burn a little energy before getting down to work might make it easier for him to focus. And if he goes potty before a session, he won't be distracted by that need.

## Heel

The concept of heeling—when a dog walks in lockstep with his owner—began with hunters needing to keep their dogs under control either on or off lead. Because most hunters were right-handed, they carried the gun in their right hand and had the dog walk at their left side. This tradition continues today, although what we hold in our right hand is the dog's leash, not a gun, and we're walking our dogs for the exercise and pleasure of seeing the beauties of nature or the sights along a bustling boulevard. There's still good cause to have your dog heel on your left side, even if you're not a hunter, as by doing so you put yourself between him and oncoming traffic when there's no sidewalk. (However, if you plan to train your dog in agility, he should get used to walking on your left *or* right side.) In addition to keeping our dogs safe when walking against traffic, we teach them to heel so that they won't pull us off our feet—which could result in our being injured, our dog's being injured or killed while dashing across a street, our dog's tangling with another dog, or our dog's jumping up on a child who forever after would be terrified of German Shepherds. Teaching the dog to obey the *heel*

command can prevent any of these scenarios from coming true. For this, the *heel* command deserves a 21-gun salute.

*Heel* may be safely practiced while walking your dog at night as well as in daylight. You may purchase a lighted collar cover that attaches easily to your dog's leash or collar for nighttime visibility up to 1 mile (1.5 km). During daytime walks in the park or a safe place without heavy foot traffic, heeling should not be a rigid rule. Life is too short for your dog not to stop and sniff the trees and grass. Have him heel for a bit, then release him from the command by saying "Okay"—the word you will use to release him from any command. And always remember that before giving any command, you must have your dog's attention.

### How to Teach It

1. Holding your dog's leash in your right hand, have him standing on your left side with his shoulder next to your leg.
2. *Heel* is an action command, so say your dog's name followed by the word "Heel" and begin walking purposefully (stride out rather than saunter).
3. If your dog should walk in front of you or pull on the leash, immediately stop

The *stay* command instructs your Shepherd to stay where he is until you release him by saying "Okay."

walking. At first he won't understand why you did, but over time he will. Anytime he forges ahead, you may say "Ah-ah" or remain quiet. But do stop walking

4. After stopping, guide him back into position and get his attention by repeating Step 2. If your dog is reluctant to learn *heel*, you may encourage him to stay in step with you by pausing every few yards (m) to give tiny treats. But being out walking is a treat in itself, and most dogs don't need to be treated while learning to heel.

## Stay

The *stay* command instructs your Shepherd to stay where he is until you release him by saying "Okay." This is a big step in building on the bond you already share—a bond that will always be dependent on your leadership. Learning to stay on command also helps a dog remain composed in a wide range of situations, a few of which he might prefer not to experience—such as being at the vet's. Of greater importance is that being trained to stay where he is until you give the release word will keep him from running out an open door at home, the vet's, or in the car without your permission. Another bonus comes with teaching your dog *stay*: his composure and even temperament will enable people who don't particularly like being in the company of large dogs to feel relaxed in his presence. You can command your dog to stay when he is standing, sitting, or lying down. But when you are teaching the command, you will have him sit. (So, effectively, he is also learning the *sit-stay*.)

After your GSD has learned *stay*, for the rest of his life you will want to give the command before he steps out the door of any building, gets out of a car, or steps into an intersection. Don't be discouraged if *stay* seems a little difficult for your Shepherd to master, especially when practiced away from home. If he is newly adopted, he may feel anxious when you're not close to him. And if you've had him from when he was a wriggly puppy, his GSD mind may be wondering how he can protect you from harm if he's not right next to you. But you're the leader. You know what's best. Hence, your dog must learn *stay* and not question the command—that is unless he sees someone run up to you and try to snatch your handbag. Then your dog may break *stay*.

### How to Teach It

1. Begin teaching *stay* by having your dog sit on your left side by your left heel.
2. Holding the leash slack in your left hand, command "Stay" and hold your right hand—palm open—in front of your dog as a visual signal. (This is called the blocking motion.)
3. Step out in front of your dog but close to him, and stand facing him for just a few seconds, then quickly walk around him (again staying close), and stand by his right side, where you began.
4. Praise and treat him for having stayed put, then repeat the exercise. But this time move just a little farther away when walking in front of him. Stay close when walking around his back, though, or he may think that you are walking away.
5. As your dog becomes more confident with staying still while you are in motion, you

will be able to extend the leash and increase the distance as you walk in front of and around him.

## Down-Stay

Normally you would not put your dog in a *stay* while he is standing and make him remain in that position over a long period. It would be tiring and possibly stressful for him, especially if he is an older dog. Being in a *sit-stay* for any length of time could also be tiring for your Shepherd. But giving him the *down* command followed by *stay* will put him in a position he can remain in for quite a while without being uncomfortable. In fact, he may fall asleep in a *down-stay* at home, which is just what you would want him to do if the book club was meeting at your house or you were practicing for your oboe lesson. After teaching your dog the *down-stay* in a class setting, your trainer may in subsequent weeks have you reinforce the command by adding distractions. When your dog knows that he is to maintain a *down-stay* even if you clap your hands, whistle, pet him, or drop a treat a few feet (m) from his nose—he will have mastered a very useful command.

### How to Teach It

1. Put your dog in the *down* position, then stand on the leash close to his collar.
2. Say "Stay" without using his name ("stay," by definition, can never be an action

Giving your dog the *down* command followed by the *stay* will put him in a position he can remain in for quite a while without being uncomfortable.

command) and give the blocking motion with your right hand.

3. Praise and treat your dog every few seconds for as long as you keep him in the *down-stay*. To avoid luring him out of the position, lean down to put treats between his paws or carefully drop them between his paws. Be especially generous with praise and yummies if there are distractions while he's in the *down-stay*.

4. The first few times you work on *down-stay*, keep your feet on the leash to prevent your dog from getting up, and don't make him stay in the position for more than a minute or two. Release him with your cheerful "Okay" and proudly pet him for being such a good student.

5. Work on the *down-stay* daily. When you are confident that your dog understands the command and is comfortable with it, you may increase the length of the sessions. Do this in increments of 20 or 30 seconds. You may also add distractions during sessions at home, such as having a neighbor walk a dog nearby, just as your dog probably experiences at training classes.

## Sit-Stay

The *sit-stay* command can be used to good advantage in numerous situations. Many dog owners command their dog to sit and stay before crossing a street, getting in and out of a car, and entering or leaving a building. *Sit-stay* will keep a large dog from taking up lots of space in an elevator. When used in a veterinary clinic's waiting room, *sit-stay* contributes greatly to a relaxed atmosphere. And there are countless people who sing the praises of dog owners whose pups, large or small, are trained to be in a *sit-stay* anytime a visitor enters their home. Now *that's* doggy politeness.

## How to Teach It

If your dog has already been taught *sit* and *stay*, he knows *sit-stay*. In fact, trainers in every obedience class I've taken dogs to (that's eight classes in six cities in three states) taught *stay* with the dogs sitting. But you can build on what your dog already knows by teaching *sit-stay* from a distance and following through with "Come".

1. Using a long lead instead of your dog's leash, put him in a *sit-stay* using verbal and hand signals, then back up a few feet (m) farther from him than you have done before. If he breaks the *sit* to come to you, gently guide him back to where he was, again put him in a *sit-stay* using voice and hand signals, and back up as far as you did on the first try.

2. When your dog has held the position for several seconds, smile and cheerfully say his name and "Come" while making the sweeping arm motion that signals the *come*. When he comes, have him sit again, facing you, then treat, praise, and pet him. Wow, is he smart!

3. After a few successful sessions teaching *sit-*

A well-trained dog will be easier to live with than an untrained dog.

*stay*, lengthen in increments the distance you put between you and the time he remains in the position. Always release him from a *sit-stay* by signaling verbally and nonverbally for him to come to you. When he gets to you, have him sit. Then praise him lavishly.

## Stand

The *stand* command is useful in many situations, as any veterinarian or dog groomer would tell you. You'll have a much easier time with his daily grooming if he stands still to be brushed. Giving him a bath certainly will be

easier with him standing. Getting him into a harness if he uses one or into a raincoat for potty breaks in a downpour will be a breeze with him in the standing position. If he has a foot injury, you will need him standing while you soak the foot in medication prescribed by his vet or while you put a bootie on the foot before taking him outside. If for any reason you need to lift him, you will want him to stand first. And of course, any dog who struts his stuff in a show ring knows to stand when told and to hold the position until released.

### How to Teach It

1. If your dog is lying down, gently slide your hand under his belly until he starts to stand up. As soon as starts to move, say his name and "Stand." When he's all the way up, cheerfully praise and treat him.
2. If he is sitting, you may either slide your hand under his belly and proceed as above or face him holding an enticing treat close to his nose, then slowly pull it away. The moment his fanny is off the floor, say his name and "Stand." Again, praise and treat him when he is standing.
3. Release him from the command by saying "Okay."
4. Practice the *stand* command from both the sitting and lying down positions. But always be certain that you have your dog's attention before giving the command. You don't want to say "Fido, stand" when Fido is half asleep.
5. After your dog has mastered the stand, you may combine it with the stay. Just put the palm of your hand in front of his face, and without using his name, say "Stay." Step away from him using your right foot, and take only a few steps before turning to face him. If necessary, repeat "Stay," but remember to speak calmly and not sound frustrated.

## Leave It

*Leave it* means "don't touch that" and is taught to keep your dog from either licking or picking up something that can harm him or from picking up and playing with something you don't want ruined, such as your new silk scarf. But never mind the scarf; one lick of antifreeze can kill your dog. Teach *leave it* for your Shepherd's safety.

### How to Teach It

1. Have your dog on leash. In your hand and pocket, have especially yummy treats for when he obeys the command—which he will not want to do.
2. Throw something interesting that isn't his (a piece of cloth or a tissue just barely scented with butter or chicken grease should interest him) on the floor or ground as a lure.
3. Walk your dog near the item, and when he shows interest, give the command "Leave it" without saying his name, then quickly walk away. He'll follow but reluctantly and only because he doesn't have a choice. However, the moment he looks at you, you will praise and treat him, and he'll probably forget about the object—which you will pick up and dispose of so that he can't get it later.
4. Repeat this sequence frequently, always rewarding your Shepherd with very special treats for not trying to get what you don't want him to have. Ultimately he will become used to obeying *leave it*, and praise will suffice for his reward if you happen not to have a treat in your pocket. But if you do, give it up for the wonderful dog who faithfully obeys all of your commands–even *leave it*.

## Drop It

Because you can't always see what your dog is going to grab, there will be times when it's

## Multi-Dog Tip

If you have two dogs, you may choose whether to have both walk on your left side—or one on the left and the other on the right. If both were originally trained to walk on the left, one can be taught to switch sides. (I've done that twice and it was easy both times.) But the dog who joined your family first should not have to switch sides.

too late to say "Leave it" and you will have to command "Drop it." The purpose of *drop it* is to have your dog immediately relinquish from his mouth something that shouldn't be there. Basically, he's learning that what's his is yours, and if you want it he must give it to you. This goes for his favorite toy as well as the box of chocolate fudge someone left on the coffee table. Teaching *drop it* and frequently practicing the command can be lifesaving if someday he actually does get hold of chocolate, snatches up a wild mushroom from the yard, or grabs a partially decomposed critter in the park— which to him might be the equivalent of your winning the lottery. Have especially yummy treats in hand when teaching *drop it*, and be generous with praise. You won't use anything unsavory to your senses while teaching your Shepherd this command, so what you accept with your hand will not test the depth of your love for him. But every time he obeys *drop it* is a demonstration of his love and trust in you.

### How to Teach It

1. Offer your dog a toy. After he has taken it, hold a treat in front of his face. With your free hand reach for and take the toy while

The purpose of *drop it* is to have your dog immediately relinquish an object from his mouth.

saying "Drop it." Give the command in a calm but firm tone. Don't sound sharp, as you may instinctively do if someday you see something potentially poisonous between his jaws.

2. As the exchange is made, reward and praise him. Do several repetitions. For practice, you may "plant" objects in the yard, wait for him to find them, then give the *drop it* command and make the exchange. Ultimately, your praise will be enough of a reward.

## Watch Me

*Watch me* is a helpful command because training your dog to do anything when his attention is elsewhere is impossible. (Having

written this, I'm wondering whether right now there isn't a genius GSD somewhere proving me wrong.) Teaching your dog to pay attention to you is important for training sessions and will be useful long after he has been trained. It was in the best obedience class I ever took a dog to that the trainer had us bring the index finger of our right hand to our nose and say "Watch me" to our dogs. It's always good to have a hand signal for a command, as well as words, and teaching *watch me* requires the hand signal. There's one caveat, though. If you haven't raised your Shepherd from early puppyhood, don't stare too long while looking him in the eye to get him to watch you. The day will come when you can happily look deep into each other's eyes, but until an adult dog has been with his owner long enough to be joined heart to heart, he may see staring as a challenge and become nervous or aggressive.

## How to Teach It

1. With your dog in a *sit* and yummies in your hand, stand in front of him and say "Watch me." When he looks in your direction, treat him. (Keep the treats in your pocket, not in a bag you're holding or your dog might be more focused on the bag rather than on you.)

2. Have another treat in your hand and this time move it up to your face while saying "Watch me." When he makes eyes contact with you, praise and treat.

3. Gradually require your dog to look at you for longer periods before giving him the treat.

4. In due time (but not too soon), your dog will be so used to looking up at you when you say "Watch me," all he'll need for a reward is your praise.

Watch me is a helpful command because training your dog to do anything when his attention is elsewhere is impossible.

# CHAPTER 10

# GERMAN SHEPHERD PROBLEM BEHAVIORS

Problem behaviors can occur in any breed, and the well-bred and socialized GSD is not prone to them more than other dogs. But like other breeds that were developed for working and that form close bonds with their families, the GSD will engage in unwanted behaviors if left alone and bored much of the time. Oftentimes unpleasant behaviors begin in puppyhood and continue into adulthood. Or they may crop up suddenly, seeming to have come out of nowhere. There's always a reason for them, though, and sometimes several reasons—including that the dog isn't feeling well. If your Shepherd has a behavior problem that can't be traced to a medical condition and isn't being helped by obedience training with positive reinforcement, it's time to talk with a canine behaviorist. There are many sources for finding a professional behaviorist, and one is your veterinarian. Your breeder also may know of a good behaviorist, or if your Shepherd was adopted, the rescue or shelter might be able to recommend one. You may want to consult several behaviorists before choosing one for your dog, and the Internet offers many reputable sources for getting help. Among them are:

- The American Veterinary Society of Animal Behavior (AVSAB), which is made up of veterinarians and other people who hold a Ph.D. in animal behavior or a related field. Go to www.avsabonline.org and click on the American College of Veterinary Behaviorists for a list of board-certified veterinary behavior specialists.
- The Animal Behavior Society (www.animalbehavior.org), which promotes and encourages the study of animal behavior, offers a public listing of Certified Applied Animal Behaviorists (CAAB) and Associate Certified Applied Animal Behaviorists (ACAAB).
- The International Association of Animal Behavior Consultants, Inc. (IAABC) states on its website that "members have diverse practices but believe that animals matter, and so do animal-owner relationships. They understand that animal behavior consultants can help manage and modify problem behaviors and strengthen relationships." Go to www.iaabc.org and click on Find a Consultant.
- Some veterinary colleges have behavior clinics. Among them are the College of

Veterinary Medicine, Cornell University (www.vet.cornell.edu), Purdue University School of Veterinary Medicine (www.vet.purdue.edu/animalbehavior/), Cummings School of Veterinary Medicine at Tufts University (www.tufts.edu/vet/behavior), and the University of Minnesota Veterinary Medical Center, Animal Behavior Services. (Go to www.cvm.umn.edu/vmc/aboutvmc/smallanimalspecialties and click on Animal Behavior Services.

- Finally, the website of the American Society for the Prevention of Cruelty to Animals (ASPCA) offers a Virtual Behaviorist (www.aspcabehavior.org) that provides advice on solving many dog behaviors.

And don't forget the value of reading up on any difficulty you face in life. A friend of mine who is a certified dog behavior consultant has shelves of books on problem behaviors in dogs. She strongly recommends *How to Behave so Your Dog Behaves*, by Dr. Sophia Yin, and *Parenting Your Dog*, by Trish King.

The GSD will engage in unwanted behaviors if left alone and bored much of the time.

## AGGRESSION

Aggression, the most common problem seen at animal behavior clinics, usually begins when a dog is around 18 to 24 months of age. It's a scary situation that once recognized cannot be allowed to continue. Aggression usually stems from a dog's feeling that he is, or should be, the leader of the pack. This is called dominance aggression and is expressed by the dog's baring his teeth, barking, snarling (his nose will be wrinkled), growling, snapping, or biting when anyone tries to get him to do something he doesn't want to do or tries to correct his behavior. He may exhibit dominance when spoken to, touched, or stared at. He may also be protective of his food, toys, and sleeping areas—which is called resource guarding. A nonaggressive dog will not do this, as he accepts that the food, toys, and sleeping areas belong to you and he enjoys them at your pleasure. Nor will he ever look at you or anyone else who's not a threat to him with raised hackles, ears up and forward, and tail up and stiff.

Aggression cannot be shrugged off, not even if a few minutes after your dog growls at you he behaves as if nothing happened. It did happen, and it wasn't the same as your dog's being naughty at first but in short order doing what you told him to do because he knows you're the boss. That isn't aggression, just obstinacy before the dog gives in. And unless pushed beyond his limits by pain or cruelty, a nonaggressive dog will always give in.

There are other forms of aggression besides dominance aggression, which is when the dog elevates his social status to leader of the pack. Fear-motivated aggression, usually the result of poor socialization, occurs when a dog thinks that he's in danger of people or of dogs (as my Charlie was before being intensely socialized in a puppy day care). Whether the aggression is motivated by dominance, fear, or protectiveness—which can include protecting his people from outsiders—any aggressive dog is potentially dangerous.

## How to Manage It

First, you will want to rule out medical causes for your dog's behavior by having him thoroughly examined by his vet. If the vet doesn't find anything amiss physically, seek professional behavioral help. Stemming aggressiveness in a dog isn't a do-it-yourself project, and aggression never goes away by itself. In fact, while aggression in a dog is treatable and can be controlled, it isn't curable. The techniques you'll be taught by your behaviorist will be tools for keeping aggression at bay the rest of your dog's life. It's up to

you to use them. Remember that the safety of people, other dogs, and your own dog—who may ultimately have to be euthanized if his aggression isn't controlled—depend on your taking precautions, and that you are liable for any harm your dog does. The behaviorist may suggest that your dog wear a muzzle when out in public. There's nothing shameful in this, and you can train him to like his muzzle by slipping tiny treats to him whenever he wears it. If he is possessive of certain belongings, you can prevent the problem by not allowing him access to them. Do the same if he's possessive of a certain part of your property. If your dog barks warnings at passersby when he's in the fenced yard, he should be confined to a part of the yard where he won't see people out walking. And if your dog is still intact, spaying or neutering may be helpful. Intact males may be more prone to dominance and territorial or protective aggressiveness. Female dogs who are in heat may exhibit aggressive behavior that is not otherwise their normal behavior. Neutering or spaying does not have to be done when the dog is still a puppy. Animal shelters "fix" adult dogs all the time. This kind of fix won't

## Training Tidbit

A dog can't have too much training, and he can't learn too many commands. If puppy training in a classroom setting is followed by intermediate training classes and then advanced training classes, you will have the dog of your dreams. And your dog will have the kind of owner that every dog deserves.

eliminate established aggressiveness in a dog, but it is likely to help.

Before hiring a professional behaviorist or behavior consultant, ask what training devices and techniques are used, as different trainers have different approaches. One thing all good professionals in this field have in common is using a variety of behavior-altering techniques. They appreciate that every dog is unique, and a one-size-fits-all approach doesn't work. Also be certain that under no circumstance will harsh physical or emotional punishment will be employed.

## BARKING (EXCESSIVE)

Barking is a mode of canine communication that we appreciate at times but don't want to let get out of hand. You certainly want your dog to bark a warning when a suspicious stranger is on your property or when a fire breaks out in the basement while you're upstairs. A dog's barking anytime the doorbell rings is appreciated by many people, myself included. But this loud barking is not to be confused with aggressive barking, which is low pitched and often combined with growls. The only time aggressive barking is acceptable is when there is no doubt that danger is at hand. I've never heard aggressive barking from one of my dogs and hope I never will. In fact, I've heard little to no barking from any Shepherd I've owned or met socially. Even GSDs I meet in the shelter are less likely to bark when visitors enter the kennel than are many other breeds. Most barking is an announcement saying "I'm bored! Let's do something! Play with me!" You won't hear this frequently and maybe not at all if your dog gets plenty of attention and exercise. If a neighbor dog is in the habit of barking, your Shepherd may bark back. Should this continue, it may accelerate to a major annoyance for anyone living within hearing distance.

Barking is broken into different modes. There is excitement or play barking ("You're home! You're home!"), barking from separation anxiety ("Come back! I can't stand the loneliness!"), barking from being startled by something unfamiliar ("What's that noise?"), protecting the home barking ("Stay off our property–or else!"), and attention-seeking or self-identification barking ("I'm over here! Bark if you can you hear me!"). Whatever

Some dogs bark due to separation anxiety.

causes persistent barking, it's annoying and you want it stopped. To do this, teach your dog that being noisy never gets the result he wants and therefore is unrewarding

## *Want to Know More?*

For a more detailed discussion of canine cognitive dysfunction, see Chapter 13: Care of Your German Shepherd Senior.

your arms over your chest while turning away from him. This method is the cold-shoulder ploy. Your dog may not stop barking immediately, and in fact may bark even louder,

behavior. At the same time, teach him that being quiet is always rewarding. Be consistent and never give him what he wants unless he's quiet. Otherwise, he'll continue trying to get his way by barking. The goal is to make him want to be quiet because when he is, life is more pleasant for him. There are two ways to go about it.

## How to Manage It: Method 1

1. If your dog barks to get your attention, ignore him completely. Don't touch him, say anything, or make eye contact, as all of these are attention-giving actions.
2. When he realizes that you are not going to respond to his barking, he'll stop doing it. This may take several minutes—because in the past his being noisy got your attention.
3. As soon as he stops barking, give a new command, "Quiet," and immediately reward him with praise, petting, and a treat. Now he has your attention—all because he was quiet. He doesn't know the command yet, but when you've repeated this procedure a number of times—often saying "Quiet" when he already is quiet, then treating him—he'll catch on that being quiet is rewarding. Ultimately, your praise and attention will be all the reward he needs.

## How to Manage It: Method 2

Another method to use when your dog barks in your presence is to say "No bark" and cross

but when he's frustrated enough by your ignoring him, he will stop. Although none of my Shepherds were barkers, I now have a dog whose excitement barking whenever he knew we were going for a walk or car ride was maddening. That is, until I used the cold shoulder ploy to teach him we weren't going anywhere until he was calm and quiet. It takes time, but it works.

## CHEWING

Dogs begin chewing on objects in puppyhood to help their baby teeth break through and to make their gums stop hurting. During this period of their life we give them appropriate objects to chew, just as we do for teething babies. At least that's what we should do. But because puppies are so darned cute and we're so enamored of them, we sometimes neglect to teach them what is and is not theirs to chew—until the television remote has been destroyed. Other reasons why mature dogs engage in destructive chewing include boredom, insufficient exercise, separation anxiety, and something in or outside of the home that is making them fearful. Destructive behavior due to separation anxiety or fear-related issues (especially the latter) may require consultation with a behaviorist. An old dog who has not been destructive and suddenly becomes so may have a health issue that needs looking into. Shockingly inappropriate chewing was the first clue that an elderly dog of

Stop problem chewing by encouraging your GSD to chew on appropriate items.

mine had canine cognitive dysfunction (CCD). Otherwise, stopping inappropriate chewing while encouraging appropriate chewing should be fairly easy. Remember that chewing is a desirable activity that promotes healthy teeth. Select all of your dog's toys with care, and praise him when he picks one up to chew on.

## How to Manage It

1. Keep your dog confined to one room with fresh water and safe, desirable toys (but nothing you don't want chewed) when you're not home or able to keep an eye on him.

2. Spend quality time with your Shepherd. Play stimulating games such as fetch, using his favorite toys. Physical and mental exercise are the keys to ending boredom for us as well as for our dogs. Take long walks but don't wear him out on a hot day. (No one has ever refuted that a tired dog is a good dog, but you must keep safety in mind.) There's no harm in using bitter-tasting spray products, available at pet supply stores and online, to stop inappropriate chewing. Just be sure that you don't inadvertently spray one of his toys.

3. When you catch your dog chewing on something he shouldn't have, say "Wrong" or "Ah ah" and offer him a terrific chew toy instead. (This would be a good time to practice the *give it* command.) When he takes his toy, praise him lavishly. Try putting peanut butter or large dog biscuits in a durable rubber toy, or give him a flavored nylon Nylabone to gnaw on. Get your dog to love his own toys so much that yours will seem boring to him.

## DIGGING

For dogs, to dig is instinctive, not a learned behavior. But the instinct is much stronger in

Use a durable toy, such as a Nylabone dura chew, to keep your dog from chewing on inappropriate objects.

some breeds than others. Because the German Shepherd was bred for herding, not digging out game, teaching your GSD not to dig up your flowerbed or create a gaping hole in the lawn should not be difficult. Unless, that is, he's left alone in the yard much of the day with nothing to do and starts digging out of sheer boredom. If you can't be outside with him, provide him with chew toys or interactive toys with treats stuffed inside them. Another kind of digging some bored dogs do, with potentially dire results, is to dig as a means of escape. If you find evidence of digging next to the fence, you must find a way to shore up the fence or put barriers between your dog and the fence. Better yet, stop inappropriate digging (and your dog's having muddy paws) by giving him his own really swell digging area where, amazingly, the digging leads to toys and treats.

## How to Manage It

1. Choose a place in a cool part of the yard, dig a nice big hole in it, and fill it with a mixture of sand (dogs love digging in sand) and pine bark nuggets, which are long lasting, or some other suitable material that won't hurt your dog's feet and will be easy to replace.
2. Teach your dog that this is the *only* place to dig in the yard because it's actually a treasure trove. One day he will find large biscuits in his digging place. Another day he'll find a tennis ball. Another day a Nylabone. You, of course, will have to do some digging when he's inside the house.
3. The first reward he finds in his new digging area should be only partially planted. Leave a bit showing so that he'll know right away that it's there. After you've planted it, bring him outside, show him his digging spot, and happily say his name and "Dig!"
4. When he uncovers his reward, praise him

with "Good dig!" Repeat the procedure frequently until he doesn't need your guidance. Watch him while he's outside as much as you can so that if he digs somewhere else you can catch him at it. Say "Wrong" or "Ah ah," take him to his digging area, give the *dig* command, and follow up with praise when he obeys.

5. If he continues digging in inappropriate areas, consider using deterrents such as pepper or a small amount of citrus or ammonia (diluted with water). You can also buy commercial products to create a scent your dog won't like or that are intended to

It's quite common for Shepherds not to jump at all except to catch a flying disc or greet their owners after a long absence

interfere with an animal's sense of smell. But from what I've read, these are usually not very effective. If there are one or two particular off-limits areas that your dog simply can't resist digging in, covering the area with landscape rocks, stepping stones, or a piece of furniture will solve the problem.

## JUMPING UP

Jumping up on people is yet another problem that usually begins when the dog is an adorable little puppy, then carries into adulthood when he's a great big dog who can unwittingly knock you off your feet. To the dog, who doesn't know anything about concussions, he's just giving you the loving greeting you deserve. And one could argue that if we don't train puppies not to jump up in greeting, then we do deserve the consequences of having a 100-pound (45.5 kg) dog come flying at us in joyous greeting. Fortunately, though, it's quite common for Shepherds not to jump at all except to catch a flying disc or greet their owners after a long absence. And because they are prone to being aloof with strangers, they're even less likely to jump up on people outside their family. Still, not all Shepherds are the same, and some will jump up on people they don't sleep next to. So it just makes sense to retrain such dogs not to jump up on anyone. As with aggressive behavior, a dog's owner is responsible for any harm a dog inflicts by jumping on someone, even if the harm is unintentional.

### How to Manage It: Method 1

1. When training your dog not to jump up on people, you will want a command to use. Some people choose *off*, but if that's the command you use to keep your dog off furniture, choose something else. *No jump* addresses the issue and has a solid ring to it.

2. Give the command the moment your dog's front feet are off the floor. As you do, walk forward—or into—the jump. (Don't back up, as this is seen as a retreat and puts the dog in charge of the situation.) By walking forward, though, you put the dog off balance, and he has no choice but to lower his front feet to the floor. When he does, pet and praise him.
3. If your dog jumps up before you can step forward, simply take his front paws in your hands and slowly walk forward. Dogs don't like walking backward on two feet, and your Shepherd will feel relieved when you let go and he gets to be on all fours again. Praise him quietly and pet him gently, as you don't want him to stir up more excitement.

### How to Manage It: Method 2

Another way to manage jumping up is giving the dog the cold shoulder.

1. You must act quickly, folding your arms over your chest the moment your dog starts to jump.
2. After quickly turning away from him, stand still as a stone until he too is still (and

standing on all fours), then turn to greet him with soft praise and petting.

Whichever method you choose—the cold shoulder or walking him backward—you may have to do it a number of times before he decides once and for all that jumping up on people really isn't fun.

What you must not do when teaching *no jump* or *off* is to lift your knee to your dog's chest when he jumps. That was a popular method in the dark ages (before training with positive reinforcement), but it is hurtful. So is pinching a dog's front toes while walking him backward. And yelling or pushing the dog away with your hands is both futile and detrimental to your relationship with him. Another no-no is withholding attention after he's abandoned the jump and is standing on all fours. You

may be exasperated by his not having learned yet that jumping up is forbidden, but if a moment ago he was jumping and now he's not jumping, he's a good boy. Along with praise and petting, a nice treat would help remind him that even though he's not allowed to jump, you love him to pieces.

## LEASH PULLING

Sometimes even a well-trained dog who knows *heel* and usually obeys the command simply can't resist the urge to pull on leash. It could be from excitement as you approach the place he wants to be, because there's another dog up ahead, or because he sees or smells a critter and his prey drive overcomes his be-a-good-boy drive (which he does have, even on a bad day). But leash pulling by a large dog can

Lack of sufficient exercise may be the culprit in many problem behaviors.

Sometimes even a well-trained dog who knows how to heel will submit to the urge to pull on leash.

cause mayhem, such as your falling and being injured, losing your grip on the leash, and your dog's possibly running into traffic. To prevent bad things from happening on walks, teach your dog that pulling on leash doesn't get him anywhere—at least not where he wants to go.

## How to Manage It

1. When your dog pulls, don't pull back, as all this would do is make him pull harder— and he would win. Instead, you have three choices. You can surprise him by walking backward, and when he turns to look at you, reposition him and command him to heel again. Or you can swiftly turn around and go the other way, giving him no choice but to follow, or stop walking and with

both hands hold the leash against your mid-section—your center of gravity. When your dog realizes he's not going anywhere, he'll stop pulling and you can put him in the *heel* position again.

2. To prevent your dog's wanting to pull, vary your pace when you're walking. Jog for a bit—that'll be surprising and fun. Change directions for a minute, then change back. Stop walking and practice *sit-stay* or *down-stay* and reward him lavishly for obeying. Then resume your walk. He'll wonder what you're going to do next and will be focused on you, not on the destination or the possibility of seeing another critter.

3. Because the GSD can be a very strong puller, you may want to consider using a

Gentle Leader Head Collar or an anti-pull harness for walks. These options will give you more control over your dog. After you've retrained him to heel, you can go back to using a plain leash.

# NIPPING

Nipping, or mouthing, is what your dog did when he was a very young puppy playing with his littermates. Later he may have mouthed and nipped at children when playing with them. Even adults (you, perhaps?) may have thought at first that his nipping was all in fun. This is how a puppy behavior becomes an adult behavior, and being nipped at by an adult dog is not fun. In addition to being unpleasant, it's a dangerous behavior to allow because it can lead to genuine aggression and real biting. The dog who nips and gets away with it has no choice but to consider himself the top dog—or boss—in his family. But you can put an end to his misconception by teaching him in a humane way that you, everyone else in the family, all your friends, and everyone he encounters under normal circumstances outrank him. He won't feel less loved when under any circumstances, including playing with children, he can't get away with nipping.

He'll actually feel more loved because he won't get scolded, shouted at, or pushed away when he's hurt someone.

## How to Manage It: Method 1

1. The first option is to spray a non-toxic but bitter-tasting liquid on the areas of your body your dog frequently nips at. This is usually the hands and arms or bare feet or heels (especially with children).
2. Hold out your hand for the dog to mouth. He'll recoil in disgust.
3. Repeat this a number of times until he decides that nipping at people is unpleasant.

## How to Manage It: Method 2

1. If your dog gets around the bitter liquid approach by nipping other parts of your body, or nipping when the spray has worn or been washed off, use the "shake can" option.
2. To do this, half fill a small, tight-lidded container with pebbles, marbles, or pennies.
3. When your dog tries to nip, say "No nip" or "Wrong" and shake the can hard.
4. The noise will surprise him and he'll back away from you. When he does, wait for him to settle down before giving him attention. He will learn that nipping is unrewarding—and even a little scary.
5. Make sure you're consistent with your command. If there are young children in the house, don't let them participate in this training, as they could accidentally drop the shake can on the dog or confuse him by misusing it.

# CHAPTER 11

# GERMAN SHEPHERD SPORTS AND ACTIVITIES

G erman Shepherds love the outdoors, excel at many sports, yearn to learn and please their people, and generally travel well. In this chapter we'll talk about many ways to have fun with your Shepherd while at home or wherever your fancy takes you. We'll also look at a number of sports in which your dog can participate, and we'll talk about keeping your dog well, safe, and content when engaged in a sport or traveling.

## ACTIVITIES

As dog lovers, we live in wonderful times. Nutritional choices and veterinary care just get better and better. And a wealth of activities—social, competitive, contributing to society—or enjoying the wonders of nature are ours and our dogs to have. One of the nicest things about getting your dog involved in a sport or activity is that when the excitement is over he will still be thrilled to play fetch with you in his own back yard. Activities never spoil a dog; they just bring out the best in him.

### Camping

Going camping with your dog can be a great experience that both of you will want to do again and again. Choose a time that isn't

terribly hot for this adventure, and take an emergency kit plus all essential daily needs with you—including an ample amount of potty bags. Even if you'll have good access to water, consider taking gallon (4 l) jugs of water to cool your dog down in the case of overheating. You may also want to attach a bell to his collar to warn off unsuspecting wild animals. Keeping your dog on leash will prevent a lot of possible problems, including a skunk encounter, but you may want to take Skunk-Off just in case. Dogs are allowed in campsites at national parks, monuments, and forests. Most state parks allow dogs, but phone or check the park's website to make sure before heading out.

Another kind of camping, and an excellent way to build your relationship with your Shepherd, is to go to a camp for humans and dogs—which is called a dog camp. Dog camps provide a wide range of activities, some just for fun and exercise and others that are more serious. There are camps that offer seminars on training techniques, behavior patterns, and alternative health care such as massage or acupuncture. Before signing up for any dog camp session, find out exactly what is being offered. Look at the accommodations,

Going camping with your dog can be a great experience.

including the dining room, and inquire about the foods served. You will want to know what educational training the camp staff has had for working with dogs. Also, is there a veterinarian on the premises, and if not, what veterinarians do they work with, and how far is the nearest animal emergency hospital? If the camp welcomes children, find out what activities are available for kids. Also ask whether the camp requires dogs to be vaccinated and whether proof of a current rabies vaccination is required.

As with any other vacation you and your dog take together, having a great time at a dog camp depends largely on knowing what to expect when you get there. For many people, the experience of a dog camp includes forming friendships with like-minded people and their canine companions. This is why so many people return with their dogs to the same camp year after year. One woman who has been going to the same camp for several years told me it's like being at a family reunion.

## Canine Good Citizen® Program

The Canine Good Citizen Program (CGC) was developed by the American Kennel Club (AKC) in 1989 to promote responsible pet ownership. Basically, a Canine Good Citizen—of whatever breed or breed mix and whatever age—is a dog with good manners both at home and out in society. To receive his CGC certificate, your Shepherd will need to take ten tests. But before he does, you'll need to sign a pledge affirming that you'll take care of your dog's health, safety, exercise, training, and quality of life. Plus you will show responsibility by cleaning up after your dog in public places and will never let your dog infringe on the rights of others.

The tests that your dog will take to show what a good citizen he is are, in the order they're given: calmly allowing a friendly stranger to approach him and speak with you; letting the stranger pet him; allowing someone other than his owner to groom him; walking politely on a loose leash to demonstrate that his owner is in control; walking through a crowd to show that he can be polite and comfortable in public places where there's a lot going on; showing that he obeys the commands *sit*, *down*, and *stay*; coming when called after you've walked 10 feet (3 m) from him and then turned to face him to give the command; demonstrating that he can be polite toward other dogs; showing calm confidence when faced with distracting situations; and finally, that when left with a trusted person other than yourself, maintaining his training and showing good manners. If all this sounds part exhilarating and part frightening to you, then you know how I felt when my Charlie—the "tough guy" who as a puppy had fear aggression—took the test. He was calm as

For your Shepherd to earn the Canine Good Citizen certificate, he will need to take ten tests. In the last one, he will remain still while you walk 10 feet (3 m) away from him, then come to you when you turn around and give the *come* command.

could be through all ten parts, while I could scarcely breathe.

Participating in activities and sports with your dog will help keep both of you physically and mentally fit.

If you enjoy doing volunteer work and your Shepherd is of an even temperament and likes meeting people, the two of you can visit people in a variety of institutions where care is provided.

## Therapy Work

If you enjoy doing volunteer work and your Shepherd is of an even temperament and likes meeting people, the two of you can visit people in a variety of institutions where care is provided. For anyone who ever had a dog in his or her life, the comfort gained from touching and being touched by one is a tonic for body and soul. Many people who never even considered living with a dog will light up when therapy dogs come visiting. All your Shepherd needs to do to achieve this effect is to stand or sit still to be petted and perhaps demonstrate a few of his obedience skills for the enjoyment of his new friends. And should he smile or gaze warmly into a patient's eyes, he will have made that person's day.

The Delta Society is a nonprofit organization dedicated to improving people's health and well-being through positive interaction with animals. One of the programs offered by the Delta Society is the Pet Partners Program, which screens and trains volunteers and their pets for visiting hospitals, nursing homes, rehabilitation centers, and schools. Visit www.deltasociety.org to learn about the various programs offered and the society's Human-Animal Bond Resource Center.

Therapy Dogs International, Inc. (TDI), the oldest and largest therapy dog organization in the United States, certifies dogs that are at least a year old, have a health-record form signed by a veterinarian, and have earned the Canine Good Citizen certificate. Your dog will also need to be tested and evaluated for behavior around people who use service equipment, such as a wheelchair or crutches. TDI also serves parts of Canada. For more information and to learn about Children Reading to Dogs, a TDI program that uses dogs to help children learn to read, visit www.tdi-dog.org.

## Walking/Jogging

Walking your dog isn't classified as a sport, but if the two of you stride out on a regular basis, you may consider it the sport of fitness. Walk your dog for health, recreation, and to make him feel comfortable in a wide range of surroundings. You can even take walking a step further by joining or creating a dog-walking club, which will transform walking into a highly social activity.

Wherever you walk, protect your dog. Keep him on leash and away from traffic. Don't take long walks or jog with him in hot weather. Also protect him by not walking in tall grasses or among other plants, such as burdock, that have awns (nicknamed "stick tights"), which are bristly fibers that can stick to your dog's body. Smaller seeds from various plants such as buzzard, spear, or feather grasses may even get into his nose, between his eye and eyelid, or into the skin between his toes. Seeds that cause the most problems are shaped like tiny darts with a sharp point and a long tail. Small swellings may result from a dog's being pricked by awns or seeds, and if the plant part isn't quickly removed, it may burrow farther and reach an internal organ. Inspect your dog closely if he has walked in or brushed against possibly offending plants. (At the same time, inspect him for ticks.) Matted hair can be a sign that your dog has grass seeds stuck to him. If a seed is in the ear canal, he may shake his head, rub or scratch the ear, and hold his head at a tilt. If the seed is under

the eyelid there may be redness, discharge, or tears. This is serious, as the seed can cause a corneal ulcer resulting in loss of vision. Your dog would probably chew on areas where seeds were attached to his skin, and if one was in his nose he would sneeze and paw at his nose. Swallowed seeds can stick at the back of the throat, causing inflammation. And there's worse: life-threatening abscesses can occur if seeds or awns are inhaled and manage to enter the lung or penetrate other organs.

Is any of this worth a walk or jog among plants that aren't found in a well-groomed park

German Shepherds make great jogging and hiking companions.

with walking paths? Not to me it isn't, and I'm certain it's not to you either. Enjoy walking and jogging with your Shepherd, but do it safely. If you'll be out in warm weather for more than 30 minutes, take water along. In case your dog's paws get muddy, you may want to keep extra water, a mild soap suitable for dogs, and a towel in the car so that you can clean between his pads before the ride home.

## SPORTS

Choosing the right sport for your dog will depend not only on what you think the two of you will enjoy but also on his physical condition (and perhaps yours too), how far and how often you are willing to travel, the amount of time you can devote to training and competitions, and how much you feel

that you can spend on a sport. Study up before making your choice. Talk to people engaged in the sport. If it's a vigorous sport, discuss it with your dog's vet, who may even suggest changes in your dog's nutrition as he expends more energy than he used to do. Above all, start slowly. Your dog will need to work up to the level the sport requires. In competitions or when training, don't let him overdo it or become overheated. And always remember the rule for preventing bloat: no exercise the first hour after a meal and no strenuous exercise for two hours after eating.

### Agility

Agility, which began in England in 1978, is today one of America's fastest-growing dog sports. It's challenging both physically and

Agility is a challenging sport in which a dog must navigate a timed obstacle course.

mentally, making it ideal for a Shepherd in good condition. In agility trials, dogs compete by off-leash running through a series of obstacles to determine which entrant will complete the course the fastest. The owner, or handler, runs alongside the dog while directing him to negotiate ramps, tunnels, a see-saw, and a line of poles that he must weave through. This is all done within a specified time, and the dog must not miss an obstacle or knock anything over. In the United States, three major organizations are involved in agility: the AKC, the North American Dog Agility Council (NADAC), and the United States Dog Agility Association (USDAA). Without a doubt, agility builds confidence in dogs and is a great way for you and your dog to exercise together. But it is arduous. To engage in it, you must both be in good physical condition.

## Canine Freestyle

Training your dog in canine freestyle will give you a dance partner who won't ever say "Let's sit this one out." Nor will he want to dance with anyone except you—that is, unless someone cuts in holding irresistible treats. Freestyle is basically creating a dance routine, teaching it to your dog the same way you teach him anything else (using commands and rewards), and then together performing the routine to music. Whether you dance at home exclusively for your own pleasure, or enter competitions, freestyle will deepen your bond with your Shepherd, reinforce his training skills, and give him ample cause to be proud of himself. Everyone loves a dog who can dance!

To learn all about freestyle, visit the Canine Freestyle Federation, Inc. (CFF) at www. canine-freestyle.org, and the World Canine Freestyle Organization (WCFO) at www. worldcaninefreestyle.org. Also, to see how wildly popular this sport has become and

how far you can go with it, visit www.youtube. com and search for "canine freestyle." You will be amazed at the versatility of the performances. Be sure to watch videos from freestyle competitions at Crufts. If you can look at offerings from Crufts Freestyle Heelwork to Music without wanting to get up and dance with your Shepherd, freestyle is not the sport for you.

## Conformation

Conformation, the sport of dog showing, is extremely popular in many countries and nowhere more than in the United States and United Kingdom. A dog whose reproductive organs are intact and who is registered with the AKC, Kennel Club in England, or the Canadian Kennel Club (CKC) may participate in shows sponsored by his club. But if your breeder did not deem your puppy to be of show quality, conformation probably would be disappointing for you. While it's true that any AKC-registered dog can be entered in a dog show, it's also true that every judge has the right to withhold a ribbon. However, if your dog is of show quality, conformation can be a very rewarding sport for the two of you, as well as the rest of your family. It can also be stressful, though, as it requires a lot of

Conformation is the art of dog showing.

dedication, training, and travel. Then there's the sure fact that sometimes—or oftentimes—you will expect your dog to win points toward a championship and he will not. On top of all that, conformation is expensive. So before jumping in, attend some shows in your area, look carefully at what goes on, and then decide whether the sport is for you and your dog. If you think it is, get opinions on whether your pup really is of show caliber, as gorgeous isn't enough. If people in the sport think that he has the right stuff, your next step should be to take advantage of the AKC's Exhibitor Mentoring Program. This will pair you and your Shepherd with an experienced GSD fancier. Or if you're considering purchasing a show-quality Shepherd, the program can match you with a breeder. You may have to wait in line for a

show-quality puppy, but while you do you can study the sport.

## Obedience

If you and your dog enjoy adding commands to your repertoire, showing off his exemplary manners, and being out with like-minded dogs and their people, consider competing in AKC obedience trials. The first step would be to visit a dog show that includes obedience trial competitions to see whether this is for you. You may also find out where the dogs train and get names of trainers who are in, or close to, your area. Obedience has three levels of competition: Novice, Open, and Utility. The Novice level is designed for dogs who are proficient in basic commands from heeling both on and off leash to maintaining a *down*

## Want to Know More?

For information on basic obedience skills that you will need for the CGC test, see Chapter 4: Training Your German Shepherd Puppy.

position for three minutes. The Open level requires the dog to follow commands either by voice or hand signal and has more complicated exercises, including an exciting "retrieve over high jump." And when you reach the Utility level of obedience, your Shepherd will know how to respond to many hand signals—including a directional signal to fetch a glove and return it to you. He will demonstrate his ability to sniff out your scent among a pile of articles. Of course, your scent is the best scent in the world to him, so this exercise will be one of his favorites. There are obedience clubs promoted by the AKC throughout the United States, and obedience clubs promoted by the CKC can be found throughout Canada.

## Search and Rescue (SAR)

Search and rescue dog teams are available around the clock and every day of the year when anyone of any age becomes lost in woods, a wilderness area, or has just wandered away from a hospital or their home. SAR teams also search for victims of natural disasters, fires, plane crashes, drowning, and any other circumstance that can cause the disappearance of a person, living or dead. In the tragic wake of the

German Shepherds are among the breeds most suitable for search and rescue work.

earthquake that ravaged Haiti in January, 2010, numerous countries from around the world dispatched SAR teams to the stricken nation.

German Shepherds are among the breeds most suitable for search and rescue work. Of course, all SAR dogs (also called sniffer dogs) and their owners/handlers must be highly trained. Both dog and human must also be physically fit and able to work outdoors in any weather conditions. If you think that search and rescue is a good fit for you and your Shepherd to participate in, you'll need to train arduously for about a year, after which you'll be evaluated as a team before being sent on a real mission. It's not just about your dog's sound temperament, stamina, and sniffing skills, though. You would have to train at many things, including first aid with CPR, land navigation, wilderness survival, and using maps, a compass, and radio communication. Adult dogs as well as puppies may train for SAR, and throughout the United States there are always new units being formed. To learn more about this invaluable service, visit the website of the National Association for Search and Rescue (NASAR) at www.nasar.org.

## Training Tidbit

You can train your dog to enjoy car travel by taking him on frequent rides to parks outside your community. Go a little farther each time, with each "trip" including a good walk. This will help prepare him for when it's time to go on a really long car trip.

## Skijoring

One of the fastest growing sled dog sports, skijoring (the word is Norwegian for ski driving) combines cross-country skiing with dog mushing, and GSDs are good candidates for this exhilarating sport. In skijoring, you ski with your dog pulling you. Many people take up skijoring for the sheer pleasure of exercising their dog while enjoying a winter wonderland and later train to enter skijoring competitions. As with all sports in which you can engage with your dog, skijoring requires some training, and you and your dog will need to learn dog-sledding commands. Both of you will also need to be in good physical shape before becoming skijorers. As of this writing, there are skijoring clubs and sled clubs that support skijoring in ten states, from Alaska in the west to Maine in the east. Visit www.skijornow.com for links to these and other skijoring organizations, including the International Sled Dog Veterinary Medical Association (ISDVMA).

## Schützhund

*Schutzhund*, a German word meaning "protection dog," defines a dog sport enjoyed by people of all ages, in tiptop shape or with disabilities, and is ideal for a family sport. It's also suitable for a wide range of dog breeds but is mostly associated with German Shepherds. This is evidenced by the United Schützhund Clubs of America (USA) stating that its membership is "for the German Shepherd Dog," and that the purpose of Schützhund is to demonstrate the Shepherd's intelligence and utility. There are three parts of a Schützhund trial: the tracking phase, obedience phase, and protection phase. Dogs who perform in these trials demonstrate their trainability, courage, endurance, mental stability, and ability to scent. The German Shepherd Dog Club of America-Working Dog Association (GSDCA-

Dogs who perform in Schützhund trials demonstrate their trainability, courage, endurance, mental stability, and ability to scent.

WDA) sponsors Schützhund trials throughout the United States. It also chooses a team in open competition to represent the GSDCA at the World Union of German Shepherd Dog Associations (WUSV) world championship.

## TRAVEL

Anytime you travel with your dog, even if it's just for a weekend, plan ahead so that the trip will be as stress-free and as safe as possible. For a longer trip, a vet visit before you go would be wise, especially if lots of activity will be involved. Make a list of everything your dog needs for his comfort and health. Packing for him really is more important than packing for yourself, as you don't need food for all of your meals, bowls, toys, and a bed

from home. Don't forget any medication he takes, his medical records (including proof of vaccinations), contact information for veterinarians and emergency clinics near where you'll be staying, your doggy first-aid kit, and a generous quantity of potty bags. Pack an ample supply of his food and his favorite treats, as the brands he's fed may not be available where you're going. Also take bottled water or water from home with you, as the water at your destination or along the way may not agree with your dog. In case of carsickness, ginger snaps are good to have on hand. And in case your Shepherd gets lost, have current pictures of him, plus identifying information and phone numbers to call if he is microchipped or tattooed.

## By Car

Ideally, when traveling by car with your Shepherd you will have him in a crate attached to the back seat by a bungee cord or restrained in the back by a harness or doggy seat belt. This is to keep him from flying forward during a sudden stop or if there's an accident. Don't get a barrier made of nylon mesh or metal to keep him in the back seat, because mesh isn't likely to hold up in an accident, and his being thrown against metal would seriously injure him. Equally dangerous, or more so, is letting your dog ride in the front seat, as a deployed air bag can kill him. If

there are young children in the car, explain to them the importance of behaving calmly and not squabbling so that their dog will not be stressed. You can encourage them to pet and speak softly to him, but when he is sleeping, remind them not to disturb his rest. Of great importance is that they not unsnap his seat belt or open his crate until you give the okay. And most important of all is that they understand the danger of opening a car door before the dog is on leash—with the leash in *your* hand. And just as you would not leave children in a parked car, don't take that risk with your dog. One could argue

If you are traveling with your GSD by car, he should be safely secured with a doggy seat belt or in a crate.

that dog thieves are less likely to try to steal a grown GSD than most other breeds, but it can happen. Besides, heat kills. Your dog could perish from heatstroke even with the car parked in the shade. Don't think that cracking the windows will make a difference, as the temperature in your car can still be deadly hot.

## By Plane

If your vacation allows a choice between car and plane travel, your Shepherd will fare better on the open road than above the clouds. Because of his size, he will have to fly cargo. Not knowing what was going on, where you were, or where this madness would lead to, he could not help but be stressed. If you must travel by plane and want your Shepherd with you, be mindful of weather when planning the trip. Airlines don't accept dogs in cargo if the temperature anywhere the plane will land is expected to be below 45°F (7.2°C) or above 85°F (29.4°C). Also consider that there can be delays or canceled flights, putting your dog in the position of being crated for long periods.

The kennel you ship your dog in must be airline approved and have absorbent padding. To keep him hydrated during the flight, you can attach a pail filled with frozen water to the inside of the crate. (If it's not frozen, it will spill during loading.) Unless absolutely necessary, don't sedate your dog before he flies, as evidence shows that sedation can increase the risk of injury or even death. Also, if you can't see your dog being loaded on the plane, ask the counter agent to call the ramp to make sure that he is on board. Of equal importance, after the plane takes off, ask a flight attendant to make certain that your dog is unloaded from cargo after the plane lands. Then ask again when the plane has landed. I stress this because once when I had landed in Los Angeles and was told where to wait for my two dogs to deplane, I waited to no avail. And while I was waiting, my dogs were flying to Vegas.

Another option, if you don't want to drive to your vacation destination, is for you to fly with a traditional airline and your dog to fly Pet Airways, which began service in 2009 as the first airline exclusively for pets. Your Shepherd will fly in the main cabin, be given potty breaks during the flight, and at 15-minute intervals be monitored for his comfort. However, at the time of this writing, the airline flies to just nine states.

Although there are legitimate concerns about traveling by air with a dog too large to fly coach, plane travel is something that a dog may become used to and not bothered by. Manhattan, the inimitable GSD show champion, flew in the cargo hold of an airplane almost every weekend for many years without having it adversely affect him. But Hatter enjoyed a temperament that could withstand stress, and as a frequent flyer he was accompanied by James Moses, one of the most expert handlers of all times. One can imagine that when Moses cheerfully told Hatter to have a good flight, Hatter obeyed.

## Lodging

Wherever you go, arrange for pet-friendly lodgings and confirm your reservation before setting out. Also, ask about extra pet fees or deposits, where your dog can be walked, and whether he's allowed in the lobby. Some lodgings allow dogs in smoking rooms only, so if this would be a problem for you, be sure to ask. You'll also want to know in advance the rules of places you visit with your pup. And if he is prone to even the slightest separation anxiety, don't ever leave him alone in the room. Even if he can be left alone in the room, make it as short a time as possible, and have the "do not disturb" sign on your door.

You can find pet-friendly accommodations by contacting the chamber of commerce or visitor's information center in the area you'll be visiting, or by checking online directories such as www.petswelcome.com. There you can search by state, route, or hotel chains. There's even a list of lodgings that welcome large dogs. Another source is the AAA book *Traveling With Your Pet.* Be sure, though, to get the current edition. Also, if your dog lies on the bed or a chair, having a lint roller or pet hair magnet to use before checking out would be thoughtful and appreciated by the cleaning staff.

## If You Can't Take Your Dog With You

The time may come when you must, or will want to, travel without your dog. If you have a family friend or relative nearby who would like having him for a houseguest or would be willing to be your houseguest (only without you there), that may be the ideal solution. Otherwise, you have two good choices: hiring a pet sitter or boarding your dog.

### Boarding and Pet-Sitters

Good boarding kennels abound, and your veterinarian would probably be happy to recommend one. So will friends of yours who are happy with the facility where they board their dogs. There's one in my town that I praise to the moon and back. But boarding isn't for all GSDs. Shepherds can take guarding their home and protecting their owners very seriously, so for some, being boarded is highly stressful. Also, a senior Shepherd that's never

You can find pet-friendly accommodations by contacting the chamber of commerce or visitor's information center in the area you'll be visiting, or by checking online directories.

been boarded before could become ill from separation anxiety at a boarding kennel—even one with a "people" bed and television for his enjoyment. Not having experienced being boarded early in life, he has no way of knowing that you'll come back to get him. For a dog of any age who is prone to separation anxiety, consider in-home care with a relative, friend, or a professional dog-sitter who will provide you with references. Your vet or breeder may be able to recommend someone who will come to your home. This was how I found a dog-loving and reliable couple to stay with my GSDs after my Joey became so dejected at a boarding kennel that the owner worried about him the entire four days he was there. After that experience, our vet recommended the in-home sitters upon whom we subsequently relied, and Joey never again grieved at our leaving him.

Another way to find an outstanding pet sitter in your area is through the National Association of Professional Pet Sitters (NAPPS). After interviewing the sitter, tell her everything that should be known about your dog. Then write it all down so that nothing will be forgotten. Include a list of your dog's daily schedule and of any unusual habits or quirks he has. Write your cell phone number, the phone numbers and addresses of your vet, the nearest emergency vet clinic, and where you'll be staying—as cell phones can go on the blink or get lost. Also provide the sitter with written verification of up-to-date vaccinations.

### Doggy Day Care

You don't have to be going away overnight to need someone to provide care for your Shepherd. If he's highly energetic and gets bored easily or is prone to separation anxiety when left alone for several hours, doggy day care—which is much like day care for young children—may be just the ticket for your pooch. Doggy day care is operated out of a staffed commercial facility or a private home, with each offering its own benefits. A private in-home daycare will have fewer dogs for the provider to attend to, and your dog will be in a home environment. This may be a better option if your dog is aloof toward other dogs but warms easily to people or if he requires extra attention because of a health problem. A commercial day care can have up to 20 dogs, but the staff, trained in caring for dogs (and in preventing aggression from breaking out), will provide outdoor play and perhaps indoor games as well. With either option, your dog gets hours of socialization, and that in itself is a benefit.

PART III

SENIOR YEARS

# CHAPTER 12

# FINDING YOUR GERMAN SHEPHERD SENIOR

For many people wanting to add a German Shepherd to their family, adopting a senior is the best choice, with the pros far outweighing the cons of such a decision. If you're thinking of adopting a senior, though, don't be fooled by a dog's numeric age or the fact that at seven a Shepherd is considered a senior. It's true that your senior will be far less energetic and needy than a puppy or young adult, and you won't have to make major changes in your lifestyle when he moves in. But that doesn't mean that he can thrive on snoozing the whole day through. Rather, compare his being seven or older to a person aged 65 or older. Sixty-five is when the United States government considers us to be seniors. Do we then stop exercising, getting together with friends, enjoying being out in the wonders of nature? Of course not. And like us, dogs whose senior years include love, mental stimulation, exercise, and socialization tend to stay young until they are exceedingly old. In fact, a Shepherd well beyond the age of seven can be a puppy at heart when enjoying his walks and games of fetch with you. But compared to a real puppy, the senior will be a different animal, one who sleeps more and when awake requires just

a fraction of your time that a puppy would require. In this chapter we will look at the benefits of adopting a senior and how to go about finding one.

## WHY ADOPTING A SENIOR IS A GOOD IDEA

The question really is how one decides if getting a senior instead of a puppy or adult dog is the right choice. Sometimes, though, the answer comes before the question is even asked. Following is an example of how this instantaneous knowing may occur.

Let's say you've been thinking about getting a Shepherd and are in your local animal shelter because a friend alerted you to the fact that the shelter had several GSDs on the adoption floor. Excited about this, you do a walk-through, looking at all the available dogs, not just GSDs, because you're a genuine dog

## *Want to Know More?*

If adopting a younger adult is more your cup of tea, see Chapter 5: Finding Your German Shepherd Adult for more information.

## By the Numbers

When boarding two dogs who are closely bonded and used to being together day and night, try to arrange for them to share an extra-large kennel or a suite the size of a small bedroom. If the boarding kennel of your choice can't provide this or has a policy against it, ask that the dogs be walked together and have play periods together. Boarding is much easier on a dog when he's with his canine sister or brother.

lover. Seeing a couple of GSD puppies chewing on their raised plastic bed makes you smile—and consider how much work raising one of those puppies would be. All that training! No, that isn't for you, so you continue looking. There's a senior Shepherd—nine years old. He's sitting down but looks up at you with a thoughtful expression. A beautiful dog. Serene looking. Nine is much too old, though, so you move on, and for several minutes you admire a snoozing adult Shepherd who was just neutered. His cage card says that he is three years old, housetrained, good with kids, and walks nicely on leash. Now this Shepherd is a definite possibility. But somehow you can't stop thinking about the senior you gave only a quick glance to before walking by. Drawn by those intelligent, inquiring eyes; enchanted by the notion of giving an old dog a good home; oblivious now to everything but the close bond you and he could form, you turn and go back to his kennel. Your eyes meet and he stands up. This is your dog. You're sure of it. How

fortunate that you got to the shelter before someone else adopted him. You hurry from the kennels to the adoption desk to proclaim that you want this wonderful dog. And you hadn't even been thinking of all the really good reasons to adopt a senior.

## SENIOR CONSIDERATIONS

But before discussing the many positives in adopting a senior GSD, let's dispense with the few negatives.

### The Negatives

The one that probably comes right to mind is that the Shepherd's life span typically falls between 11 and 13 years, so at best a dog adopted at age seven will be with you just six years. However, the number of years any dog will be with you, even a puppy who hasn't yet cut his teeth, is unknowable. In a lifetime of living with dogs, I have had several who lived well beyond their expected life span. I've also had dogs whose lives ended much too soon. But no matter how much or how little time you are given to love and nurture a dog, ultimately you are grateful for having had him in your life.

When considering whether to adopt a senior, you may also be wondering—in spite of what the shelter or rescue says about a particular dog—whether he is homeless because he has a health or behavioral problem. Believe me that when this is the case, any reputable shelter or rescue will put it out on the table. If my shelter is typical of shelters throughout the country—and I like to think that it is—a problem of any kind is stated in detail on the shelter's website and on the dog's kennel door. If it is a health or behavior issue, a veterinary write-up, with specifics and adoption restrictions, is available at the adoption desk. The dog is listed on Petfinder.com as "Exceptional Owner Wanted," with the reasons detailed. But as discussed in Chapter 5, the reasons why dogs of any age lose their homes are more likely to be about problems the owners have, not problems the dogs have. Moreover, the majority of Shepherds that have been owner surrendered to my shelter have been reported as housetrained. Nor have any of the shelter's five campuses ever found evidence that housetraining is a challenge with GSDs.

But don't senior dogs run up higher veterinary bills than do younger dogs? Not necessarily. Veterinary care is needed at all life stages of any breed, and sometimes care is less costly for an older dog than for a youngster. I've had pet insurance for nearly all of my dogs and have lost money on only one, a Shepherd who lived to a ripe old age without ever realizing she wasn't young anymore. Still, it's very important to consider the cost of ownership before acquiring a dog of any age. Dogs are expensive. Preventive care is a must. Excellent nutrition and a wide variety of supplies are other ongoing expenses. And certainly a senior Shepherd may acquire senior illnesses that are expensive to treat. So before adopting a senior, you may want to get a veterinary health report on the dog to help you

Many German Shepherds surrendered to shelters are already housetrained.

Senior dogs offered for adoption by rescues are likely to have had obedience training.

decide whether your financial situation will support this commitment.

## The Positives

Now for the pros of adopting a senior—in addition to those I've already sprinkled in with the cons. Senior dogs offered for adoption by rescues or shelters have already had training in house manners and are likely to have had obedience training. They know all about riding in the car, walking nicely on leash, and going to sleep when you go to sleep. They've long since given up the habit of chewing on chair legs. Most are very good with children. Many are cat safe. Senior German Shepherds are, in fact, a known commodity: intelligent, eager to bond with their new owners, almost always quiet, not destructive, and grateful to have a real home again.

And if you yourself are a senior, there are extra benefits in bringing a senior Shepherd into your home. Did you know that people who live with pets may have significantly lower systolic blood pressure and cholesterol levels

*Training Tidbit*

Senior Shepherds can be trained in many activities. In particular, a laid-back senior who enjoys being with people is an ideal candidate for therapy work.

than those who don't? It's true, and I think we can agree that living with a calm and loving senior Shepherd would be more likely to lower our blood pressure (whether we're seniors or not), than would a puppy or an always-up-for-more exercise adult. *Between Pets and People: The Importance of Animal Companionship*, a book by Alan Beck and Aaron Katcher, shows how living with pets can help ward off depression and loneliness. Again, I think that relaxing with a senior Shepherd after you've had a grinding day at work, followed by freeway gridlock,

Senior German Shepherds have a lot to offer potential adoptees.

## Multi-Dog Tip

A newly adopted senior Shepherd is likely to bond quickly with another dog in the home. In fact, adding a senior to an already pet-inhabited home may be much easier on everyone than bringing in a puppy or adolescent.

would be much more likely to make you feel good about life than would chasing after a puppy or taking an adult dog to intermediate training classes.

## HOW TO FIND YOUR SENIOR SHEPHERD

One way to find a senior Shepherd to adopt is to visit the American German Shepherd Rescue Association (AGSDRA) at www.agsra.com and click on Rescues by State. As of this writing, there are GSD rescues in 42 states and Washington D.C. Another source for finding your senior is to visit www.petfinder.com. I did this, searching for senior German Shepherd Dogs of either sex, and came up with animal shelters and rescues throughout the country.

A bill passed by the Congress in 2000 made it possible for civilians to adopt retired military working dogs—many of whom are GSDs. To find out how you can add a retiring senior veteran to your family, visit www.militaryworkingdogadoptions.com. Most of the pictures on this very moving website are of Shepherds.

# CHAPTER 13

# CARE OF YOUR GERMAN SHEPHERD SENIOR

The care you give your senior Shepherd can make those golden years deeply satisfying for you as well as your dog. Schedule biannual checkups even when he is healthy, and monitor his weight while continuing to feed him a tasty diet that meets his nutritional needs. Give him the exercise he requires without letting him overdo it. As with older people, older dogs with an inactive lifestyle can lose muscle mass and tone, making exercise more difficult for them. But with routine exercise that isn't taxing, your dog's digestive system, heart, and *joie de vivre* will benefit, as well as his muscles. A walk around the block or in the park can provide socialization in addition to exercise. Now is the time to indulge your dog in anything he enjoys that is beneficial to his health. Skijoring and agility may be out, but German Shepherd meet and greets and visiting friends of yours who love him too are in.

## WHEN IS THE GSD A SENIOR?

Like dogs of most other large breeds, the GSD is considered a senior at age seven. Yet many Shepherds who have celebrated their seventh birthday and perhaps a few more don't show their age in any way that would make an observer say "Now that's an old dog." In fact, when you look into a senior Shepherd's clear, healthy eyes or witness his fluidity of movement as he runs or trots across the lawn, it's tempting to think that the experts on canine aging erred in consigning a seven-year-old Shepherd to the senior category. But they had their reasons. However subtle, there are changes in a Shepherd who is seven or older, and by knowing what they are and anticipating them before they are recognizable, we can help our senior dogs to have a happy and fulfilling old age.

## Signs of Aging

Signs of aging in a dog usually begin subtly, as they do in humans; also as in humans, over time they can be numerous. They can be benign, such as slowing down and sleeping more hours of the day, or they can signal illness. Behavioral changes such as irritability in a normally placid dog, confusion in familiar surroundings, or separation anxiety when a dog has never had it before call for a vet visit. Look for changes in your dog's gait, how he gets to his feet after lying down, and any other signs of difficulty in movement. It's a good idea

Like dogs of most other large breeds, the GSD is considered a senior at age seven.

to keep a list of anything new that you notice in your dog so that it can be reported to his vet.

Many signs of aging in dogs are the same as those seen in people. Your Shepherd's skin may become thinner and drier. Constipation can result from a decrease in gastrointestinal motility, which often is caused by inactivity but also can be a sign of serious illness and must be reported to his vet. A decrease in his ability to fight off infectious diseases is normal, and this makes keeping your senior up to date with his vaccinations very important. If your housetrained senior starts having accidents indoors even though he is taken outside more often than he used to be, it could be from changes in eating or drinking habits. But it also can signal important health problems. So too

can bad breath, which often stems from dental disease.

An aging dog may lose all or some of his sight and hearing. If this happens to your dog, children in the family and children who visit your home must be made to understand the situation and taught not to startle him in any way. If the dog is blind, no one should approach and touch him without first speaking to him. Vision loss usually is caused by changes inside the eyeball. An excellent book that can help owners help their dogs is *Living With Blind Dogs: A Resource Book and Training Guide for the Owners of Blind and Low-Vision Dogs,* by Caroline D. Levin. And a product called The Blind Dog Hoop Harness is, for the vision-impaired dog, the equivalent of a

If your adopted senior was allowed on furniture in a prior home but you prefer that dogs stay off the furniture, try to compromise by choosing a sofa or large chair for him to sleep on and covering it with his own quilt. Otherwise, put cushy dog beds in several rooms of your home and sit on the floor beside him while he adjusts to keeping off furniture.

walking stick for a vision-impaired human. Hearing loss can be caused by degeneration of an ear's internal structure, but if your dog appears to be going deaf, you will want to find out whether the cause is an infection, a growth in the ear, or just a buildup of wax. For books on living with and training a deaf dog, visit www.deafdogs.org. I did and was amazed by the activities, from agility to therapy work, in which a deaf dog can participate.

While writing this chapter I asked a friend what she loves best about her aged GSD, Rosie, who has scarcely any hearing left. Without hesitation my friend replied, "She always looks me in the eye when I talk to her. She seems to understand everything I say."

Well, that's a German Shepherd for you.

## FEEDING

It probably won't be necessary to change your dog's food simply because he is a senior. If he isn't underweight or overweight, still enjoys exercise, and doesn't have health problems, you obviously are providing him with a well-balanced diet that includes high-quality protein—so why change it? You will want to keep an eye on his weight, though. Some seniors do have trouble keeping weight on, but being overweight is a much more likely concern, with obesity being one of the main health problems of older dogs. If your dog's activity level has decreased significantly, you may have to curb his calories. But he shouldn't be fed a low-protein "senior" diet unless your vet recommends it, as too little protein can cause muscle wasting and weight loss.

By exercising your senior, you will keep him mentally fit while helping him burn calories and maintain musculature. However, even if he is able to continue with his regular diet, you may need to give him a smaller quantity. Also, if he eats three or four small meals a day instead of two large ones, he'll burn calories more efficiently. And if he's of good appetite and is overweight, you'll want to help him lose weight without denying him the pleasure of frequent eating. (This is what we want for ourselves when we put on a few pounds [kg] we don't need.) So don't stop giving your boy treats to reward good behavior and show him how much you love him; just give smaller but still nutritious treats that aren't high in calories.

Appetite in any species is a key to health, and gradual loss of appetite in your senior Shepherd merits as much concern as does overeating. His indifference to food could be caused by a diminishing sense of smell or taste. If this is the case, one way to make his meals more appealing is to warm them. Stir the food after taking it from the microwave to make sure that it isn't hot enough to burn the tissues of his mouth; to be on the safe side, touch the food with your finger. You can also look for healthful foods that may tempt an older dog to eat more. One that I've had luck with is green tripe. (You may have to hold your nose until you get used to the smell.) If your dog appears to want to eat, and then doesn't—or if he takes a bite of food and then drops it—he may have dental pain, so have this confirmed or ruled out by his vet. Speaking of dental health, if for years your pup has been fed dry kibble as part of your protocol for keeping his gums healthy, try moistening the kibble now to see whether that's more palatable to him. (You can be extra diligent about brushing his teeth—perhaps doing it twice a day since it takes so little time.) By mixing in a little cooked chicken, ground beef (but minus the fat drippings, which can cause pancreatitis), or chopped hard-cooked eggs, you can turn plain kibble into gourmet fare. Also, a really old dog who has lost interest in his food may find it a lot tastier when it's given as treats. You wouldn't have dreamed of feeding your dog by hand when he was young and frisky, but why not do it now?

For a dog of any age, not eating can signify the onset of serious illness. Therefore, anytime your dog ignores his food bowl for more than a day, tell your vet. And because an older dog is more prone to constipation, you may need to add more fiber to your dog's diet. Home cooking is an option, and I haven't met a dog who doesn't enjoy a home-cooked diet. But any major dietary change you make for a senior dog should be discussed with your vet.

## What to Feed

If your senior Shepherd was adopted from a shelter or rescue after being there for a while, you can find out what his diet consisted of and keep it the same while he adjusts to his new home. Even if you feel that what he was previously fed isn't a high-quality diet (and let's face it, many shelters and rescues have limited resources), or if the shelter or rescue reports that your dog didn't seem to like his food all that much while he was there, changes should be made gradually. Even then he may experience loose stools. This isn't of concern unless it continues for more than 24 hours. Any time diarrhea persists that long, whether or not there's been a change in diet, you should call your vet. By following your adopted dog's schedule for eating and walking when he was between homes, at least for the first week or two, you may prevent tummy upsets. And by all means, keep his diet just as it was if you are impressed by the quality and see no reason to change it.

Mix something appetizing, like cooked chicken, into your dog's food bowl to stimulate his appetite.

## Feeding Schedule

How many times a day you feed your senior can be the same as when he was younger, or it can be more often if frequent feedings will help keep him at an optimum weight or help with his digestion. Of course, it also depends on your schedule, as you can't be expected to come home from work in mid-morning or the afternoon to feed him. But however often he's fed, you want to control the content of his diet, so make certain that other members of the family aren't slipping him extra food. Children like sharing their food with dogs, especially when the food is something they don't want to eat themselves and Mom isn't watching. (The Boxer I grew up with had lots of fresh-cooked and canned vegetables—all from my plate.) Also make certain that your dog doesn't have access to another pet's food. Cat food in particular is not healthful for dogs, being too high in fat and protein for them. And free feeding really isn't a good idea for your senior, even if he's underweight.

## GROOMING

Careful grooming of your senior will help keep him healthy while indulging him in his favorite pastime: being close to and touched by you. And now that he's older, you will want to be extra gentle when grooming him, especially if he has aches anywhere. Try not to move him in any way that may be uncomfortable while brushing his coat or teeth, trimming his nails, or cleaning his ears. When bathing him, be sure to keep him from getting chilled. If he has arthritis, he won't be comfortable standing for an extended period, and sitting even for a short while may be difficult also. If this is the case, do as much grooming as you can with him lying down. You can't bathe him lying down, but bathing doesn't need to be done often and shouldn't be. Nail trimming

does need to be done frequently, especially if the nails aren't being worn down by activity as they were when your dog was younger. But nail trimming is easily done with him lying on his side—especially if you use a Dremel-type tool and have someone helping keep him calm, comfortable, and devouring small treats if he's so inclined. You also needn't trim all of his nails in one session. Many dogs (including all who have shared their lives with me) are touchier about having the nails on their front feet trimmed than the nails on their back feet. If your dog feels this way, it may be easier to do the front feet one day and the back feet another day. You can use the same approach when brushing him, which will make perfect sense if by lying on his side to be brushed he'll be more comfortable.

One of the benefits of grooming sessions is that they're a means of checking for problems: small tumors or growths, changes in the skin (that may or may not signal internal problems), thickening of the foot pads, broken or brittle nails, and redness or discharge from the eyes (evidence of dry eye, which can be treated by an eye ointment). A discharge or odor from an ear will be noticed while you gently clean his ears, as would ear mites. Discovering such an odor or discharge is very important, as it could be caused by an infection, and your dog's immune system may not be as strong as it once was. Likewise, fleas or ticks can do more harm to older dogs than young ones. And if your dog has even just one tick or flea, careful grooming should reveal the parasite.

## HEALTH CARE

Health care for your senior Shepherd is not all that different from when he was a puppy or adult. You monitor for changes and remain scrupulous about his nutrition and veterinary care.

### Preventive Care: Senior Checkups

Preventing serious problems isn't always possible; cancer happens, as do other diseases that can afflict dogs of any age or breed. So do breed-specific illnesses happen, such as degenerative myelopathy in German Shepherds and hereditary myopathy in Labrador Retrievers. But veterinary care—both routine and whenever a problem is suspected—can add years to a dog's life through detection of curable or treatable diseases.

In the first three years of your Shepherd being a senior, twice-yearly checkups should suffice. But when his age is in the double digits, you may want to change to three checkups a year, giving your vet a chance to find anything amiss while it's in an early stage. In between these visits, don't put off seeing the vet when problems occur. Unless your dog has enjoyed routine dental care throughout his younger years, he's almost certain to experience dental disease in older age. Even after years of having his teeth brushed routinely, he may develop dental problems that in old age can be life threatening.

Brush your senior's teeth gently, but do brush them, and if while you do he shows discomfort or anything looks amiss—such as increased redness of the gum line—schedule a dental checkup. An intact male should have his prostate gland checked at every routine physical exam, as he is at very high risk for prostate disease. Although rarely cancerous, it results in an enlarged prostate, which can cause problems with urinating and defecating. Breast cancer in an unspayed older dog is as common as it is in humans, so if your senior is female and unspayed, her mammary glands should be checked at each physical.

Preventive health care for your senior also includes regular exercise. His days of engaging in rigorous sports may be over, but as long as he is mobile and feeling well he should enjoy the outdoors and not be limited to his own back yard. Just because he can no longer jump into a car doesn't mean that he can't go places with you. Ramps and folding steps for large dogs are available from many online stores. Your senior may be very skeptical about getting on the ramp at first, as was a 13-year-old dog of mine, but don't give up and don't look or sound as if you share his skepticism. Having one person at his head (but not pulling him by his collar or leash) and one at his rear is helpful. When my dog finally decided to go

Preventive health care for your senior also includes regular exercise.

for it, he didn't walk the ramp—he ran up. Whatever works!

## Senior Illnesses

The illnesses listed below often affect dogs in their later years, just as they do people. Even when there is no cure, there are ways to help preserve quality of life.

### Arthritis

Osteoarthritis, commonly called arthritis, is a degenerative joint and cartilage disease that's common in older dogs (just as it is in older people), with large breeds being the most prone to it. Arthritis is often accompanied by hip dysplasia, and it frequently occurs in dogs with a history of infection or who have had an earlier injury. But it is usually simply the result of ordinary wear and tear on the bones and joints. The disease can be debilitating or may only cause the dog to suffer slight stiffness. Dogs with arthritis may have difficulty lying down or getting up, going up and down stairs, jumping into the car, or walking. They may favor one leg and when symptoms are greater than stiffness are likely to whimper or cry out when making a sudden movement. Diagnosis is made by a physical exam that may include X-rays. Your vet may recommend supplements such as glucosamine and chondroitin, as well as pain relievers if necessary.

A dog who has trouble getting to his feet and walking probably won't go to his water bowl as often as he should. If you notice that he's not drinking as much as he used to, you can help prevent dehydration—which would further impair his health— by buying a few more water bowls and putting them near his beds or anywhere else he likes to sleep. If he hasn't drunk for a while, you may want to bring the bowl to him. After he drinks, give him a gentle kiss and tell him he's a good boy.

Acupuncture (see Chapter 8) is known to have helped many dogs as well as cats live comfortably with arthritis. Canine hydrotherapy, too, can be very beneficial— reducing the pain of arthritis and increasing the dog's mobility. However, at the time of this writing, it is an unregulated industry. Beverly W. McCartt, a member of the American Canine Sports Medicine Association (ACSMA), suggests that should you decide to take your dog to a canine hydrotherapist, you ask the therapist what training she has had, especially in canine anatomy and the musculoskeletal system, and for how long she has trained. You also will want to know whether she is familiar with the various orthopedic and neurological disorders that dogs are prone to. If the therapist mentions a specific program, check to

## Want to Know More?

To find out more about hip dysplasia, see Chapter 3: Care of Your German Shepherd Puppy.

see whether there's a website where you can read about the program. McCartt cautions that some places train their people for just one week. Others, though, offer an intensive program consisting of several units of learning, and some programs teach both hydrotherapy and acupressure. A qualified hydrotherapist is likely to receive referrals from veterinarians and will stay in contact with the treating vet. A big red flag arises when a practitioner suggests or promises to cure a degenerative disorder or terminal illness.

### Canine Cognitive Dysfunction (CCD)

Canine cognitive dysfunction goes by several names, including cognitive dysfunction syndrome, old dog syndrome, senility, and doggy Alzheimer's disease. It is in fact an age-related disorder that causes deterioration of the cognitive abilities and is the equivalent of Alzheimer's. The many symptoms of CCD include aimless wandering, changes in sleep patterns, confusion, loss of housetraining, and staring at walls. None of this reflects

## The Bottom's Up Leash

A product named the Bottom's Up Leash (www.bottomsupleash.com), but called the "butt leash" in my house, can help a post-surgical dog or one with weak hindquarters eliminate comfortably, go up and down stairs safely, and enjoy his daily walks. There also are wheelchairs and harness systems for helping dogs who are temporarily or permanently handicapped. And an excellent source for information on pain management in dogs is available at www. morrisanimalfoundation.org, website of the Morris Animal Foundation—the world's largest nonprofit foundation dedicated to funding research to benefit animals.

normal aging, and as with Alzheimer's disease in humans, what exactly causes canine cognitive dysfunction remains unknown. There is medication for treating CCD. It can make a difference, but it is not a cure. The other treatment is an abundance of love. My Chapstick, nicknamed Happy Chappie, had CCD in the last year of her life. Fortunately, her symptoms were minimal and happiness never left her.

## Cataracts

A cataract is an opacity or cloudiness in the lens of the eye. There are different kinds of cataracts, each with different causes. Late onset cataracts, often called senile cataracts, occur in dogs over six years of age but are seen much less frequently in dogs than in humans. Diabetes mellitus can cause cataracts, and when this occurs it's usually in both eyes. Trauma—with something penetrating the eye and damaging the lens—is another cause. If your dog has a cataract, you probably will notice the most common symptom, which is lens cloudiness. The dog can't see through the part of the lens that's cloudy, and if the entire lens becomes involved, he will be blind in that eye. When a dog shows cataract symptoms, tests are required to determine the cause. Cataracts can be treated successfully by surgical removal performed by a canine ophthalmologist. If your regular vet isn't able to recommend an ophthalmologist in your area, the Canine Eye Registry Foundation (CERF) offers a list of American College of Veterinary Ophthalmologists (AVCO) diplomats. Visit www.vmdb.org/history.html and click on ACVO Clinic List.

Another age-related eye condition your senior might have is nuclear sclerosis, a normal change that usually occurs in the lenses of both eyes. The condition gives the eyes a bluish-

When a dog shows cataract symptoms, tests are required to determine the cause.

gray look and may affect the dog's vision, but not to a significant degree, and treatment is not required. Cataracts, which have a white appearance, are a different story. The word "cataract" means "to break down," and this breakdown can result in partial or complete blindness.

## Congestive Heart Failure

The most common heart problem in dogs is congestive heart failure (CHF). A dog of any age can develop CHF, but usually it strikes older adult or senior dogs who are overweight. It also can be caused by heartworms or by a hereditary weakness of the heart. Dogs with CHF can have both fluid in their lungs, which causes stressful coughing, and a problem with mobility. The symptoms are many and almost painful to read about. Among them is fainting, which is common, as is the dog's having trouble catching his breath. A swollen abdomen from the fluid can cause a potbellied appearance, and the dog may stand with his front legs wide apart and his neck extended and lowered in an attempt to get more air into his lungs. There's no cure as yet, but there are treatment options that include medication, nutritional changes to control weight and salt intake, and supplements, all of which your vet will discuss with you. Lifestyle—especially routine exercise and optimal nutrition—are key factors in preventing an otherwise healthy dog from getting CHF.

### Cushing's Disease

Hyperadrenocorticism, commonly known as Cushing's disease, occurs in older dogs (and humans, cats, and horses) as a result of the body's producing too much of the hormone cortisol, which is produced and stored by two small glands, called adrenals, that sit on top of the kidneys. Although there are a number of possible causes for Cushing's disease, abnormal functioning of the pituitary gland is the most common. The disease is seen more frequently in dogs with hypothyroidism (underactive thyroid).

Symptoms of Cushing's disease (named after Harvey Williams Cushing, a famous neurosurgeon and pioneer of brain surgery) develop slowly, which often causes early signs to go unnoticed. Symptoms can include an increase in thirst, appetite, and urination; changes in the skin, and skin infections; loss of hair; excessive panting (and reduced activity); and an enlarged abdomen that gives the dog

a potbellied appearance. Diagnosis is made through blood tests, and your vet may also use ultrasound to help detect a tumor on an adrenal gland. Cushing's is usually treated with medication only, although in some cases surgery is recommended. Dr. Ann Stohlman, a veterinarian in the FDA's Center for Veterinary Medicine, believes that dogs with Cushing's disease can still enjoy a quality life under care of a veterinarian and with an owner who follows the vet's blood work and medication schedules.

## TRAINING

Should you even try to teach an old dog new tricks, especially if he has health issues? The answer is a resounding yes. As long as he isn't overworked or made to assume a painful position (if sitting is uncomfortable for him, the *sit* command is out), your teaching him new tricks and reinforcing old ones will help keep him happy and fit. And given a choice between training a puppy or an old dog, many seasoned dog owners would choose the senior. People who work with rescue and shelter dogs often come to think that training old dogs is easier than training puppies because the seniors can stay focused longer than puppies and young dogs. Also, most seniors already have experience being trained in house manners, staying still to be groomed, behaving on walks and in public buildings, and in everyday activities, such as a game of fetch. This experience has taught them that learning to obey a new command or having a command from their younger years reinforced leads to being rewarded and feeling good about themselves. And the German Shepherd loves to work. He was bred to work; it's in his genes. So being retired from his responsibilities—which in addition to obeying commands and playing fun games with you may include patrolling the

Reduced activity is a sign of Cushing's disease.

perimeter a few times a day—will only make him feel older and possibly useless. Boredom, the result of having nothing to do, can also lead to obsessive compulsive disorder (OCD). This is found in animals and humans alike, only with different behavior patterns. You or I might wash our hands excessively, while a Shepherd with OCD is likely to chase his tail compulsively.

It's all right to retire your Shepherd from conformation or agility because of his age, as long as he still has mental challenges and a routine to follow. Of course, there are factors that may require his routine to be changed, but since change involves training, this too can be beneficial. So can obedience training in a classroom setting. If your dog already knows all of the routine commands, having opportunities to demonstrate his knowledge will make him feel good. And his being with unfamiliar dogs and people will reinforce his social skills. Just be sure that the trainer is certified, uses positive training methods, and appears glad to have an old dog in the class. And don't be surprised if, among all the younger dogs, your boy becomes teacher's pet.

Whether you train your senior at home or in a classroom setting, he may need more bathroom breaks than when he was younger. In fact, he may need them more often under any circumstances, including in the dead of night. And sometimes, either because he didn't alert you to his need or he tried to let you know but you didn't hear, you may not get him outside in time. Not all seniors have accidents indoors or unconsciously dribble in the house after urinating outside. But some do, and they should never be scolded for it. At all stages of our lives as dog owners, we must continually train ourselves to be fair.

CHAPTER 14

# END-OF-LIFE ISSUES

As much as your dog loves you and lives his life to please you, there is no way he can keep from breaking your heart. Even if he should beat the life span odds for his breed, he is canine; his life is brief. In this chapter we will look at ways to help your dog be comfortable as the end of his life nears. We will talk about home hospice for pets and about euthanasia, the act of putting to death painlessly, which must be the saddest aspect of veterinary medicine. Yet euthanasia (the word is Greek for "good death") is a merciful act that spares pets from painful diseases or conditions that cannot be cured. We also will look at ways in which we can help ourselves, our children, and other dogs in the family get through this time of grief and loss.

## WHEN IS IT TIME?

In the most unfortunate of circumstances, one knows exactly when it's time to euthanize a dog. This is when he has been in a terrible accident, or he is suffering physically and there is nothing his vet can do to make the pain go away. It's harder to know when to let your dog go, even if he is terminally ill, if physical suffering can be kept under control. In some cases, with degenerative myelopathy being an example, even without medication there may be no bodily pain. But there is emotional pain; you can see it in his eyes. Trying to determine when it's time to let go often is anguishing. In the evening we may decide it's time and that we will phone the vet in the morning; then we wake in the morning feeling uncertain again. As hard as this is, though, no one except your vet can or should tell you when it's time. But perhaps asking yourself a few questions about your dog's quality of life will help. First, does he really have a high quality of life anymore? Does he still have good days when he appears to feel relatively well and eats and drinks without being coaxed? And if he does have some days that are free of apparent discomfort, do they make up for the really bad days?

## HOSPICE AND EUTHANASIA

"Hospice" and "euthanasia" are not words we want to think of in conjunction with our dogs. But hospice can make the end of life easier for a dog, and euthanasia will spare him pain.

## Joey

My first male Shepherd, Joey, was two years old when he had his first epileptic seizure. He was not my only dog to suffer from epilepsy. A little mixed breed, whom my children named Nancy Texas Goat, endured mild seizures throughout most of her 16 years. Joey's seizures, though, were not mild, and in his fifth year the seizures were so frequent and profound that our canine neurologist, with deep compassion in his eyes, said, "You are not on earth to keep Joey alive."

I knew this but still wasn't ready. How can one ever be ready to end the life of a faithful companion who lives only to please and protect his people? Besides, Nancy stopped having seizures in her final years. Who was to say this couldn't happen with Joey? And although I didn't dare take him on walks, we still could take short car rides together.

Joey had one more seizure. When it was over, he struggled to his feet and looked around with fear and bewilderment in his eyes. I realized that he didn't know where he was, who he was, or who I was. Some minutes later, he did know. He came to me and rested his head on my lap. I understood then that I was not on earth to make Joey suffer.

## Hospice

Home-hospice care for terminally ill pets is a relatively new concept modeled on home-hospice care for people, and it has become widely available through veterinary hospitals and volunteer organizations. The Nikki Hospice Foundation for Pets (NHFP), founded by Dr. Kathryn Marocchino and headquartered in Vallejo, California, helps people locate veterinarians who offer home-hospice care. NHFP, an associate member of the National Hospice and Palliative Care Organization, also provides pet-loss support through free workshops and a 24-hour hotline and informs pet parents of hospice-related veterinary services and products. The website is www.pethospice.org.

Another organization, Animal Hospice Compassionate Crossings (AHCC), is headquartered in Idaho's Wood River Valley and states on its website (www.animalhospice.org) that it provides support, compassion, and a sense of connection. Services are offered by trained volunteers who will visit in person or by telephone, mail, or e-mail. They also offer ongoing support groups, and there is no charge for anything they provide.

## Euthanasia

Except for the dog who perishes in an accident or dies in his sleep, our beloved canine companions are gently put to rest by their veterinarian, either at home or in the vet's clinic. Your vet will explain the virtually painless procedure to you before beginning it. Sedation is brought about by an injection, followed after your dog is asleep by a second injection that causes the heart to stop. It is over in a few seconds. During the process, you may lie next to your dog if you wish or kneel beside him, and while stroking him gently tell him anything you want him to know, which probably will include that he is the best dog who ever lived.

While you can't avoid the emotional pain of losing your beloved dog, there are ways to reduce the stresses that often precede euthanasia or come afterward. First, plan ahead by deciding whether you want your dog to be euthanized at home or at the veterinary clinic. There are advantages and disadvantages to both. Home is by far the more comfortable environment, especially if your dog always felt nervous at the vet's. And having the vet come to your home would especially benefit your dog if he's so ill that getting into and out of the car would be a hardship. It would also give you some feeling of control, which helps in any time of loss and grief. But if you do prefer to have it done at the vet's—and there are good reasons to want this—the problems that may arise from your dog's having to travel or being anxious when he gets to the clinic can be mitigated by asking your vet to prescribe a mild

tranquilizer before the trip. And you can take some of the comforts of home with you, such as your dog's favorite bed, a quilt or blanket belonging to him, and his favorite snuggly toy.

One of the things you will want to know in advance if your choice is home euthanasia is whether your vet makes house calls. Most vets do not, but some who ordinarily don't will make an exception for euthanasia. If, however, your vet's coming to you is out of the question and you feel strongly about having it done at home, ask whether the vet can recommend a vet who does make house calls. Or you may be able to locate one in your area by checking the American Association of Housecall & Mobile Veterinarians (AAHV) at www.housecallvets. org. AAHV is a member organization of the American Veterinary Medical Association

No matter how much or how little time you are given to love and nurture a dog, ultimately you are grateful for having had him in your life.

Mental stimulation is a tonic for a dog nearing the end of his life. He may have limited hearing and vision, but his sense of smell is still good. Give him a few objects to sniff, one at a time, while naming them for him. When he sniffs something and appears interested, praise him. What a smart and good boy he is!

(AVMA). When scheduling the appointment, find out whether the vet will arrange for removal of your dog's remains through the organization that provides this service for veterinary clinics.

The advantages of having your dog euthanized at his vet's office include your not having memories of him dying in your home. No room in the house will contain his death, just his vibrant life and happiness. You also will have the emotional support of the vet staff. They have been through this many times. Some have said goodbye to their own dogs here. They know the heartbreak. They know how to make the procedure go smoothly. And they know how to give comfort.

To make this visit to the clinic easier for you and your dog, try to book the first or last appointment of the day, with last being preferred. This way there won't be a long wait in a room with other people and their pets. But if you must go in the middle of the day, it's likely that you and your dog will be shown into an exam room where you can have privacy while waiting for the vet. If this isn't offered, don't hesitate to make the request.

You may also want to pay the bill before

the day of euthanasia, as you will not want to stand crying at the desk when it's over. But if you don't arrange for prepayment and you are known at the clinic, you may ask at the desk whether you can come in the next day to pay. I've never had anyone say no to this request, and at some clinics the person behind the desk will sympathetically wave you off with "We'll let you know the costs."

Something else to determine in advance is what you want to do with your dog's remains. For many years now, cremation has been the preferred method, with the remains buried either on the owner's property or in a pet cemetery, or else kept indoors in an urn. If you specify at the clinic that you want your dog to be cremated alone, not in a group, his ashes will be returned to the vet clinic, where you can pick them up. Some people prefer not to have their dog cremated, wanting instead to have a whole-body burial either in their yard, a pet cemetery, or a natural outdoor setting. If whole-body burial other than at a pet cemetery is your choice, you must first check with your city, town, or state to see whether it's permissible or disallowed because of health regulations. There also may not be a pet cemetery in your area that isn't strictly for cremated pets, but you may find one within a reasonable distance by searching the member list of the International Association of Pet Cemeteries & Crematories (IAOPCC). Located in Ellenburg Depot, New York, IAOPCC is a not-for-profit organization dedicated to the advancement of pet cemeteries through public awareness programs. According to the association, there are more than 600 active pet cemeteries in the United States, with the oldest having been established in 1896. However, IAOPCC cautions that of the 600, only about 400 are "good operating businesses." The association advises that when choosing a pet

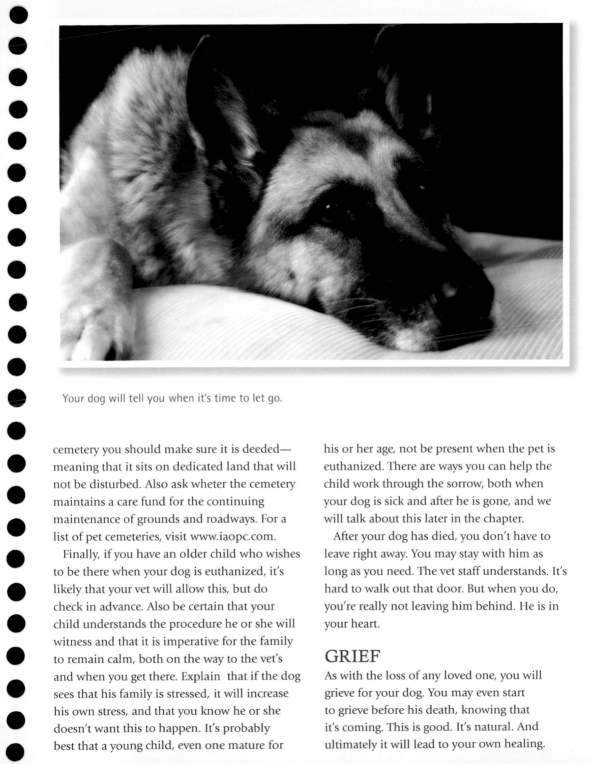

Your dog will tell you when it's time to let go.

cemetery you should make sure it is deeded—meaning that it sits on dedicated land that will not be disturbed. Also ask wheter the cemetery maintains a care fund for the continuing maintenance of grounds and roadways. For a list of pet cemeteries, visit www.iaopc.com.

Finally, if you have an older child who wishes to be there when your dog is euthanized, it's likely that your vet will allow this, but do check in advance. Also be certain that your child understands the procedure he or she will witness and that it is imperative for the family to remain calm, both on the way to the vet's and when you get there. Explain  that if the dog sees that his family is stressed, it will increase his own stress, and that you know he or she doesn't want this to happen. It's probably best that a young child, even one mature for

his or her age, not be present when the pet is euthanized. There are ways you can help the child work through the sorrow, both when your dog is sick and after he is gone, and we will talk about this later in the chapter.

After your dog has died, you don't have to leave right away. You may stay with him as long as you need. The vet staff understands. It's hard to walk out that door. But when you do, you're really not leaving him behind. He is in your heart.

## GRIEF

As with the loss of any loved one, you will grieve for your dog. You may even start to grieve before his death, knowing that it's coming. This is good. It's natural. And ultimately it will lead to your own healing.

It's possible, though, or even probable, that when your dog nears the end of his life, or has died, someone incapable of understanding the magnitude of your pain will say something thoughtless, such as, "Try to put it into perspective." Or much worse, "After all, it's only a dog." Their intent is not to hurt or belittle but to make you see reality. The problem is that your reality is something they can't understand. For this reason, it's important that you spend time with people who do understand, who share your reality, whose hearts will ache for you because they too love animals and consider dogs to be family members.

Many resources for grief support are only a phone call or website away. The ASPCA's Pet Loss Support program offers a hotline at (877) 474-3310. Pet loss support hotlines are also available from many colleges of veterinary medicine. Or visit the Delta Society at www.deltasociety.org and click on Pet Loss Resource Directory. Some animal shelters provide pet loss support groups that are free of charge, not limited to people who adopted from the shelter, and led by a trained facilitator. So you see, your options for sharing your grief are numerous, starting with family and friends and branching out to like-minded people. You'll find them everywhere.

## Explaining Pet Loss to Children

Children of all ages need an extra measure of love and support when their pet is dying and after he is gone. If possible, have your child say goodbye to her dog before he dies, and assure her that he is not going to feel pain. Before and afterward, encourage her to talk about him and let her ask all the questions she wants. Answer them in ways that are both honest and consoling. You don't want to be vague or make up a story, as the former can leave a child confused and the latter can lead to mistrust. For a very young child, any explanation of what has happened should be brief and simple, and a preschooler may need to hear the answers to her questions a number of times.

Reading with a child about the loss of a beloved pet can be beneficial.

According to the American Academy of Child and Adolescent Psychiatry (AACAP), children who are between three and five years of age see death as temporary and potentially reversible, while children between six and eight "begin to develop a more realistic understanding of the nature and consequences of death." A complete understanding of the permanence of death usually doesn't occur until nine years of age. But whatever the age of your child, share your own feelings about the family's loss. You miss his smile. It's sad to come home and not find him there. By expressing your feelings, you help your child express her own.

Reading with a child about the loss of a pet, either before or after death occurs, also can be beneficial. Many books on the topic have been written, with one of the most widely read being *When a Pet Dies*, by Fred Rogers, creator and host of the long-running public television show "Mr. Rogers' Neighborhood." Described by the Bulletin of the Center for Children's Books as a "sensitive and sensible first book about death," *When a Pet Dies* is for children between four and eight years old. A beautiful and much appreciated book for readers of all ages is *Dog Heaven* by the Newbery award winner Cynthia Rylant.

There are many ways you can validate to your child after her dog dies that he was a real member of the family and will never be forgotten. For one, with her help you can create a living memorial by planting a small garden or tree in your yard, with a plaque or gravestone bearing your Shepherd's name. You could also hold a small service for him

As with the loss of any loved one, you will grieve for your dog.

Dogs grieve too, especially when they were closely bonded to the pet who died.

and have your child write a poem, story, or eulogy—with your help if needed—to read at the service. You probably have taken many pictures of your Shepherd, and she could choose her favorite to have framed for her bedroom. She may also want to keep his collar, tags, and favorite toy in a special box. You could also help her select a German Shepherd rescue, animal shelter, or any canine welfare organization to donate to in your dog's memory. Because you know your child so well, you will think of other ways to help her get through this.

Nikki's Hospice Foundation for Pets has as its motto: *non omnis moriar*—"I shall not wholly die." When you know the time is coming for your Shepherd to leave this world or if it should happen suddenly, you can tell your child that her dog will live on in her heart and memories. This may be helpful. It definitely is true.

## Helping Other Pets Deal With Loss

Dogs grieve too, especially when they were closely bonded to the pet who died. (While the bond is usually between two dogs, it's not unusual for a dog to grieve over the loss of the family cat.) If you are a multi-pet home, it's best for your healthy dog to witness the passage of his housemate. He will then understand that his companion is no longer living, which will give him the closure he needs. Otherwise he may become depressed or anxious. I evidenced this after my Joey's progressive epilepsy reached the point that we had to let him go. He and our female, Chapstick, were very close, but we didn't take her with us on Joey's final trip to the vet's office. When we came home without him, Chapstick didn't understand his absence. For days she was fearful of leaving the house, even to eliminate, obviously worried that if she left she might not return. My husband and I learned a lesson from this. So when Charlie had to be released from his suffering, Chappie went with us. She watched as he slipped peacefully away and while we cried over him. We stayed with him a while afterward, and when we were ready to leave, Chapstick was too. That day and thereafter, she displayed no signs of fear, nor even grief. She had known for a long time that Charlie was gravely ill. She witnessed his death. She accepted it.

One day you may decide to bring a new German Shepherd Dog into your home.

## By the Numbers

The number of years a dog lives is not what matters most; it's the number of years he was loved.

## ACCEPTANCE

Grief over the loss of a pet has, for each person, its own timetable. You can't know how long it will be before you wake in the middle of the night or at dawn without missing your dog. But you should know this: You were an outstanding owner and guardian of your Shepherd. You cared for him in sickness and in health. Whether you got him as a puppy, an adult, or in his senior years, in your care he had the very best. And should the time come that you decide to bring another Shepherd into your life, that dog too will be blessed with a wonderful home.

# 50 FUN FACTS EVERY GERMAN SHEPHERD OWNER SHOULD KNOW

1. In World War I, the German army employed 48,000 German Shepherd Dogs in tasks ranging from sentry duty to hospital dogs and messengers.

2. Brindle used to be included in German Shepherd Dog colors, but it's been many decades since a "striped" GSD was surveyed.

3. The German Shepherd Dog was first exhibited in America in 1907.

4. The German Shepherd Dog was the first breed used for guiding the blind.

5. Gunter Grass, who won the Nobel Prize for Literature in 1999, wrote in his novel Dog Years about a German Shepherd Dog whose offspring became Adolf Hitler's favorite dog.

6. Horand v Grafrath SZ1 and Mari v Grafrath SZ2 were the first two German Shepherd Dogs registered in Germany.

7. Giving a GSD puppy a high-calorie diet will place increased stress on his hips.

8. Your veterinarian will vaccinate your new puppy against a range of infectious diseases and notify you whenever he is due for a shot.

9. A GSD that is neutered or spayed is protected against certain cancers and is much less likely to wander from home.

10. Most German Shepherds are black and tan or black and red with black masks and saddles.

11. Your Shepherd wants to please you. To let him know that he does, always reward him with praise, petting, or treats when he has done something good.

12. GSDs have an incredible sense of smell and can detect a gas leak 15 feet (4.5 m) under ground.

13. In 1908, the first GSD imported from Germany was registered in the United States. Her name was Queen of Switzerland.

14. The German Shepherd Dog Club of America (GSDCA) was founded in 1913 by Anne Tracy and Benjamin Throop.

15. Captain Max von Stephanitz, a German cavalry officer, developed the German Shepherd in 1899.

16. In 1927, a female German Shepherd Dog called Buddy became the first Seeing Eye dog.

17. In 1921, a GSD called Strongheart became one of the first dogs to star in silent movies. Two years later the unforgettable Rin Tin Tin became a star.

18. If your puppy is between 8 and 16 weeks old, now is the ideal time for training to begin.

19. One way to meet adoptable GSDs is to attend German Shepherd meet and greets, often held at local pet supply stores. Besides swooning over the beautiful Shepherds, you will meet dedicated volunteers who love answering questions about their breed.

20. In 1917, a German Shepherd named Filax of Lewanno—a hero of World War I who brought 54 wounded soldiers to safety—was exhibited at Westminster.

21. The German Shepherd remains the leading breed in Germany, with about 20,000 dogs whelped per year.

22. Too much fat in the diet can bring on pancreatitis, a severe inflammation of the pancreas. GSDs are prone to pancreatitis. Never feed fat trimmings!

23. Pannus, a serious eye condition found predominantly in German Shepherds, can be controlled if treated early.

24. Make sure that all chew toys you give your German Shepherd are designed for large dogs who are strong chewers.

25. If you can't count your Shepherd's ribs by running your hands over his sides, he's eating too much.

26. German Shepherds who are free fed (allowed to eat all they want, when they want it) are more likely to get hip dysplasia.

27. Brushing your GSD's coat every day will remove loose hair and help distribute natural oils that keep his coat lustrous.

28. When your Shepherd begins to blow his coat, switch from your slicker brush to your shedding blade to groom him.

29. The AKC standard gives a big thumbs up to German Shepherds born with a medium-length double coat.

30. A Shepherd's ears stand erect, but puppies under six months may have slightly drooping ears.

31. A GSD with arthritis, hip dysplasia, or degenerative myelopathy may benefit from canine hydrotherapy. It's not a cure for any health problem, but it can improve muscle mass and joint flexibility.

32. A GSD should become used to having his teeth brushed when he's a puppy. Dental health is important through all life stages and especially so when the dog is a senior.

33. To find a qualified dog trainer in your area, visit the websites of the Association of Pet Dog Trainers (www.apdt.com) and the German Shepherd Dog Club of America (www.gsdca.org).

34. Since 1984, the American German Shepherd Dog Charitable Foundation, Inc., has made it possible for tax-deductible gifts to be made for projects beneficial to GSDs.

35. A monthly heartworm preventive will also protect your German Shepherd from hookworm and roundworm.

36. If you see your dog scooting on his fanny instead of walking, the problem is probably impacted anal sacs, not worms.

37. The first Schützhund trial was held in Germany in 1901, with the purpose of emphasizing the German Shepherd's correct working temperament and ability.

38. A German Shepherd should not have strenuous exercise until his bones are fully developed.

39. After your GSD has learned to respond to the stay command, for the rest of his life you will want to give the command before he steps out the door of any building, gets out of a car, or steps into an intersection.

40. Teaching your dog to retrieve a toy is an especially fun way for him to get extra exercise in between walks. A good game of fetch isn't meant to replace walks, but your dog needs more than one kind of exercise.

41. Use hand signals as well as verbal commands when training your German Shepherd. When he obeys hand signals, the depth of your partnership with him is loud and clear.

42. Your Shepherd will win the admiration of strangers when he sits or lies down on command and remains in that position until you release him from it. A well-trained dog in a public setting is an ambassador for his breed.

43. Always discourage normal canine behaviors that can be hurtful to people. These include jumping up, nipping, and leash pulling.

44. German Shepherds are good candidates for the exhilarating winter sport of skijoring, which combines cross-country skiing with dog mushing.

45. Schützhund, a German word meaning "protection dog," defines a dog sport that is suitable for many breeds but is mostly associated with GSDs.

46. The German Shepherd Dog is one of the most suitable breeds for search and rescue work.

47. German Shepherds are highly protective of their people, making them less likely to run off than many other breeds.

48. Giving your Shepherd the down command and following it with the stay command will put him in a position he can remain in for quite a while without being uncomfortable.

49. If your GSD is a very strong puller, you may want to consider using a Gentle Leader Head Collar or an anti-pull harness for walks.

50. A senior German Shepherd who is mobile and feeling well should enjoy the outdoors without being limited to his own back yard.

# RESOURCES

## ASSOCIATIONS AND ORGANIZATIONS

### Breed Clubs

**American Kennel Club (AKC)**
5580 Centerview Drive
Raleigh, NC 27606
Telephone: (919) 233-9767
Fax: (919) 233-3627
E-Mail: info@akc.org
www.akc.org

**Canadian Kennel Club (CKC)**
89 Skyway Avenue, Suite 100
Etobicoke, Ontario M9W 6R4
Telephone: (416) 675-5511
Fax: (416) 675-6506
E-Mail: information@ckc.ca
www.ckc.ca

**Federation Cynologique Internationale (FCI)**
Secretariat General de la FCI
Place Albert 1er, 13
B – 6530 Thuin
Belgique
www.fci.be

**German Shepherd Dog Club of America (GSDCA)**
www.gsdca.org
German Shepherd Dog Club of
Canada Inc. (GSDCC)
www.gsdcc.ca

**The Kennel Club**
1 Clarges Street
London
W1J 8AB
Telephone: 0870 606 6750
Fax: 0207 518 1058
www.the-kennel-club.org.uk

**United Kennel Club (UKC)**
100 E. Kilgore Road
Kalamazoo, MI 49002-5584
Telephone: (269) 343-9020
Fax: (269) 343-7037
E-Mail: pbickell@ukcdogs.com
www.ukcdogs.com

### Pet Sitters

**National Association of Professional Pet Sitters**
15000 Commerce Parkway,
Suite C
Mt. Laurel, New Jersey 08054
Telephone: (856) 439-0324
Fax: (856) 439-0525
E-Mail: napps@ahint.com
www.petsitters.org

**Pet Sitters International**
201 East King Street
King, NC 27021-9161
Telephone: (336) 983-9222
Fax: (336) 983-5266
E-Mail: info@petsit.com
www.petsit.com

### Rescue Organizations and Animal Welfare Groups

**American Humane Association (AHA)**
63 Inverness Drive East
Englewood, CO 80112
Telephone: (303) 792-9900
Fax: (303) 792-5333
www.americanhumane.org

**American Society for the Prevention of Cruelty to Animals (ASPCA)**
424 E. 92nd Street
New York, NY 10128-6804
Telephone: (212) 876-7700
www.aspca.org

**The Humane Society of the United States (HSUS)**
2100 L Street, NW
Washington DC 20037
Telephone: (202) 452-1100
www.hsus.org

**Royal Society for the Prevention of Cruelty to Animals (RSPCA)**
RSPCA Enquiries Service
Wilberforce Way, Southwater,
Horsham, West Sussex
RH13 9RS
United Kingdom
Telephone: 0870 3335 999
Fax: 0870 7530 284
www.rspca.org.uk

### Sports

**International Agility Link (IAL)**
Global Administrator: Steve
Drinkwater
E-Mail: yunde@powerup.au
www.agilityclick.com/~ial

**The World Canine Freestyle Organization, Inc.**
P.O. Box 350122
Brooklyn, NY 11235
Telephone: (718) 332-8336
Fax: (718) 646-2686
E-Mail: WCFODOGS@aol.com
www.worldcaninefreestyle.org

### Therapy

**Delta Society**
875 124th Ave, NE, Suite 101
Bellevue, WA 98005
Telephone: (425) 679-5500
Fax: (425) 679-5539
E-Mail: info@DeltaSociety.org
www.deltasociety.org

**Therapy Dogs Inc.**
P.O. Box 20227
Cheyenne WY 82003
Telephone: (877) 843-7364
Fax: (307) 638-2079
E-Mail: therapydogsinc@
qwestoffice.net
www.therapydogs.com

**Therapy Dogs International
(TDI)**
88 Bartley Road
Flanders, NJ 07836
Telephone: (973) 252-9800
Fax: (973) 252-7171
E-Mail: tdi@gti.net
www.tdi-dog.org

## Training

**Association of Pet Dog Trainers
(APDT)**
150 Executive Center Drive
Box 35
Greenville, SC 29615
Telephone: (800) PET-DOGS
Fax: (864) 331-0767
E-Mail: information@apdt.com
www.apdt.com

**International Association of
Animal Behavior Consultants
(IAABC)**
565 Callery Road
Cranberry Township, PA 16066
E-Mail: info@iaabc.org
www.iaabc.org

**National Association of
Dog Obedience Instructors
(NADOI)**
PMB 369
729 Grapevine Hwy.
Hurst, TX 76054-2085
www.nadoi.org

## Veterinary and Health Resources

**Academy of Veterinary
Homeopathy (AVH)**
P.O. Box 9280
Wilmington, DE 19809
Telephone: (866) 652-1590
Fax: (866) 652-1590
www.theavh.org

**American Academy of
Veterinary Acupuncture (AAVA)**
P.O. Box 1058
Glastonbury, CT 06033
Telephone: (860) 632-9911
Fax: (860) 659-8772
www.aava.org

**American Animal Hospital
Association (AAHA)**
12575 W. Bayaud Ave.
Lakewood, CO 80228
Telephone: (303) 986-2800
Fax: (303) 986-1700
E-Mail: info@aahanet.org
www.aahanet.org/index.cfm

**American College of Veterinary
Internal Medicine (ACVIM)**
1997 Wadsworth Blvd., Suite A
Lakewood, CO 80214-5293
Telephone: (800) 245-9081
Fax: (303) 231-0880
Email: ACVIM@ACVIM.org
www.acvim.org

**American College of Veterinary
Ophthalmologists (ACVO)**
P.O. Box 1311
Meridian, ID 83860
Telephone: (208) 466-7624
Fax: (208) 466-7693
E-Mail: office09@acvo.com
www.acvo.com

**American Holistic Veterinary
Medical Association (AHVMA)**
2218 Old Emmorton Road
Bel Air, MD 21015
Telephone: (410) 569-0795
Fax: (410) 569-2346
E-Mail: office@ahvma.org
www.ahvma.org

**American Veterinary Medical
Association (AVMA)**
1931 North Meacham Road,
Suite 100
Schaumburg, IL 60173-4360
Telephone: (847) 925-8070
Fax: (847) 925-1329
E-Mail: avmainfo@avma.org
www.avma.org

**ASPCA Animal Poison Control
Center**
Telephone: (888) 426-4435
www.aspca.org

**British Veterinary Association
(BVA)**
7 Mansfield Street
London
W1G 9NQ
Telephone: 0207 636 6541
Fax: 0207 908 6349
E-Mail: bvahq@bva.co.uk
www.bva.co.uk

**Canine Eye Registration
Foundation (CERF)**
VMDB/CERF
1717 Philo Rd
P.O. Box 3007
Urbana, IL 61803-3007
Telephone: (217) 693-4800
Fax: (217) 693-4801
E-Mail: CERF@vmbd.org
www.vmdb.org

**Orthopedic Foundation for Animals (OFA)**
2300 NE Nifong Blvd
Columbus, Missouri 65201-3856
Telephone: (573) 442-0418
Fax: (573) 875-5073
Email: ofa@offa.org
www.offa.org

**US Food and Drug Administration Center for Veterinary Medicine (CVM)**
7519 Standish Place
HFV-12
Rockville, MD 20855-0001
Telephone: (240) 276-9300 or (888) INFO-FDA
http://www.fda.gov/cvm

# PUBLICATIONS
## Books

Borzendowski, Janice. *Caring for Your Aging Dog: A Quality-of-Life Guide for Your Dog's Senior Years.* Sterling Publishing Co., Inc., 2007.

Brandenberg, Jim. *Brother Wolf: A Forgotten Promise.* NorthWord Press, Inc., 1993.

Caras, Roger A. *A Dog Is Listening: The Way Some of Our Closest Friends View Us.* Simon & Schuster, Inc., 1992

Comfort, David. *The First Pet History of the World.* Simon & Schuster, Inc., 1994.

*The Complete Dog Book: Official Publication of the American Kennel Club. 19th edition, revised.* Howell Book House, 1997.

Davis, Caroline and Keith. *Dog Training in No Time: How to Understand and Train Your Dog in Just Minutes a Day.* Octopus Publishing Group Ltd., 2004.

Fox, Dr. Michael W. *The Healing Touch for Dogs: The Proven Massage Program.* Newmarket Press, 2004.

Gorrell, Gena K. *Working Like a Dog: The Story of Working Dogs Through History.* Tundra Books, 2003.

Morris, Desmond. *Dogwatching.* Crown Publishers, Inc., 1987.

Rogers, Katharine M. *First Friend: A History of Dogs and Humans.* St. Martin's Press, 2005.

## Magazines
### AKC Family Dog
American Kennel Club
260 Madison Avenue
New York, NY 10016
Telephone: (800) 490-5675
E-Mail: familydog@akc.org
www.akc.org/pubs/familydog

### AKC Gazette
American Kennel Club
260 Madison Avenue
New York, NY 10016
Telephone: (800) 533-7323
E-Mail: gazette@akc.org
www.akc.org/pubs/gazette

**Dog & Kennel**
Pet Publishing, Inc.
7-L Dundas Circle
Greensboro, NC 27407
Telephone: (336) 292-4272
Fax: (336) 292-4272
E-Mail: info@petpublishing.com
www.dogandkennel.com

**Dogs Monthly**
Ascot House
High Street, Ascot,
Berkshire SL5 7JG
United Kingdom
Telephone: 0870 730 8433
Fax: 0870 730 8431
E-Mail: admin@rtc-associates.freeserve.co.uk
www.corsini.co.uk/dogsmonthly

**The German Shepherd Dog Review (official magazine of the German Shepherd Dog Club of America)**
Susan Casey, Editor
2884 Oakland Drive
Sedalia, CO 80135
Telephone: (303) 660-0535
E-Mail: GSDReview@aol.com

## Websites
**Nylabone**
www.nylabone.com

**TFH Publications, Inc.**
www.tfh.com

# INDEX

# PHOTO CREDITS

## DEDICATION

In loving memory of Chapstick, Joey, and Charlie—and to Tedi Ginsburg, the wonderful breeder who brought these splendid German Shepherds into my life.

## ACKNOWLEDGMENTS

For their generous help with this book, I am grateful to Tedi Ginsburg, breeder (Asgard German Shepherds), AKC judge; Cindy Johnson, customer service director, Animal Humane Society; Muriel Lee, author, editor, AKC judge; Lee Livingood, author, certified dog behavior consultant (Lee Livingood's Clever Companions), International Association of Animal Behavior Consultants; and Beverly White McCartt, canine hydrotherapist (K9 Wellness & Fitness), American Canine Sports Medicine Association. I owe a huge debt of gratitude to Dr. Howard Steinberg—author, scientist, and longtime friend—who has unfailingly helped and encouraged me throughout the writing of this book and several others. Above all else, loving thanks go to my husband, Gary, who one day looked at me across the dining room table and said, "I think we should get a German Shepherd Dog."

## ABOUT THE AUTHOR

**Cindy Victor** grew up in Los Angeles with her dogs Nipper and Ginger. She and her husband, Gary, have lived many places and shared the love of many dogs, including German Shepherd Dogs. The author of eight novels and a breed book, *Greyhound: The Essential Guide for the Greyhound Lover*, she also has published short stories and articles in literary reviews, newspapers, and animal magazines. Cindy now lives in Woodbury, Minnesota, with her husband and their two Greyhounds.

## ABOUT THE VET

**Wayne Hunthausen, DVM,** consulting veterinary editor and pet behavior consultant, is the director of Animal Behavior Consultations in the Kansas City area and currently serves on the Practitioner Board for *Veterinary Medicine* and the Behavior Advisory Board for *Veterinary Forum*.

## ABOUT THE BREEDER

**Tedi Ginsburg** and her husband Evan, as Asgard German Shepherds, have been breeding and showing top-winning German shepherds for more than 30 years.

# NATURAL with added VITAMINS

# Nutri Dent ®MD

## Promotes Optimal Dental Health!

Visit
nylabone.com
Join Club NYLA
for coupons &
product
information

360° Design
Cleaning Action!™

**Dogs L♥ve 'em!**™

AVAILABLE IN MULTIPLE SIZES AND FLAVORS.

**Nylabone**®

*Trusted For Over 40 Years*

MADE IN THE USA